Luther on Vocation

Luther
on Vocation

GUSTAF WINGREN

Translated by CARL C. RASMUSSEN

Wipf & Stock
PUBLISHERS
Eugene, Oregon

Wipf and Stock Publishers
199 West 8th Avenue, Suite 3
Eugene, Oregon 97401

Luther on Vocation
By Wingren, Gustaf
Copyright©1957 by Wingren, Gustaf
ISBN: 1-59244-561-6
Publication date 2/19/2004
Previously published by Muhlenberg Press, 1957

Contents

Introduction

The task to which we address ourselves in this investigation of Luther's doctrine of vocation is purely historical in that its only aim is understanding Martin Luther's thought on one special point. Our study is not intended to be systematic treatment of basic principles, criticism of contemporary theology, comparison of Lutheran and Romanist thought, or comparative treatment of Luther and his followers. When Luther's own view has been made clear we shall have completed this undertaking. Having thus defined our task, we make its limits clearer by stating the way we seek to understand Luther's doctrine of vocation. Our aim is not to trace the progressive unfolding of this view in Luther through successive modifications occasioned by his various experiences and the progress of his reforming efforts. Such an investigation would have to be chronological, beginning with his earliest writings and following through to the old Luther and the Genesis commentary. It is inevitable that this will be touched upon to some degree in our study; but this will not be the regulative aim. Our aim is rather to integrate Luther's statements about vocation with his basic theology, that is, to present expressions concerning *Beruf* in the context of his fundamental concepts—law and gospel, the work of Christ, freedom, sin, etc. The correctness of an interpretation of Luther's doctrine of vocation can be shown only by its clarity and congruity with

his total outlook. Our main purpose therefore makes our
treatment of the material systematic in that our quest is
the total view of a definite historical person, Luther.

Such a systematic procedure in the study of the thought
of a historic person rests on the implicit assumption that
his basic theological position is itself unified. It is said
that this assumption is not completely valid in the case of
Luther. The position of the pre-Reformation Luther often
makes necessary a chronological treatment of the material
and attention to the historical development of his view.
For example, our discussion of his 1520 *Treatise on Good
Works,* will be concerned with a certain carry-over from
his pre-Reformation thought.[1] But the problem of Luther's
development lies outside of our main objective because of
the nature of the concept we aim to investigate—vocation.
Such words as sin, righteousness, faith, etc. have a central
place in the young Luther, as well as in the writings of
his mature and his older years. The content of such terms
changed greatly between 1516 and 1525. But the word
vocation *(vocatio)* is, in the sense he gave it, a product of
the central Reformation thesis of the mature Luther. His
doctrine of vocation presupposes that the monastic ideal
has already been overthrown from within. In his lectures
on the Epistle to the Romans, 1515-1516, we find direct
insistence that every station in society imposes its peculiar
requirement, which is neglected if one instead imitates the
legend of some holy life.[2] But such sporadic, early state-

[1] See Chapter I, sections 5 and 6.

[2] *WA* 56, 417 and 418. Here the term "status" is the ordinary one; but
on p. 417 the expression "according to his vocation" is clearly used as
applied to worldly occupation, for it refers to "uncultured people." But
there is a basic difference between this and Luther's later view, for in his
lectures on the Epistle to the Romans he regards the monastic life as a
status instituted by God.

ments never have the form of a decisively expressed proclamation; they lack the very point of his later doctrine of vocation, that is, his polemic against the solitary monastic life, isolated from the family and the life of the world. Not until the life of the cloister is judged something evil do the words *vocatio* and *Beruf* begin to appear more profusely in Luther's writings. As to the word *Beruf*, on the whole it does not appear before 1522.[3] The definitive rejection of the cloistered life had been made in *De votis monasticis,* 1521. By saying that the pre-Reformation Luther was hardly concerned with the problem of worldly vocation, we greatly simplify our task. It is generally recognized now that after his open break with the cloistered life, Luther presents a unified outlook. It follows then that statements about vocation, for example, even from different years of his work, can be incorporated into an inclusive picture. The proof of this can be supplied only by the ensuing presentation.

One further limitation of our investigation must be given. Not only does the question of Luther's psychological development lie outside of our main objective; so do questions of "effects" and "influences" from various sources.

[3] Karl Holl, *Gesammelte Aufsätze* III (1928), p. 217 *(Die Geschichte des Wortes Beruf).* What is comprehended in the concept of vocation of course appears more indefinite than in case of the word *Beruf.* Arvid Runestam has pointed out that Luther does not yet use the concept "vocation" in his 1520 treatise *On the Freedom of a Christian Man;* but the basic idea is there "ready to enter." The idea appears even more clearly in Luther's treatise of the same year, *Treatise on Good Works.* To this it is necessary to add only that in the 1519 treatise on baptism there appears a view of life in earthly orders that later becomes characteristic of Luther's fully developed concept of vocation. Cf. *WA* 2, 724f. Yet all that appears at this time is prologue. As Holl emphasizes, the concept of vocation breaks through clearly for the first time in the *Kirchenpostille* of 1522, the monastic ideal having been completely repudiated in 1521. See also *WA* 1, 451 (*Decem Praecepta,* 1518): "The first thing was to give heed to what the Lord required of you, the work of whatever office he laid on you, as the Apostle Paul says, 'Everyone should remain in the state in which he was called.' " Paul's statement is found in I Corinthians 7:20.

Luther's viewpoint is probably a transformation of medieval thought. There remains the task of tracing the lines from Luther back to scholasticism and to German mysticism. But all Luther's thoughts have significance which can be determined without dealing with sources. To take a comprehensive view of Luther's idea of vocation in relation to the rest of his thoughts is thus the delimited task we set for ourselves. As to the concept of vocation, Johann Tauler would be considered a source and basis of comparison. We can refer to Karl Holl's analysis of Tauler in "Die Geschichte des Wortes Beruf" (in *Gesammelte Aufsätze* III, 1928, pp. 204 ff). Holl's Romanist opponent, Nikolaus Paulus, an authority on the Middle Ages, as early as 1911 had written "Die Wertung der weltlichen Berufe im Mittelalter" (in *Historisches Jahrbuch der Goerresgesellschaft*, pp. 308-316). In 1925, in the same publication (pp. 725-755) he critically examined Holl's contribution, which had appeared separately in 1924, offering not the slightest objection to Holl's analysis of Tauler. Since Tauler accords a monk a higher holiness just because he is a monk, his position and Luther's are certainly not the same. And as far as the idea of vocation is concerned, no evidence of influence is to be found in Luther's marginal notes on Tauler's sermons.[4] But this question is of no importance for our task anyway. The content of Luther's doctrine of vocation can be given definitely, even without an answer to the question concerning its genesis.

The following presentation is divided into three chapters. In the chapter "Earth and Heaven," Luther's view of the two kingdoms is discussed: the realm of the law

[4] *WA* 9, 95f. Luther seems to have begun to read Tauler in 1516, and his marginal notes appear to belong to that year.

over the body on earth and the realm of the gospel over the conscience in heaven, the former temporal, and the latter eternal. These kingdoms stand side by side, and are not hostile to one another *per se*. Both the earthly and the spiritual realms are in God's hand. But, as Gustav Törnvall says on this subject, Luther's thought nearly always proceeds immediately to the juxtaposition of the kingdom of Christ and the kingdom of the devil. God and the devil do not stand side by side, but are enemies one of the other. Their mutual antagonism cuts across the two kingdoms. This facet vastly complicates Luther's view. This problem is clarified in the second chapter, "God and the Devil." It is our aim to keep the individual out of these two chapters, as far as possible. Here we are concerned with the "powers" or "orders" themselves: in Chapter I, the regimes or kingdoms; and in Chapter II, God against sin. To leave man completely out of consideration is of course impossible; and for that reason the third chapter, "Man," will be to some extent a repetition of the two preceding chapters. Man in his vocation is in the earthly kingdom hoping for the heavenly kingdom, which comes to him here through the gospel, but which will not be fully revealed in power until after death. Thus he stands between heaven and earth. But he also stands between God and the devil. His vocation is one of the situations in which he chooses sides in the combat between God and Satan. But some repetition of the first two chapters in the third is balanced by a gain. It is good to have Luther's view set forth with the emphasis on its significance for the individual, especially now when it sometimes seems as if Luther's view of man is nihilistic. Furthermore, additional material will be presented which does not appear in the first two chapters, particularly

Luther's conception of prayer and his distinctive expression of "the time" or "the hour."

The many problems to be faced in the presentation which follows could not be comprehended in a common, inclusive formula. But there is one issue which will appear repeatedly throughout all three chapters; in a certain way, the main issue in Luther's thought on vocation is the relation between stability and mobility, between freedom and constraint. Sometimes life in vocation appears as subjection to a predetermined and fixed reality; but at other times man, through faith and love, bursts through the external and stands free and recreative over against the given. Certainly just this almost lighthearted feature in Luther's ethics lies behind his belief in God as he who is ever creating anew. The duality of stability and mobility gives its peculiar color to Luther's view of creation. The following discussion does not seek to solve this problem but it will now and then return to it, placing it in the center of Luther's faith. "Solution" might lie in the simple fact that both God and the devil are ever present. The devil uses a static vocation for his purpose, and God replies with free new creation. The devil uses man's freedom to promote anarchy, and God replies by setting compelling barriers against freedom. But more about this in later parts of our discussion. For the present our juxtaposition is not God versus devil, but earth and heaven.

Earth and Heaven

1. *The Earthly Kingdom*

Vocatio can mean different things. It can refer to the very proclamation of the gospel, through which human beings are called to be the children of God. It can also be used as meaning the work which each one does as farmer, craftsman, etc. This use of the term occurs in I Corinthians 7:20, where it is said that each shall remain in the same vocation *(klēsis)* in which he was called. Whether Luther is right in his interpretation of *klēsis* as signifying one's outer status or occupation is a question we need not answer here. It is to some degree a third use of *vocatio* or *vocatus* when the term is used to designate the call to the office of preaching. For in that case it is not the office as such which is called *vocatio* but the action by which one rightly enters the office.[1] So too the word *Beruf* has more than one meaning; but Luther uses it most often as outer status or occupation. This use of the term is new with Luther. In speaking about Luther's doctrine of vocation, we always mean vocation in accord with Luther's interpretation of I Corinthians

---

[1] In a Latin work, such as his *Large Commentary on Galatians*, Luther characteristically enough speaks of the office of preaching as *ministerium*. As soon as he turns from preaching to magistrates, heads of households, servants, etc. he uses the word *vocatio*. Cf. *WA* 40^{II}, 152-153. But in German writings *Beruf* is used also as referring to the work of the ministry, e.g. *WA* 30^{II}, III (*On War Against the Turks*, 1529).

1

7:20. We do not deny that included as well in earthly vocation is the call to be the child of God through the gospel.
As far as we can determine Luther does not use *Beruf* or
vocatio in reference to the work of a non-Christian. All
have station *(Stand)* and office; but *Beruf* is the Christian's
earthly or spiritual work. Here we are inquiring only into
Luther's conception of earthly work, not vocation in any
other sense.[2]

Is there any position or occupation which is not *Beruf*,
not *Stand* in the true sense? In *De votis monasticis,* Luther
shows monastic vows to be contrary to faith, to freedom,
to God's command and love, and to reason. A monastic
vow is accordingly a vow to do evil. It must be broken,
even as a vow to steal, to lie, or to murder. "It ought not
to be argued whether you vow with good or evil intent,
when it is certain that what you vowed was bad. One ought
to be faithful to the gospel; and such vows, for whatever
cause they were made, with whatever intention, and at whatever time, ought to be forsaken with all confidence, and
subjected to the liberty of Christian faith."[3]

The entire discussion in that work has the purpose of
affirming that the monastic order is a false *Stand*, in which
no Christian with sustained faith and love can remain. But
he makes certain qualifications. If one is so humble and
simple that he can make the vow of chastity, simply because
it is respected and holy to live that way, let him make the
vow of chastity and serve God without marriage.[4] But such
persons can hardly be found; the very fact that one vows
for all time shows that he expects thus to win something

[2] We shall often have occasion to come back to the question of the relation between worldly work and faith or prayer (i.e. fellowship with God).
[3] *WA* 8, 668; cf. 664.
[4] *WA* 8, 611-12.

2

from God.[5] In a sermon in his *Kirchenpostille,* on I Corinthians 7:20, Luther raises the direct question as to what it means to have a vocation. He answers that you occupy a station *(Stand),* you are husband or wife, son or daughter, boy or girl. Then he stresses the greatness of the responsibilities involved in these external relationships; if one had four heads and ten hands he would still be unable to fulfil them all. It is striking for example that being a chaste and moderate young person is part of one's vocation as son or daughter.[6] Certainly the Ten Commandments are conceived as applicable under the term *Beruf.*

In immediate connection with this reference, Luther goes on to mention the prince, the bishop, the prelate, who are servants and have vocations, even if the last two do not fulfil them, but rather say masses without care for people. Somewhat later in this sermon Luther goes the whole way, and declares that the orders of pope, bishop, priest, and monk, "as they are now," are sinful orders like robbery, usury, and prostitution.[7] Just orders, such as are ordained by God or those whose existence is not contrary to God's will, are husbands and wives, boys and girls, lords and ladies, governors, regents, judges, officeholders, farmers, citizens, etc.[8] In his work about the blessed order of soldiers, in 1526, he emphasizes that the soldier's life is a ministry of love and a vocation. "So, because it is from God that a soldier receives his fitness to do battle, he may serve therewith, serving with his skill and craft whoever desires his services; and he may accept wages for his labor.

[5] *WA* 8, 620.
[6] *WA* 10$^\mathrm{I}$, 1, 308f. Cf. Werner Elert, *Morphologie des Luthertums* (1930), II, p. 65.
[7] *WA* 10$^\mathrm{I}$, 1, 317.
[8] *WA* 10$^\mathrm{I}$, 1, 317.

3

For his too is a vocation which issues from the law of love."[9]

If I find myself an occupant of some of these life stations which serve the well-being of others, I must not entertain the slightest doubt of God's pleasure, but believe the gospel. The significant thing is not whether I enter such a station as one who is sinful and worthless. The issue is whether the "station" itself is sinful or not.[10] The sin of the person himself is judged and forgiven in heaven, where there is no question of station, office and vocation, but only about the heart. On earth, on the other hand, one must give thought to office and station, not to the sin of the heart.

Therefore a person must avoid stations which are sinful. But the same reservation that appears in *De votis monasticis* crops up again in the *Kirchenpostille:* if one can avoid making the life of the cloister a matter of right and wrong and have no thought that one is made holy by being a monk, let him remain in the cloister, exercise his faith there just as elsewhere in the world, and love his neighbor.[11] This is really, in principle, a negation of monasticism, modified by outward conditions which soon passed when the hesitant left the cloistered life. When after 1532 Luther's sermons were reissued, this statement about remaining in the cloister was eliminated.

A vocation is a "station" which is by nature helpful to others if it be followed. It is important to emphasize the fact that vocation is not confined to an occupation, but includes also what Betcke calls biological orders: father, mother, son, daughter. Every attempt to differentiate between the sphere of the home, where personal Christian

[9] *WA* 19, 657.
[10] *WA* 10^{I}, 1, 316-317.
[11] *WA* 10^{I}, 1, 493.

4

love rules, and the sphere of office, where the more impersonal rules of vocation hold sway, immediately runs afoul of Luther's terminology. The life of the home, the relation between parents and children, is vocation, even as is life in the field of labor, the relation between employer and employee. In anything that involves action, anything that concerns the world or my relationship with my neighbor, there is nothing, Luther holds, that falls in a private sphere lying outside of station, office, or vocation. It is only before God, i.e., in heaven, that the individual stands alone. In the earthly realm man always stands *in relatione,* always bound to another.[12] From this it is clear that every Christian occupies a multitude of offices at the same time, not just one: the same man is, for instance, father of his children, husband of his wife, master of his servants, and officeholder in the town hall. As stated in passages we noted in the *Kirchenpostille,* all these are vocations.

To understand Luther's views as to such life stations, we might begin with a passage which Holl has discussed. "All stations are so oriented that they serve others."[13] As an example of how work in all such stations is conducive to the good of others, Luther points to a mother who cares for her children, and a father who must arise in the morning and labor to give support to his family. Holl uses all statements like this in support of his familiar thesis that central in Luther's ethics is reason that is Christian in character. *Lex naturae* is only another term for the Christian commandment of love. If worldly orders are worldly, lacking in Christian faith, they are ethically empty. When Luther uses examples from these life stations, he always

[12] *WA* 32, 390f (*The Sermon on the Mount,* 1530-32).
[13] *WA* 15, 625.

chooses examples of love; that is, says Holl, always examples of "Christian morality." This interpretation is incorrect.

The real point in the Luther passage quoted above is the contrast between purpose and practice. "All stations are intended to serve others. But we go now this way and now that." [14] Here we come across what for Luther is the decisive contrast between God's self-giving love and man's egocentricity. The human being is self-willed, desiring that whatever happens shall be to his own advantage. When husband and wife, in marriage, serve one another and their children, this is not due to the heart's spontaneous and undisturbed expression of love, every day and hour. Rather, in marriage as an institution something compels the husband's selfish desires to yield and likewise inhibits the egocentricity of the wife's heart. At work in marriage is a power which compels self-giving to spouse and children. So it is the "station" itself which is the ethical agent, for it is God who is active through the law on earth.

What is effected through these orders of society is not due to an inner transformation of the human heart. The corruption of the heart is amended in heaven, through the gospel of Christ. There the human being is a "single person" and there inquiry is made into his inner wickedness, even if on earth it has been ceaselessly repressed and hindered from outer expression. On earth and in relation to his neighbor he fills an "office"; there the main point is that creation is sustained, e.g., that children receive food, clothing and care. This work of love God effects on earth

[14] Holl must have noticed that the words "we turn everything upside down" contain a meaning which is troublesome to his interpretation of Luther. Luther's meaning makes "all stations" the subject, not we who occupy these stations, not Christians by their moral behavior.

through the "orders"—the order of marriage, of teacher and pupils, of government, etc. Even persons who have not taken the gospel to their hearts serve God's mission, though they be unaware thereof, by the very fact that they perform the outer functions of their respective stations.

One human being may not take the life of another; but God is free and does so. He does it through the offices of judge and executioner. To the judge God says, "If you do not kill and punish, you shall be punished"; for then the judge would fail his vocation.[15] Man must not look on a woman to lust after her; but in the "station" which God instituted for the propagation of the race, God himself effects desire thereby.[16] A minister must not condemn anyone; but the office of preaching does so. "I have often said that the office of preaching is not ours but God's; but it is not we but God who does whatever is God's."[17] This line of thought is not limited to Luther's *Exposition of the Sermon on the Mount*, 1530-32. We meet it in the same form in his treatise *Whether Soldiers Too Can Be Saved*, 1526, and in his *Kleiner Sermon von dem Wucher* in 1519.[18] This treatise of 1519 is the clearest contribution Luther made to the idea of the effectiveness of these orders themselves as instruments in God's hand, regardless of personal quality. There Luther discusses certain statements in Matthew 5, which say that one must not resist evil. He considers the objection that if we were to obey such injunctions, only

[15] *WA* 32, 382 (*The Sermon on the Mount*, 1530-32).

[16] *WA* 32, 382f.

[17] *WA* 32, 398. Not all who occupy the office are devout, but God does not inquire as to that; "be the person whatever he is, the office is nevertheless right and good, and not of man but of God himself." *WA* 32, 529.

[18] "It is not man but God who hangs, tortures, beheads, strangles, and does battle. These are all his works and his judgments." *WA* 19, 626 (*Whether Soldiers Too Can Be Saved*). Cf. *WA* 6, 4 (*Von Dem Wucher*).

knaves would survive, and all would end in social chaos. He replies that the temporal sword sees to it that things do not go that way. Because there is rigorous government, man can take the Sermon on the Mount in earnest. Through the temporal sword God himself protects his children. It is misunderstanding to think that people are divided into two groups, one of which (judges, executioners, etc.) resists evil and does not obey Christ's word, while the other, escaping such responsibility, can be Christian. The paradox rests with God: it is *he* who forcibly resists evil through the offices of judge and executioner, and commands all persons not to resist evil as individuals, even though they be judges and executioners. For that which the office does is not part of man's account, but of God's.[19]

Luther's idea of office constitutes an important element in his rich concept of creation, which is peculiarly concrete and vital. The birds, which sing even though they do not know what they are to eat, are an example for us. God pours out his gifts, seeds, herbs, and edible creatures. Our only care ought to be what we should do with all the good that God has made, so that it may benefit our neighbor. But instead we worry how we can get as much as possible for ourselves; and thus we put ourselves athwart creation's generous stream.

In his sermons of 1525, Luther interprets Christ's command against being anxious, as he refers to the lilies and the birds. Note, for instance, the reference to the wool and the sheep (p. 418): "He gives the wool, but not without our labor. If it is on the sheep, it makes no garment." God gives the wool, but it must be sheared, carded, spun,

---

[19] Thus Luther sharply distinguishes between the office and the person. Cf. *WA* 19, 655-656.

8

etc. In these vocations God's creative work moves on, coming to its destination only with the neighbor who needs the clothing.[20] Vocations differ from us: farmers, fishers, and men of all orders, who handle creation's wares, carry God's gifts to their neighbors, even if their purpose is not always to serve. God is active in this. There is a direct connection between God's work in creation and his work in these offices. Silver and gold in the earth, growth in the creatures of the forests, the fruitfulness and unquenchable generosity of the soil, all is the ceaseless work of the God of creation, which goes forward through the labors of mankind.[21] God creates the babes in the mother's body—man being only an instrument in God's hand—and then he sustains them with his gifts, brought to the children through the labors of father and mother in their parental office. "Even though a father is an instrument of procreation, God himself is the source and author of life."[22]

God himself will milk the cows through him whose vocation that is.[23] He who engages in the lowliness of his work performs God's work, be he lad or king. To give one's office proper care is not selfishness. Devotion to office is devotion to love, because it is by God's own ordering that the work of the office is always dedicated to the well-being of one's neighbor.[24] Care for one's office is, in its very frame of reference on earth, participation in God's own care for human beings.

[20] *WA* 17I, 414-418.
[21] *WA* 15, 368-369 (*Psalm 127*, 1524).
[22] *WA* 40III, 210f. Cf. *WA* 10II, 304 (*Vom ehelichen Leben*, 1522), *WA* 15, 375 (*Psalm 127*, 1524), and *WA* 40III, 254f.
[23] *WA* 44, 6 (*Commentary on Genesis*, 1535-45).
[24] *WA* 32, 459 (*The Sermon on the Mount*, 1530-32).

So vocation belongs to this world, not to heaven; it is directed toward one's neighbor, not toward God. This is an important preliminary characteristic. In his vocation one is not reaching up to God, but rather bends oneself down toward the world. When one does that, God's creative work is carried on. God's work of love takes form on earth, and that which is external witnesses to God's love. If we note properly how much good God bestows upon us, both through his direct creation and through all his created orders, we shall know the truth that he forgives sins. "God has shown the forgiveness of sins in all his creation." But in dealing with the forgiveness of sins we enter another realm, the eternal, heavenly kingdom.

2. *The Kingdom of Heaven*

In no other writing does Luther set forth vocation with such force as in his *Kirchenpostille*. But there, more clearly than anywhere else, vocation is rejected as a means to man's salvation and status as child of God. In heaven, before God, vocation has as little to contribute as do good works. Good works and vocation (love) exist for the earth and one's neighbor, not for eternity and God. God does not need our good works, but our neighbor does. It is faith that God wants. Faith ascends to heaven. Faith enters a different kingdom, the eternal, divine kingdom, which Luther considers just as evident as the earthly realm, with its offices and occupations through which God carries on his creative work. In the heavenly kingdom Christ is king, and there his gospel alone rules: no law, and therefore no works. What Luther means by faith and its kingdom in heaven, in contrast to works and their realm on earth, is not clear

10

apart from his view of law and gospel, spiritual and earthly rule, faith and love. For the present we must give a more general description of the heavenly kingdom. We begin with references in Luther in which vocation is, so to speak, barred from heaven and applied to earth. First we speak of the passage recently noted in the *Kirchenpostille*.[25]

When a monk or a nun hears that the vow of the cloistered life cannot contribute to salvation, he or she may leave the cloister for the lay status, in order to be saved there. That would be like living under the tragic misapprehension that one would have to be a shoemaker to be saved, and then fall into the delusion that it is by being a tailor that he can gain heaven. The work of Christ is victory over the law in any form: good works lead to salvation by neither one route nor the other. The conscience alone, through faith in the work of Christ, is freed from a false faith. Christ frees neither the hand from its work nor the body from its office. The hand, the body, and their vocation belong to earth. There is no redemption in that, but that is not the idea. The purpose is that one's neighbor be served. Conscience rests in faith in God, and does nothing that contributes to salvation; but the hands serve in the vocation which is God's downward-reaching work, for the well-being of men. From the viewpoint of faith, vocation has no relevance. As soon as any outward quality of life claims a place in conscience or in heaven, claiming to be a condition for God's forgiveness, the immateriality of vocation must be emphasized. "The faith and the Christian station are so free a thing that they are bound to no special orders, but are above all orders, in all orders, and through all orders; wherefore there is no need for you to take up or leave any station in order to be saved. . . . It is all free, free."[26]

This is the meaning of the famous statement about prince and emperor as *einzele person* before God. "So the emperor, when he turns to God, is not emperor but a single person, like any other human being before God. But if he turns to his subjects, he is emperor as many times as he has subjects. Thus we must speak about all authorities. When they turn themselves toward the authority that is above them, they themselves have no authority. But when they turn to those who are under them, they are therein clad with authority."[27] God dispenses all stations and offices that they may operate downward; but he confers no authority over against himself.

The truth is that the need of others is an absolute imperative in the life of a Christian concerning love, works, vocation, but it is counted as nothing before God. Faith's realm in heaven and love's realm on earth must not be confused; but neither is inconsequential. Cf. the remarkable passage in *WA* 34[II], 27: Here below man must obey rulers, love his wife. "Such works have their place in this life. In the other life we shall not have wife or child, and offices will have come to an end. There all shall be alike. Therefore the law shall not hold sway there." Here we see that faith's realm is a future kingdom, a kingdom after death; but vocation's realm is in the present, and will come

[26] *WA* 12, 126.

[27] *WA* 19, 652-653 (*Whether Soldiers Too Can Be Saved*, 1526). Cf. 661, where the thought about the soldier's station is summarized. One is saved, not as a soldier, but only as a Christian. Obedience in one's vocation is rendered, not for the sake of heaven, but because the cause is good. In death the soldier has to trust in God's grace, not in his death as a soldier. Therefore before battle the soldier ought to commit himself to God's mercy, for Christ's sake, before he takes his weapon and goes to his task.

to an end. Faith's kingdom is a realm in which all are alike; but vocation's world is full of grades and differences.

When anyone, be he emperor or craftsman, turns to God in faith, or, more concretely, in prayer, he is without the outer support which "station" gives in relation to others. Here one does not stand *in relatione*, or meet with another human being, as one does in his vocation. Each is alone before God. Before God the individual is as alone as if there were only God and he in heaven and earth.[28] Before God not only does station vanish, but also every work stands as sinful and worthless. Therefore all those qualities are wiped out which differentiate among men on earth. What makes the difference on earth is the structure of many offices, with their respective works. But in heaven all are alike. There all simply receive, and receive alike, the grace of God. Thus equality in the heavenly kingdom depends only on the fact that it is the kingdom of Christ, ruled by a divine gift, the gospel, not by law.

When one presents works before God in the kingdom of heaven, God's order is disrupted in both realms. Since the reign of Christ is in giving, and in grace and the gospel, to proffer gifts here is an attempt to depose Christ from his throne. A human being lets his works compete with the King of heaven. At the same time, his neighbor on earth is neglected since his good works have clearly been done, not for the sake of his neighbor, but to parade before God. Faith is revoked in heaven, and love on earth. Neither God nor one's neighbor receives that which is properly his. "Thus they corrupt both of them, faith and love. . . . They

[28] *WA* 7, 566 (*The Magnificat,* 1521). Being alone means that one does not come with an accompaniment of good works. Cf. *WA* 8, 66 and 79. Before God there is only one kind of righteousness, i.e. faith; before God there is only the righteousness of God.

deny their works to their neighbor and direct them to
themselves. . . . Then faith cannot continue."[29]

Here we espy the work of the devil, through which works
are forced up to heaven, salvation by the law, which is both
blasphemy of God and scorn of one's neighbor, an impure
performance of vocation (on earth). The devil's work is
in direct contradiction to God's, and ever competes with
it throughout man's world. When God battles with the devil
for the life of man, his instrument is the gospel, which
effects faith in man's heart; and faith is channeled to one's
neighbor in works of love.[30] Works belong to the earthly
realm, in service to others, directed downward in vocation
which bears altogether the stamp of the earthly realm. And
vocation is most purely and really served when through the
gospel it has become clear that vocation has nothing to do
with salvation. God receives that which is his, faith. The
neighbor receives that which is his, works. To break down
the faithfulness which God effects in man's vocation is one
of the devil's greatest desires. A weapon that serves the
devil well, to this end, is the cloister and the splendid saintliness that does not concern itself with vocation. Luther
points this out forcefully in De votis monasticis. We shall
return later to the dualism between God and the devil. We
refer to it here simply to clarify the way in which the
heavenly kingdom is, in the will of God, distinguished from
the earthly.

We may point out that this demarcation between earth
and heaven is the main point in two of Luther's central
writings: *Large Commentary on Galatians* and *The Bondage of the Will*. "We set up, as it were, two worlds, one

[29] *WA* 8, 363.
[30] *WA* 8, 363. Cf. 372.

heavenly *(coelestis)* and one earthly *(terrenus)*. Each has its own kind of righteousness. The righteousness of the law is earthly, concerned with earthly affairs and consists of our doing of good works *(facimus bona opera)*. . . . The heavenly, passive righteousness is not of ourselves; we receive it from heaven. We do not produce it but receive it in faith *(non facimus, sed fide apprehendimus)*."[31] This concept of the two kingdoms underlies all statements in that work that aims at correct differentiation between law and gospel. It is stated directly, repeated, and driven home. "So these things ought to be noted: that you place the gospel in heaven and the law on earth; that you call the righteousness of the gospel heavenly and divine, and the righteousness of the law earthly and human."[32] Even where reference is made only to law and gospel, what Luther says can be comprehended in the picture of the two kingdoms, and by that be made most vital.

But it is even more impressive that the distinction Luther makes in *The Bondage of the Will* between "things which are above us" and "things which are below us" is exactly the same as that just noted between earth and heaven. Here Luther declares that man lacks free will in that which is above him, but has free will *(liberum arbitrium)* in that which is under him. We must learn to use the term free will in such manner that "free will in man is admitted not toward that which is above us, but only in what is below

[31] *WA* 40[I], 46 (*Commentary on Galatians*, 1535).

[32] *WA* 40[I], 207. Likewise, he writes this again and again, on the succeeding pages, 208-210. On page 214f, it is stated that the law is to rule the body (i.e. on earth), while conscience, i.e. faith, abides with Christ *in sublimi monte*, without the law. The distinction is also emphasized, on page 393f, between the righteousness of heaven and of the state. It appears even more clearly on pages 469f and 544f. Cf. 622-664, and also *WA* 40[II], 37-38, where the terms "before God" and "before men" are used, meaning the same as "in heaven" and "on earth."

us." That is to say, will is free, not before God, but solely in earthly matters.[33]

The terms "superior" and "inferior," which he uses at the beginning of this treatise, Luther interprets later when he treats of a peculiarly difficult passage in Sirach. He divides human beings into two kingdoms, *duo regna*.[34] In the one kingdom man acts freely, concerning the things which are below *(puta in rebus sese inferioribus)*. With the introduction of our foregoing idea of the earthly kingdom we see the reason: in this realm man is to perform works, as it is filled with office and vocations and constant labor, and here man's freedom is active, thereby being an instrument in the hand of God who thus carries on his creative work. But—the passage in *The Bondage of the Will* continues—in the other realm *(altero vero regno)* man is not left to his own free will. There the *servum arbitrium* obtains. As we mentioned before, man is not to effect anything there. This is the essential characteristic of the kingdom of heaven. There is no place for vocation, works, or love as man's accompaniment. Only faith may enter. All the rest is placed on the earthly level, where his neighbor needs it. In a kingdom wherein man is not the doer, but one who only receives, his will is not free; it is bound. If freedom of will ascends to heaven, it is an infraction of the divine order, a work of the devil, identical with the circumstance mentioned above in which works are thrust up before God, not addressed to one's fellow-men, freely, directly and simply. Free will thus exists before God only as evil.

Therefore it is entirely natural for Luther, in *The Bondage of the Will*, to speak of man's co-operation with God,

[33] *WA* 18, 638.
[34] *WA* 18, 672f.

cooperatio. This co-operation is limited entirely to the sphere that is "below," "under us." Not only in *The Bondage of the Will* but in other writings as well, Luther speaks about God's continuing work of creation through man's work in his various stations. We meet this in Luther's exposition of *The Sermon on the Mount*, in his treatises about soldiers and about the 1525 Peasant Revolt; also in both Latin and German versions of his exposition of Psalm 127, and in the *Commentary on Genesis*. Everywhere in these writings, as in *The Bondage of the Will*, there is the same clear differentiation of the two realms.[35] If man lacks free will before God in the heavenly realm, but has a certain freedom of will concerning things and humans in the earthly realm, then the very idea of co-operation, confined as it is to the earthly, is in fact a greater emphasis on the truth that man is not free before God, but that all power is God's.

In the conclusion of his writing against Erasmus, Luther again returns to the distinction between the two different lines of man's action, which must be kept distinct in considering the freedom of the will. "We are not inquiring . . . into our situation on earth *(super terram),* but into our situation before God in heaven *(in coelo coram deo).* We know that man has been made master over those things which are below him *(inferioribus),* over which he has right and freedom of will. . . . But what we are inquiring about is whether he has freedom of will before God. . . . Hear John the Baptist, that no one can receive anything except it be given him from heaven *(nihil accipere posset, nisi donetur ei de coelo).* Therefore the freedom of the will comes to nothing."[36] In that statement every word is im-

[35] The chief reference to co-operation, in *The Bondage of the Will,* is found in *WA* 18, 753-754.
[36] *WA* 18, 781.

17

portant. *Inferiora* is equated with earth, with the realm of works. There free will operates. Freedom of will is denied in heaven before God because heaven is the realm of divine giving, where man can only receive, but not offer good works. As we shall see, the bondage of the will in this sense does not at all mean mere passivity: man can receive from God only in prayer, and prayer is struggle, just as faith is struggle. Man turns himself upward toward God in prayer and faith; and the very action of both of these demonstrates our bondage of will before God. We can only take or receive from God. If one who prays begs God for something but does not receive—and that too is possible—that also demonstrates the bondage of his will.

The continuity of thought between his other writings and *The Bondage of the Will* on this point is clearly shown in his argument against Erasmus (*WA* 18, 767-768). There it is explained that the realm of the free will is the realm of the law, in which righteousness according to civil law is possible; but the will is bound in relation to the gospel, the righteousness which is bestowed apart from works of the law. "To illustrate, the free will has power through its own efforts to move forward in one way and another in manifest good works or in the righteousness of civil or moral law; but it cannot move up to the righteousness of God. . . . For Paul clearly distinguishes these two kinds of righteousness, ascribing one to the law and the other to grace, saying that the latter is given without the former and without man's own works" (p. 767f). The good that man does on earth is God's creation, and it is to be directed toward his neighbor. Before God the good is not man's but God's.[37]

[37] *WA* 38, 373.

THE KINGDOM OF HEAVEN

Only before one's neighbor does the good done appear as coming from him who does it. Through this we can understand the concept of man as "mask" of God.

These statements agree fairly literally with the oft-repeated thesis of Luther's *Large Commentary on Galatians*. In it the line of thought leads directly to the earthly and spiritual kingdoms. But before we deal with these, we must devote some attention to the fact that the heavenly kingdom is a kingdom beyond death, a coming kingdom. We have already called attention to what Luther says (*WA* 34^{II}, 27) about the difference between life on earth and life in heaven. On earth one must heed the authority of government and parents, be a good spouse and a good neighbor. In heaven man has neither wife nor children, for all offices leave off, and human beings are all alike, since the rule of law is put away. The realm of vocation is temporary. It is only in the present, short life that we are concerned with the endowments and responsibilities of office. The transitoriness of vocation can be called another aspect of the fact, already stated, that vocation has nothing to do with salvation. The gospel, as the promise of salvation, is also the promise of eternity, of a kingdom which will never pass away. On earth we receive from God gifts which are transitory; but in the heavenly kingdom we receive God himself, who never passes away. "His good things are merely gifts that last but for a season; but his grace and regard are the inheritance which lasts forever, as St. Paul says in Romans 6, 'The grace of God is eternal life.' In giving us gifts, he gives but what is his, but in his grace and his regard of us he gives his very self."[38]

Faith cannot lay hold of an external good, or of a gift;

[38] *WA* 7, 751 (*The Magnificat*, 1521).

for the gift will pass away. But faith must rise up to God himself and rest in him; faith is entrance into heaven. Love is rightly at home on earth, in the transitory world, where man cannot trust in anything, because love will be misused and betrayed.[39] The earthly realm is destroyed little by little, and little by little created anew by God in nature and in all offices. In this realm we live *now,* under the rule of the law. If this were the only world, the gospel would be an empty word and without meaning. "All the things which God would have done on the sabbath are manifest signs of another life after this. Why is it necessary for God to speak to us through his Word, if we are not to live in a future and eternal life?"[40]

The gospel is thus an eschatological message, in the sense that it promises something that belongs to the future, life after death. This is evident in Luther's way of differentiating between *iustitia civilis* (civil righteousness) and *iustitia christiana* (righteousness in Christ). Civil righteousness is promoted by the law and is relevant in courts, in general, before man, as an adequate righteousness. Righteousness in Christ is a given righteousness, and can be said to consist of the forgiveness of sins. Luther distinguishes these two kinds of righteousness in this way: *iustitia civilis* has its function on earth up till the hour of death; but then all *iustitia civilis* becomes sinful. The forgiveness of sins is the only righteousness that is enduring. "Thus man is to be viewed in the light of two kinds of righteousness. Let him live honestly in outward relations, that he may have a tranquil life. But when the end of this life really comes, let

[39] *WA* 18, 651-652 (*The Bondage of the Will,* 1525); and *WA* 50, 567 (*On Councils and Churches,* 1539).
[40] *WA* 42, 61 (*Commentary on Genesis,* 1535-45).

20

him know of what kind his true righteousness is. For there
his works become sins. Then let him learn to say, 'If I had
never done a good work, nevertheless I believe the article
on the forgiveness of sins.' There nothing ought to be
thought of but the remission of sins."[41]

In death man crosses the threshold into the other kingdom, which is not subject to the conditions that obtain on
earth. Through the gospel of the forgiveness of sins there
is proffered to us a righteousness which is valid for eternity, and which faith already receives on earth. In time
and among human beings on earth, on the other hand,
forgiveness of sins does not obtain as righteousness in fact;
here one must take man's deeds into account. It is entirely
right and in harmony with God's will that on earth a righteousness of works is demanded. But that outer righteousness is transitory, like all else on earth. It does not reach
as far as heaven. At the very gate of heaven, in the hour
of death with its anxiety, it totters and collapses.

So the kingdom of God is given us as a promise. When
faith accepts that promise and believes it a true word of
God, eternal life begins here on earth, but everything which
lies on this side of death is only a weak beginning. Reality
is first encountered in the resurrection. Life based on civil
righteousness is of such character that it must always seek
to escape death, which brings such righteousness to naught.
On the other hand, a life built on faith reaches forward
to death and awaits it, looking forward to the revelation
of righteousness in Christ.[42] Thus righteousness lies ahead of

[41] *WA* 29, 572 (*Sermons*, 1529; Poach).

[42] *WA* 32, 468 and 469 (*The Sermon on the Mount*, 1530-32). Also,
very clearly, *WA* 2, 278f and 734f; for example, "So then, the life of a
Christian, from his baptism to his grave, is nothing but the beginning of
a blessed death; for in the last day God will make him new altogether."
728 (*Treatise on the Sacrament of Baptism*, 1519).

faith, and faith awaits it. It is no contradiction of this to say that righteousness is before faith, that it is, so to say, prepared and evident through Christ. For the work of Christ has already been effected before our time, and nothing is lacking in that righteousness which Christ has acquired by his death and resurrection, but which he has not yet fulfilled in us. That will be realized only in our death and resurrection, which are still to come. Thus faith stands between two resurrections, the resurrection of Christ, which has already taken place, and our own resurrection, which lies before us. These two resurrections Luther links together in his own special way. The resurrection of Christ is "not complete" before our resurrection has come. Believers are the body of Christ; the body of Christ is not risen until they who are his are raised. Therefore to say that faith looks *forward* is not to deny that it is faith in the work of Christ. The work of Christ stretches over both the past and the future. He arose on the third day, and he arises anew wherever faith is awakened. The resurrection from the dead which he has begun with the birth of faith in a person, he will completely "fulfil" in that person's death and resurrection in heaven. Toward that glory of Christ faith looks forward.[43]

When Stomps, from the point of view of his philosophy, takes up consideration of Luther's thought, it is this future quality, the forward reach of faith, which he points out in his view of the relation between faith and knowledge according to Luther. This is the point of value in this philosophical treatment, which otherwise expounds much that is not true

[43] Cf. *WA* 56, 372 (*Commentary on Romans*, 1515-16).

to Luther. But he makes a good observation in the following definition: faith looks to things which are invisible and unknowable; but they are invisible and unknowable "not because they are basically unknowable, but because they are *not yet* visible, *not yet* knowable. Faith directs itself to that which is to come—Faith is the proper way to wait."[44] It is on earth that man believes in the kingdom of heaven, for it has not yet come with power. But in the resurrection world faith no longer exists. There one sees that in which he has believed.

"When he [Christ] names only those who come into this world, he indicates that he speaks only of that light of faith which shines and helps in this life; after death no one is enlightened by it. It must occur here through faith in the man Christ, but without his deity. After this life we shall see, not through his humanity and by faith; we shall behold his unveiled deity, openly manifest in itself."[45]

3. *The Spiritual and Earthly Governments*

Up to this point we have spoken of two kingdoms, without talking about the governments through which these two kingdoms carry on. Luther himself hardly ever does so. It is only because the kingdoms are ruled by God that they continue. God daily maintains outer temporal peace and tolerable life on earth through worldly government, and access to heaven through spiritual government, both "against the

[44] M. A. H. Stomps, *Die Anthropologie Luthers* (1935), p. 121. Cf. also W. von Löwenich, *Luthers Theologia crucis* (1929), pp. 112-115.
[45] *WA* 10^I, 1, 222 (*Kirchenpostille*, 1522). Cf. *WA* 18, 784 (*The Bondage of the Will*, 1525).

23

devil," *adversus Diabolum, carnem et mundum.*[46] Should
the kingdoms be left to themselves for a moment, they would
be overthrown by the power of evil and destruction.

In his treatise *Whether Soldiers Too Can Be Saved,*
Luther shows what he means by the two governments. "For
he [God] has set up two kinds of government among men.
One is spiritual, through the word and without the sword,
through which men might become devout and righteous,
so that along with this righteousness they might receive
eternal life. This righteousness he administers through the
Word which he has committed to his preachers. The other
is an earthly government through the sword, in order that
they who refuse to be made devout and righteous unto life
eternal shall by such earthly government be compelled to
be devout and righteous before the world. This righteousness he administers through the sword. Though he does not
reward this righteousness with life eternal, he nevertheless
insists on it, in order that peace may be maintained among
men; and he does reward it with temporal gifts."[47] This
statement fits very easily into the picture we have given
of Luther's view. One righteousness is righteousness for the
world, not for eternal life, and is rewarded with *zeitlich gut*
(the things of this world). Here we see again the earthly
kingdom, to which our vocation is relevant, and in which
God ever produces external benefits for the maintenance
of life. Accordingly all this belongs under earthly government. Its work is a kind of righteousness, a righteousness
of God, and yet a transitory righteousness which does not
reach life eternal. The other righteousness, the righteous-

[46] See the classic reference concerning church, school, home, town hall
and castle in the treatise *On Councils and Churches,* 1539; *WA* 50, 652.
[47] *WA* 19, 629.

ness which is given, is bestowed through the gospel, which has acquired the office of preaching as its instrument on earth. In the church just such a "spiritual rule" operates, and here the kingdom of heaven appears in an external way, for hereby the door is opened to eternal life.[48]

Earthly government presents a variegated content. Luther usually divides its work into two "hierarchies," political economy and domestic economy (the family). A third "hierarchy," the church, alone constitutes the spiritual government. In the domestic economy one is father, mother, boy or girl. Here again we come across certain of the vocations about which the *Kirchenpostille* spoke. The list is completed in the political economy, represented in all the down-reaching ramifications of rulers, from the prince to him who handles the sword, the soldier or the executioner. Over all of this wide field God's government is carried on against the devil, against all evil which emerges among men and aims to bring forth evil deeds. Beside the sword of government is the rod in the fatherly hand for the correction of the child.[49] All this is comprehended in the law, God's law, and its civil use, its *usus civilis*. "Here [in external matters] whether you are preacher, ruler, spouse, teacher, disciple, there is not time to hear the gospel but the law; here you must fulfil your vocation!"[50] Law and the sword *(lex* and *gladius)* belong together. Law and voca-

---

[48] The office of preaching, as an office, is clearly one office among others; and it does not belong to that kingdom in which other orders have no place. Even the office of the ministry is a *Beruf* subject to the conditions of a vocation. Nevertheless through this particular vocation God carries out something distinctive and totally different from all other vocations.

[49] *WA* 32, 316-317.

[50] *WA* 40[I], 210 (*Commentary on Galatians*, 1535).

tion belong together. Vocation falls within the kingdom of the law.[51]

From the long quotation cited from *Whether Soldiers Too Can Be Saved* (p. 24), we might decide that earthly government is to rule over one group of people (the evil) and the spiritual government over another group (the Christians). That view is suggested too in Luther's *Treatise on Secular Authority*.[52] But it is obvious that this statement is an abbreviated mode of expression, like "The Christian needs no law." In reality, a Christian is of course a sinner even while he is righteous, and as a sinner he is subject to the law. In the first part of our discussion we adduced quotations from Luther in which he affirms that the body is ruled on earth by the law, while the conscience or faith is in heaven from which the law is barred and only the gospel rules. Luther often emphasizes the simultaneity of these two governments over one and the same person. "With the Spirit in the paradise of grace and peace, and with the flesh in the world of toil and cross," a Christian lives his life. "So as the law holds sway in the flesh, the promise rules most graciously in the conscience. When you have thus recognized the proper sphere of each, you walk most securely with the promise in heaven and the law on earth, with the Spirit of grace and peace in Paradise and in the body of works and the cross on earth."[53]

The two governments do indeed encompass different

[51] *WA* 19, 629 (*Whether Soldiers Too Can Be Saved*, 1526). Also cf. *WA* 40[I], 429f concerning the civil or political use of the law (*Commentary on Galatians*, 1535), where Luther says it is "to curb the barbarous and wicked." He specifically refers to the force which government exercises. This is to be seen clearly in *WA* 40[I], 479-485.

[52] *WA* 11, 229-281. See, for instance, page 249: "Here we must divide the children of Adam, all men, into two classes: the one belongs to the kingdom of God, the other to the kingdom of the world" (1523).

[53] *WA* 40[I], 469 (*Commentary on Galatians*, 1535).

THE SPIRITUAL AND EARTHLY GOVERNMENTS

groups of people, since some do not have the gospel, yet live under earthly government; but even after the gospel has freed the conscience, man is still subject to worldly government of law in his earthly vocation, the two governments thus signifying "two different positions for people," as Törnvall says. The law is really embodied in external ordinances which require work and deeds *(iustitia civilis);* and the gospel is similarly embodied in the church, which proffers the forgiveness of sins *(iustitia christiana).*[54] Now we ask whether there is any inner connection between these two governments.

The answer is twofold. There is a connection from above, from God's point of view, and a connection from below, from man's point of view. The former we have already spoken of. Both governments are expressions of God's love. In his vocation man does works which effect the well-being of others; for so God has made all offices. Through this work in man's offices, God's creative work goes forward, and that creative work is love, a profusion of good gifts. With persons as his "hands" or "coworkers," God gives his gifts through the earthly vocations, toward man's life on earth (food through farmers, fishermen and hunters; external peace through princes, judges, and orderly powers; knowledge and education through teachers and parents, etc, etc). Through the preacher's vocation, God gives the forgiveness of sins. Thus love comes from God, flowing down to human beings on earth through all vocations, through

[54] The signs which show that the church is present are "baptism, sacrament, and the gospel." *WA* 6, 301 *(On the Papacy at Rome,* 1520). Through these means the forgiveness of sins is given; wherefore it can be said that "the whole church is forgiveness of sins." *WA* 2, 722 *(Treatise on the Sacrament of Penance,* 1519). Here man is to be reminded that the forgiveness of sins is heavenly righteousness, which is effective after death. Thus the church is an eschatological reality, whereas business and civil order are relevant to the present life.

both spiritual and earthly governments. This can also be a connection between the two governments from man's point of view, if he ponders what he receives through the faithfulness of others to their vocations. He receives the good gifts of God's love through both prince and preacher.

But we find a connection between the two governments on the horizontal plane too. This emerges if man looks at his position in his own vocation, not asking what he receives, but what he is to do, what God requires of him. Vocation is law and commandment, a synthesis of God's commands to the person who occupies the particular place on earth that his offices indicate. Thus in his vocation the law comes just as close to him as does the gospel in its incarnation in the church. Both law and gospel press themselves home upon man in tangible earthly form, the law through vocation (domestic life, officialdom, labor, kinships, talents with correlative stations), and the gospel through the church, where the Word is preached and the sacraments are administered immediately before men. The church always points, at least primarily, on towards eternity, up toward heaven. Vocation points to the present, to the present day, to this world. Here we discover a firm and definite connection, from the point of view of the individual.

Baptism is the church's fundamental sacrament. In baptism the recipient is buried with Christ: he must die with him that he may rise and live with him (Rom. 6). This takes place day by day through the putting to death of the old man and the rising of the new man out of sin.[55] This is completely effected in death, when the body of sin withers, and God's new creation appears in the consummation. Therefore man ought to rejoice in death. But instead he

[55] *WA* 2, 727-728 (*Treatise on the Sacrament of Baptism*, 1519).

28

fears death. The old man does not want to die and leave the world of sin; on the contrary, he wants to live in it as long as possible. God must help man to die daily. For that reason God has ordained many different orders, in which man is to discipline himself and learn to suffer and die. In this connection Luther again refers to his amply differentiated vocations, all supplied with the same divine mandate, "trouble and toil."[56] In one's vocation there is a cross—for prince, husband, father, daughter, for everyone—and on this cross the old human nature is to be crucified. Here the side of baptism which is concerned with death is fulfilled. Christ died on the cross, and one who is baptized unto death with Christ must be put to death by the cross. To understand what is meant by the cross of vocation, we need only remember that vocation is ordained by God to benefit, not him who fulfils the vocation, but the neighbor who, standing alongside, bears his own cross for the sake of others. Under this cross are included even the most trivial of difficulties, such as: in marriage, the care of babes, which interferes with sleep and enjoyment; in government, unruly subjects and promoters of revolt; in the ministry, the whole resistance to reformation; in heavy labor, shabbiness, uncleanness, and the contempt of the proud. All of this is bracketed with the high and holy cross of Christ; but then that too was deep in humiliation when it was erected.

In *An die Pfarrherrn wider den Wucher zu predigen* (1540), Luther says that a Christian must suffer (e.g. p. 400), and continues, "I ask where our suffering is to be found. I shall soon tell you: Run through all stations of life, from the lowest to the highest, and you will find what you are looking for" (p. 404). Then follows a realistic

[56] *WA* 2, 734 *(ibid.).*

description of a day in Germany about 1540, of peasants, burghers, nobles, etc. He then sums up. "Therefore do not worry where you can find suffering. That is not necessary. Simply live as an earnest Christian, preacher, pastor, burgher, farmer, noble, lord, and fulfil your office faithfully and loyally. Let the devil worry where he can find a piece of wood out of which to make a cross for you, and the world where it can find a branch out of which to make a scourge for your hide" (412).

In the final sentences the allusion to Christ's cross is manifest. Behind this entire view of Luther's lies the concept of vocation's work as divine love's coming down to earth, the same love as was in Christ. No person who lets the work of his vocation go forward without grudging will escape troubles, hatred, and persecution.[57] This view of vocation will be met often in our study.

The crucifixion of Christ was followed by his resurrection on the third day. One is baptized not only that he may die with Christ; but also that he may arise with Christ; not only unto the crucifixion of the old nature in vocation, but also to the resurrection of the new—through faith in the gospel, by which the life-giving Spirit is given. With the latter (the gospel, faith, the Spirit, the new creature) our next section will deal. Here it is referred to only in a summary way, because it includes the answer to our question about the connection between earthly and spiritual government from the point of view of the individual human being. The Christian is crucified by the law in his vocation, under the earthly government; and he arises through the gospel, in the church under the spiritual government. Both of these take place on earth; but both are directed toward heaven.

[57] *WA* 51, 325f.

Through both the individual is incorporated into Christ; through vocation, into his cross, and through the church, into his resurrection. Christ is king in heaven, in the kingdom beyond death. That is the destination toward which a Christian is to be carried along. Baptism is therefore completely fulfilled only in death, as we saw in Luther's explanation of baptism.

Here we find a new possibility in what Luther says about the two different directions of faith and works. The true love is the love of Christ directed, even as his body is crucified, to men of death and to robbers. The human being who in his vocation serves his fellow-men fulfils his task out of love for Christ, and receives the same poor measure of gratitude as Christ did. This is the only way love of Christ can be real. Every attempt to select a gathering of holy and unworldly people for service has the result of forcing love—and that is not the love of Christ. In the cloister where such compulsion rules, Christ is accordingly not present with his love. Christ is excluded whenever the ordinary neighbor is excluded. And furthermore, since faith is simply the presence of Christ, this means that in the cloister faith is impossible. Where Christ is excluded it is not possible for man to have faith. In the cloister man is forced to perform works which are a substitute for the works which he should "pour out on his neighbor, in love," in the world at large. His works are done for a reason other than the purely earthly aim of being of service to his neighbor; his aim is now to make himself holy. That is to seek justification before God by works. Faith is wiped out.

Accordingly, in *De votis monasticis*, Luther declares that when God wants to save a monk, he compels him to occupy himself with earthly things. That is how God dealt with

Bernard of Clairvaux (Luther has in mind Bernard's comprehensive political activity), and the same thing has happened in other cases. It was that kind of miracle by which they were saved from languishing in the cloister, with its cooped-up and fictitious love.[58] In that way marriage has the function of compelling one to work for the good of others. And when that happens, man generally stands empty-handed and helpless before God; that is to say, faith then has a chance to be born.

Christ is present with men in these works, since they serve others. And he is also present there bringing forth faith. Faith and works are never to be divorced. If a person begins in faith, works immediately leap forth, for faith is Christ. If a person begins with works that are really good (that is, works that serve others, the works of his vocation), he sees immediately that out of inner necessity faith mounts up to God, for such works empty one so completely that one cannot go on without God. This emptying is the "cross," Christ's cross and man's cross, for these two are the same, since Christ is also present. But on the other hand, the consolation of faith is the power of the Christ who is risen.

All his life the monk is supplied with food, clothing and everything else, provided by the labors of others out in the world, and put at the disposal of the cloistered inhabitants in the form of gifts and endowments. So the monk is secure, without perils or cross. To seek such a station in life is to try to escape the common trials of mankind, to "avoid looking up to heaven, expecting daily bread from God, and trusting God to provide sustenance."[59] As soon as one leaves the cloister and marries, such cares approach, that is, such

---

[58] *WA* 8, 628.
[59] *WA* 12, 106 (*Exposition of 1 Corinthians 7*, 1523).

occasions for faith, for trust, for practice of faith. In the cloister faith has "no room, no place, no time, no occupation, no exercise." But marriage is of such character that it "teaches us and compels us to look to God's hand and grace, and simply drives us to faith."[60]

We have noted above that vocation is so constituted that it is conducive to the well-being of neighbors; it serves others (love). Now we see that it also compels one to look to God, to lay hold of his promise (faith). Man is thereby put into right relation both to earth (love) and to heaven (faith). God's complete work is set in motion through vocation: he changes the world and he sheds his mercy on hard-pressed humanity. As soon as vocation is abandoned, God loses hold of man, both faith and love cease, and, since there is no free will before God, the devil, that objective power that opposes God, has gained control of man.

This view of vocation cannot be emphasized enough. Through vocation God's presence is really with man. As the God of the law, he places himself above man's self-will, and drives man to prayer, which is answered by God's love and care. In vocation works are constrained to move toward one's neighbor, toward the earth; and faith alone, trust, prayer, all without works, ascends heavenward. In all this one is incorporated into Christ; the cross in the vocation is his cross, and the faith which breaks forth from that cross in the vocation is his resurrection.[61] This latter point

[60] *WA* 12, 106. Cf. *WA* 32, 511-512, where prince, judge, husband, boy, and girl are called true monks and nuns on account of the weight of their cross, while those who inhabit cloisters are said to be playing foolishly with the cross (*The Sermon on the Mount,* 1530-32).

[61] On the point of man's sharing in the crucifixion and resurrection of Christ, see, for example, *WA* 5, 128-129 (*Operationes in Psalmos,* 1519-21), *WA* 1, 112-113 (*Sermo in Die S. Thomae,* 1516), and *WA Deutsche Bibel* V, 628 (*Preface to Romans,* 1529). The last-named reference speaks of baptism exactly as Luther did in 1519 (*WA* 2).

33

we shall discuss in the next section about faith and love. But before that perhaps certain additional characteristic citations ought to be given, in which emphasis is given to the risk in all earthly life in the service of others.

In *Heerpredigt wider den Türken*, of 1529, Luther speaks of the "cross" which "profits man unto salvation" and in which "faith is to be exercised and sustained."[62] It was possible that the cross which God would let many bear at that time (1529) was imprisonment by the Turks, with consequent servitude under harsh conditions and in a foreign land. As long as resistance to the Turks is possible, resistance is one's vocation (this is a major point in the entire treatise). But if one be taken prisoner, then the Turkish master becomes one's neighbor and rightful lord over one's body: then faithful service to him is one's vocation. That is where one must bear the cross. This is what Jacob did in Haran, Joseph with Pharaoh, the children of Israel in Assyria, the children of Judah in Babylon. This was the experience of Christ and all the saints. Christ permitted Pilate and Herod to do to him what they would.[63] When Luther speaks of earthly labor, a striking gladness rests upon the very hardships that underlie his words. In these simple difficulties on earth there is fellowship with God's Son, who was mocked and buffeted. So, for example, one sees how Luther strives, in a sermon of 1531, to express the enigmatical fact: he who loves his neighbor is smitten on the mouth, and his purpose does not prosper; but in his very failure God is close by upon earth, active and strong.[64]

[62] *WA* 30[II], 193 (1529).

[63] *WA* 30[II], 193 and 194.

[64] *WA* 34[II], 181. This thought is even clearer in Luther's exposition of *The Magnificat*.

At times Luther seems to feel that earthly life as such helps man toward faith and love. But right away he sees that the worldly man, just as well as the monk, can turn away from all concern for his neighbor and make himself comfortable for his own sake, so that he no longer stands in need of faith in God. Observations such as these lead Luther to make concrete proposals for reforms of the life of society, in which, for instance, certain forms of business, etc. are condemned. Of special interest in this connection are Luther's statements about usury.

The kind of businessman who lives by lending money at interest to working people, is to Luther extremely objectionable, as objectionable as a monk. His position is quite like that of the monk: entire security for himself without the least labor (therefore no place for faith) and without regard for his neighbor (no place for love). He who receives the loan and accedes to the demand that he pay interest has to labor to make the principal productive; but in that labor he stands ceaselessly under the power of God *(Gottes Gewalt)*, amid a thousand dangers; death, sickness, water, fire, storm, hail, thunder, rain, wild beasts, and evil men.[65] The lender would certainly become aware of his insecurity if he himself, by his own toil, tried to make his money productive, instead of lending it. But he avoids insecurity by demanding a fixed interest on a given date (with the threat that otherwise he will deprive the borrower of his property which he has put up as collateral). In that situation the lender cannot pray in earnest that God give him daily bread; that necessity he himself has taken care of far in advance. Any person who does not know what insecurity is does not know

[65] *WA* 6, 56 (*Grosser Sermon von dem Wucher,* 1520).

35

what faith is.[66] Luther's proposal is that the lender receive
interest, not on the principal of the loan but on the profit
it earns for the borrower during a year. If catastrophe befall
the borrower, the lender will receive nothing.[67] If things turn
out well for the borrower, they also go well for the lender.
Both are in the same boat. The advantage to this perhaps
somewhat utopian proposal is that the rich person shares
the insecurity and is thereby driven to faith, while he enters
into real fellowship with the poor person, and is thereby
driven to love. Thus he is brought closer to a right relationship with both God and his neighbor. It is the same point
of view as the one Luther presents when he rates marriage
above the cloistered life. In marriage both faith and love
are promoted, whereas they are stifled in the cloister.

Through earthly and spiritual government God drives
men to good works and to faith. The earthly life as such
compels one to work for the good of one's neighbor, and
awakens prayer for help from God, as we see Luther has
said in contrasting marriage with the monastic life. Thus
there is a strong pull in all earthly orders to serve others.[68]
On the other hand, Luther can give heed to a concrete
form of earthly life, and propose reform to foster the same

[66] *WA* 6, 8 (*Kleiner Sermon von dem Wucher,* 1519). Cf. *WA* 15, 299,
where it is emphasized that God will keep us in continual uncertainty
about the future. This is the way God continues to be God. See also p.
300, "For that same reason, in the Lord's Prayer, he has bidden us to pray
only for our daily bread today.

"For we are to live and labor in fear, knowing that there is no time
when either life or goods are certain; we are rather to expect and accept
everything from his hands, for that is what true faith does" (*Von Kaufsshandlung und Wucher,* 1524).

[67] This is the position taken in *Kleiner Sermon von dem Wucher,* in
1519 (*WA* 6, 8); it is fully developed in the *Grosser Sermon* the next
year. (*WA* 6, 57). Luther's thought follows the same line when he condemns monopoly in *Von Kaufsshandlung und Wucher* in 1524 (*WA* 15.
299f, for example).

[68] *WA* 15, 625.

pull—love to one's neighbor and faith in God—as we have witnessed in what he says about usury. When the worldly order is reformed in the right way, its reform is in harmony with the pull God has built into it. This is manifestly not a static characteristic of earthly orders; it must ever be guided forward by law. Here an active quality enters into the realm of vocations which makes unchanging conservatism impossible. One might ask why such reshaping of the orders should be needed. The answer is apparent in the sight of measures resorted to by the greedy businessman, whose dealings are contrary to both faith and love. Here Luther sees a direct expression of the "power of darkness," or the devil: the usurer is in the hands of the devil.[69] In earthly orders God and the devil are both actively at work. Therefore these orders never stand still. They are always corrupted because men depart from God's will. But they are improved and reformed anew by God, among other things, in true Christian faith and love.

4. *Faith and Love*

In the foregoing we have repeatedly touched on faith and the new man, but always in particular ways. As man is crucified by the law, through the cross of his vocation, he is made alive and raised through faith in the gospel. As works go forth toward one's neighbor and the world, faith reaches up to God, to heaven. As works have this life in view, faith stretches forward to life after death, away from

[69] *WA* 15, 293 (*Von Kaufsshandlung und Wucher*); *WA* 6, 60 (*Grosser Sermon von dem Wucher*, 1520). In *An die Pfarrherrn wider den Wucher zu predigen* (1540), this dualistic aspect is very marked. See, for instance, *WA* 51, 340, "Everyone who lends and takes back more than he lent sins against God as a usurer. Even if he in that way does a service, he does it to the accursed devil."

the present. In his *Sermon vom Leiden und Kreuz,* of 1530,
Luther lays special stress on the forward-looking character
of faith.[70] The same idea is found in the often-repeated concept of *vivificatio* as the living Christ himself, since the
new man's *vivificatio* is resurrection, in the same way as
the old man's *mortificatio* is crucifixion. Thus the life of the
new man is resurrection and transition to heaven, just as
was the resurrection of Christ. It is therefore significant
that the concept of "transition" in the lectures on the Epistle
to the Hebrews includes three things: the resurrection of
Christ, our transition here from the old man to the new,
and our future bodily decease.[71] Bodily death is the death
of the old man and the life of the new, but it is also transition from earth to heaven.

The concept of justification also has an eschatological
meaning. The forgiveness of sins, as justification, implies
that it is only through the forgiveness of sins that man can
stand in the judgment—that is, the final judgment. Thus
the forgiveness of sins is the same as eternal life. Since it is
faith which receives the forgiveness of sins, faith is seen
to have an eschatological dimension. The righteousness of
faith means, in this connection, that conscience is free and
unafraid through the gospel, even though sin continues in
our bodies. Luther links the fearless conscience to the resurrection of Christ. Through the cross of Christ we come to
know our sin, making conscience tremble; but through the
resurrection of Christ the conscience is set free, since the

[70] *WA* 32, especially 31-36. The idea is basic to the whole treatise, and
cannot have been added by a later editor, as has been suggested.

[71] *WA* 57, 218, 223, 232. As to the line of thought see 131, "Anyone
who fears death, or is unwilling to die, is not Christian enough. He is
lacking in faith in the resurrection, and loves this life more than the
future." See also p. 132 (1517-18).

resurrection is victory over sin.[72] The sin over which Christ triumphs is our sin, the sin of all who believe. And the power of sin which Christ takes away is its power to accuse, the ability of sin to speak against us in the judgment after death.

Concerning this orientation of faith away from the world, Luther lays hold of faith at once when he interprets Psalm 102:8, about the bird alone on the housetop. With real poetic power he applies this reference to faith and its situation between heaven and earth. The world is like the sleeping house, on whose roof man climbs—he is not yet in heaven, but neither is he on earth. He hovers "alone in faith" between the life of this world and eternal life.[73] Very revealing too is the distinction between soul and spirit in *The Magnificat*. The soul gives life to the body and busies itself, not with the incomprehensible, but with things that fall within the competency of reason. But the spirit is a habitation for faith and the Word of God, and its activity is to "lay hold of incomprehensible, invisible, eternal things."[74]

In another context Luther specifies the corruption of the cloistered life, saying that it "entices man," i.e., away from faith, and "dissipates him upon temporal and external things." But through faith he breaks away from the external and earthly, and flees naked to God. "There is nothing higher or more inward in character than faith; for it clings to God's Word and is stripped naked of everything which is not the Word of God."[75]

[72] *WA* 2, 139-140 (*Sermon von der Betrachtung des heiligen Leidens Christi,* 1519).

[73] *WA* 1, 199 (*Die Sieben Busspsalmen,* 1517). The exposition is the same in the second edition, 1525 (*WA* 18, 511).

[74] *WA* 7, 550-551 (1521).

[75] *WA* 12, 107 (*Exposition of I Corinthians 7,* 1523).

Faith flees from the world and from works, from the law to the heavenly kingdom of the gospel. We ask now: how is it possible for such a faith to be active in love, i.e., in works toward our neighbors on earth? In other words, why does this faith willingly descend to the realm which is otherwise ruled by law, the realm of works, the earthly kingdom?

In two studies of Luther's concept of vocation which were made in the current century, Luther was criticized on just this point, and it was the chief criticism in both cases. Eger returns to this point again and again in stereotyped formulations in *Die Anschauungen Luthers vom Beruf* of 1900: Luther has affirmed that faith and love hang together, but he has never demonstrated it. "Serious consequences followed from the theoretical lack of a systematic relationship between justifying faith and the fulfilment of vocation in the service of love." Luther is satisfied with the "affirmation that the one cannot be without the other." Therefore all work in the vocations becomes something that runs its own course, side by side with faith and relationship with God. Vocation does not get its character from faith, but exists as a ready-made, inflexible entity. So too, Schifferdecker, in his *Der Berufsgedanke bei Luther,* of 1932, says, "The necessary inner unity between faith and the power proceeding therefrom for action in vocation Luther has not been able to establish." Vocation threatens to become an independent sphere, with given unchanging norms. Is that true to Luther?

It is true that faith flies from works and rests in God. But of that repose in God Luther says, "Only he who has experienced this, and none other, can realize how strongly such a trust draws one away from the evil and drives one

to the good."[76] That is important, because it shows that
faith's activity in the direction of works is entirely unexpected. In him who has received the gospel in his heart,
there dwells love for his neighbor, a fact at which he is
surprised. If Luther had shown by logical principles how
faith must express itself in love, as Eger and Schifferdecker
desire, he would not have developed his view more system-
atically. Rather, he would have replaced the reality of God
with an intellectual construction and denied the miraculous
character of something which is a miracle. Luther knew
very well what he was doing when he merely asserted the
relationship between faith and love without proving it. That
faith is coupled with love is in fact the same miracle as
that in which God became man. God is blessed in his
heaven. Why did he come down to earth in Christ who
loved people and suffered death on the cross? God is like
that. Faith is blessed in its heaven. Why is it that faith
does not stop there, but becomes love which is concerned
about a neighbor? Faith is God, and God is like that.[77]
In his *Large Commentary on Galatians,* faith and the deity
of Christ are placed together this way on one side. "Faith
is the divine nature of works and it is poured out in works
even as in Christ the divine nature is poured out in the
human." On the other side he sets love and the humanity
of Christ. When faith works in love, it descends and is
incarnated, as God became man in Christ. "Therefore faith
forever justifies and makes alive, but it does not remain
alone, i.e. idle . . . but it is incarnated and becomes man,
that is, it does not remain idle or devoid of love."[78] "Makes

[76] *WA* 5, 459 (*Operationes in Psalmos,* 1519-21).
[77] *WA* 36, 423f.
[78] *WA* 40^{I}, 417, and 427.

41

alive" is bracketed with "justifies," not with works! *Vivifi-catio* is resurrection, and thus it is transition from earth to heaven. To come down to earth is another thing, in-carnation.

Through faith we become sons of God, he says in his *Fastenpostille;* but through love we serve our neighbors, just as he who is first among the sons of God took the form of a servant.[79] The love that breaks forth in faith remains for Luther, to a certain extent, something incomprehensible and unexplainable, for we cannot give any explanation or reason for God's love. When Eger and Schifferdecker looked for proof in place of affirmation, they were attempting to run down an inconsistency in Luther's thought; but significantly enough they found none.

Luther speaks of God as being present in faith, more often of Christ as active in faith, but most frequently of the Spirit. In his *Treatise on Christian Liberty,* the main thought is that a Christian lives in Christ through faith and in his neighbor through love.[80] Just as it is Christ who comes in with his gospel, so the Spirit is given when one listens in faith to the gospel, and in the Holy Spirit loves his neighbor sincerely and unfeignedly, so that he would willingly bear his burdens.[81] Karl Thieme has seen clearly this characteristic in Luther's belief. But in *Die Sittliche Triebkraft des Glaubens* (1895), he refrains from taking up this thought of Luther's that God, Christ and the Spirit are active in faith. He explains that it is his purpose in this study to make clear that love of neighbor proceeds "imme-

[79] *WA* 17^{II}, 74-75 (1525).

[80] *WA* 7, 38ff (1520); cf. *WA* 40^{I}, 229: Faith is the cloud in the heart, which veils Christ's presence there (*Commentary on Galatians,* 1535).

[81] *WA* 17^{II}, 53 (*Fastenpostille,* 1525), 10^{I}, 1, 361ff (*Kirchenpostille,* 1522), 40^{I}, 312f, and 40^{I}, 336 (*Commentary on Galatians,* 1535).

diately from faith itself," as far as that can be done from Luther's writings. That is attempting a psychological explanation. Thereby Thieme's investigation is manifestly misled, particularly on the main point suggested by the title of his work—though on other points he has much to teach about Luther's ethics. Perhaps Thieme's distorted way of explaining the emergence of love from faith helped to produce Eger's view that the relation of faith and love is very unclear in Luther's thought. It seems that modern investigators in general have difficulty with Luther's statements about God, the Spirit, and Christ being really present in the Christian's faith and love.

This can be due to a misunderstanding. It is doubtless a misinterpretation of Luther to understand his statements as meaning that the emergence of love from faith can be introspectively apprehended as a discovery of God or Christ within the soul. Man does indeed find something, but not that. He finds only that he is glad for his neighbor, and love breaks through. The forgiveness of sins is given through the gospel, and with it, "life and salvation." In faith, which accepts the gift, man finds that it is not only "heaven that is pure with its stars, where Christ reigns in his work," but that earth too is clean "with its trees and its grass, where we are at home with all that is ours."[82]

There is nothing more delightful and lovable on earth than one's neighbor. Love does not think about doing works, it finds joy in people; and when something good is done for others, that does not appear to love as works but simply as gifts which flow naturally from love. Love never does something because it has to. It is permitted to act. And earth "with its trees and grass" is the site of man's voca-

[82] WA 36, 370.

43

tion. He who has the Holy Spirit knows it by the fact, among others, that in faith and gladness he fulfils his vocation.[83] He rejoices in his labor.

When a person gladly gives his endeavors to his earthly tasks, filling his neighbor's needs and attending to his vocation, then love from God or Christ is active, then the Spirit is present. Finding love is thus the same thing as finding both neighbor and vocation to be something in which one can live with joy. Our interest is not in our love; it is our neighbor and the vocation to which our interest is directed.

In his *Treatise on Good Works*, Luther compares faith's power in love with the health of a well person.[84] A person's health shows itself in all his doings; it consists of outreaching functions, even though he who acts does not consciously ascribe his actions to his health. But when he falls ill, he notices that he is unable to do the things he formerly did. In like manner love ceases when faith ceases. Christ and the Spirit have departed. Then man stands under the law, and his vocation weighs upon him with its demands. His vocation is then a cross, not a joy.

Against Holl's differentiation between *lex naturae* and the commandment of Christian love as something higher, H. M. Müller pointed out that the *commandment* of Christian love is identical with *lex naturae*. It is not these that are to be differentiated, but the love commandment (law) and spontaneously active love (that which is specifically Christian). Franz Lau, in a critique of Müller, presses the thesis against Holl that according to Luther Christian living is only faith, not works at all, not even works in love. In

[83] *WA* 40I, 577f (*Commentary on Galatians*, 1535). And in *Kirchenpostille*, for example, Luther speaks very often about joy in vocation.
[84] *WA* 6, 213 (1520).

Lau's presentation we again see faith as flight from earth, upreach to heaven, aloneness before God, waiting for death. All this is purely Lutheran. But if we have nothing more to say, we have not completely represented Luther. Are we able to say more, to say something ethical about faith, without bringing in thoughts not true to Luther, as Holl does? If I say that in faith I receive the righteousness of God and this righteousness subsequently appears in my works for my neighbor, that would be the view Luther rejects in what he wrote against Latomus.

"Therefore I say: The law of the Decalogue is indeed good, if it is kept, i.e. if you have faith, which is the fulfilment of the law and righteousness; actually it means death and wrath to you, and is not good, if you do not keep it, if you do not have faith, however much you do its works; for the righteousness of the law, not only that of the ceremonial law, but even that of the Decalogue, is impure and has been done away with by Christ; for it is specifically the covering of the face of Moses, which the glory of faith removes. So ceremonial of whatever kind is good if you follow it, not limited to works, but kept in faith, i.e. if you perform it in the knowledge that righteousness lies not in works but in faith." [85]

Only as the old man, still under the law, does the Christian ask about the righteousness of his works. Faith and the new man knows only one righteousness: the forgiveness of sins. It is his neighbor in whom the new man finds his joy. That which takes place between him and his neighbor is not works, the righteousness of which is of concern to him; he does not ask about the worth of what he does. He sees only a neighbor who awakens gladness in him.

[85] *WA* 8, 71 (*Rationis Latomianae confutatio*, 1521).

45

In the last day everything that has been done in love for others will be made manifest (Matt. 25). On earth it is not noted, so to speak. Vocation is ethically cleansing because in modesty it helps one not to let the left hand know what the right hand does. Such inner freedom from works the monk can never have.[86]

It is the neighbor who stands at the center of Luther's ethics, not God's kingdom or God's law or "character." Vocation and law benefit the neighbor, as does love born of faith. The same God works through both, in law and vocation without his Spirit, in love born of faith with his Spirit.

Love born of faith and the Spirit effects a complete breakthrough of the boundary between the two kingdoms, the wall of partition between heaven and earth, as did God's incarnation in Christ. Man "descends from heaven like rain that makes the earth fruitful." Indeed it is expressly said that he "steps forth into another kingdom *(aliud regnum)* and does the good works his hands find to do." This kingdom is the kingdom of vocation and earthly government, where now as a new man he works "with willing spirit and joy in his vocation," submitting himself in love to stern authority.[87] This is not really a new kingdom; as an "old" man he has always lived in it, governed by law. Law, as it is embodied in the many offices, had the function, in the hand of God, to compel man to serve others, whether or not he wished to do so. His station, his vocation, operates

---

[86] Cf. *WA* 6, 45 (*Grosser Sermon von dem Wucher*, 1520), *WA* 6, 105 (*The Fourteen of Consolation*, 1520), *WA* 6, 253f (*Treatise on Good Works*, 1520), *WA* 17[II], 99f (*Fastenpostille*, 1525, an illuminating passage), *WA* 23, 345, 363 (*Ob man vor dem Sterben fliehen moege*, 1527), *WA* 8, 625f (*De votis monasticis*, 1521), *WA* 30[II], 543 (*Sermon on Keeping Children in School*, 1530).

[87] *WA* 40[I], 51 (*Commentary on Galatians*, 1535).

with coercion, without his heart. But now, in faith and the gospel, the heart has been made new. Our neighbor with his need does not press upon us against our will; rather he fills us with gladness, for it is our joy to serve him.[88] What earthly government would compel we now do freely. So love works on earth, in the realm of the law, yet it is not aware of any law. Heaven is on earth. The boundary between heaven and earth has been bridged in this descent. Faith transfers to love the freedom from law it had in heaven, so that love on earth carries with it faith's own freedom from law.

To be sure, the law seeks to bring love under its control and prescribe for it rules and suitable ways of dealing with the neighbor, which befit a Christian. The law would like to "make of love a servant girl" instead of the queen which it really is. But what chance does the law have? Its business is to compel (grudging) attention to one's neighbor. Before love which regards the neighbor as a winsome reality, the law has to step aside inoffensively.

Love "overcomes all circumstances," as Luther says ceaselessly.[89] It gladly does what vocation calls for, seeing that faithful work benefits the neighbor. With clear eye it also sees immediately when, for the neighbor's sake, old practices must give way to something new. And in love God is active with his Spirit, the same God who established social orders. Now he changes these, alters his world, and

[88] Luther uses the illustration of two good friends between whom all good things are done without rules: "There is no law, no code, no compulsion, no necessity, but pure freedom and favor." Christian love looks upon every other person as such a friend; cf. *WA* 10[I], 2, 178 (*Adventspostille*, 1522). Where pure love is lacking, the Christian is a sinner and under the law. Luther's "pessimistic" view of man rests on the fact that he has a higher conception of love than do his idealistic critics who regard a person noble if he answers attack upon himself by doing the good.

[89] See, for example, *WA* 17[II], 95 (*Fastenpostille*, 1525).

47

refashions vocation. The earthly creation is made new and living through love in the new man. God descends from heaven and transforms the earth, now here, now there, as faith and love *(Glaube und Liebe)* appear through the church's preaching of the gospel, through the spiritual realm. The task of the church includes a continuing renewal of the worldly orders, a never-ending alertness in all vocations, from the princely to the meanest labor.[90]

Luther is very modest about giving directions for reform of the world. He offers no program. There is a basic reason for this which is consistent with many aspects of his faith; he is convinced that the devil is still present as change for the better is made; and his concept of sin proclaims that there are no sinful orders apart from sinful people.[91] We will consider only a single characteristic of Luther's view, by which every ethical program is upheld.

Eger and Schifferdecker insisted that Luther never shows clearly the relation between faith and love, meaning that Luther never gives a comprehensive description of the new man's love for his neighbor and its concrete expression. In his *Adventspostille* Luther explains why he has intentionally avoided that. In his sermon on the First Sunday in Advent he defines love as giving oneself to one's neighbor. "Maybe you ask now what good works you are to to for your neighbor. The answer is that they cannot be named." Christ's work for us is not divided into parts; it is

[90] *WA* 30^{II}, 537-538 (*Sermon on Keeping Children in School,* 1530). The world is changed through the fruit which the gospel bears. In addition, the church preaches the law, which implies the inclusion of all stations and vocations in the church.

[91] Luther holds that if his proposed reform in investment for interest were adopted, selfishness would begin to express itself frightfully in the borrowers, whose hands would be left free. The struggle of the Word against the sin of man never ceases on earth; only in heaven will it end. Cf. *WA* 15, 302 (*Von Kaufshandlung und Wucher,* 1524).

an entirety which included death on the cross. Love is like
that.[92] Love discovers for itself what is of the greatest benefit
to a neighbor. It cannot busy itself with deeds prescribed
by rules of propriety without ceasing to be love. It becomes
a bondage under law, concern with one's own holiness,
which, uncertain of salvation, seeks to achieve certainty by
requiring sacrifice for a neighbor. It has names for all works,
each more formidable than the next. Such sporadic "love"
does not live in childlike faith; therefore it lacks the Spirit's
certainty. It is not love, because its first interest is not a
neighbor's need, but the salvation of one's own soul.

Further on in the same postil, Luther explains that the
only thing necessary is *Glaube und Liebe* (faith and love).
All else is left freely for love to do or not to do, as it deals
with one neighbor or another. "Especially as only faith
and love are necessary. Everything else is at your liberty,
to do or to leave undone. Therefore you may do everything in one case, and leave all undone in another, and by
so doing make yourself equal towards all."[93] This variable
action, to do or to leave undone, which freedom finds in
the law, depends upon one's neighbor. The sentence, "according to what society requires" (p. 176) has the same
meaning.

Here we see clearly the central role the neighbor plays
in Luther's ethics. Where there is love, there is no legal
rigidity. Love's action may proceed in keeping with usual
practice or against it. It acts according to a principle which
cannot be construed in advance, but which makes its decision afresh in the light of the need of the neighbor, who

[92] *WA* 10^I, 2, 38 (1522). This passage has doubtless suffered redaction,
but the thought about love's unnamed works fits very well with genuine
Luther sources.

[93] *WA* 10^I, 2, 175.

steadily changes, bearing now one burden and then another.[94] All these works, ever fresh and changing, Luther assigns to vocation, to the relation between husband and wife, parents and children, master and servant, ruler and subject.[95]

Love born of faith and the Spirit is notably obvious, though Luther shows a certain shyness about describing it in detail. He fears that such a description is in danger of being made a law which "names" all works, a substitute for the relationship to God from which his new creation will flow out through love's inexhaustible richness of discovery in all offices and vocations. Probably what Eger and Schifferdecker expected from Luther was just such a programmatic description, that is, a law for the new man. This they did not find, for the new man has no law. Only the old man has that.

5. *Cross and Desperation*

In our exposition of love born of faith, many things have been barred as not pertaining to it: anxiety about the deficient righteousness of our own works; obedience to God's command against the heart's desire; a forced friendliness toward a neighbor who is displeasing to us; and faithfulness in work which we do with distaste. Luther does not, of course, thereby simply bar all such things from the life of a Christian. He very energetically calls for them, but he warns that they shall not be called love or taken as evidence of the new man. All this, comprehended in the term law, Luther proclaims with as much force as he does the

[94] Luther's expressions as to "time" and "hour" will come in for discussion at the end of our investigation.
[95] *WA* 10^I, 2, 41.

gospel; but he preaches it for the Christian as the old man, the "sinner."

Faith, or the conscience, is in heaven; and since not law but gospel rules in heaven, no sin is there. There is sin only where there is law.[96] On earth law and worldly government rule; and there too is the body of man which must be crucified with its sinful lusts. In his *Rationis Latomianae Confutatio,* Luther discusses with warmth this double aspect of man (*WA* 8, especially pp. 103-107).

As several have noted, Luther's terminology here departs from that which he usually employs. But the line of thought is familiar from acquaintance with the *Large Commentary on Galatians:* the conscience is free, but the body is simultaneously engaged in continual battle against sin. In God, divine wrath and divine favor contend. If divine favor *(gratia Dei* or *favor Dei)* wins over divine wrath, the victory is total; *ira Dei* (the wrath of God) is wiped out. "Whom God receives in grace he receives completely, and whom he favors he favors completely. On the other hand, against him with whom he is angry he is completely angry."[97] In man "below," *corruptio naturae* (corruption of nature) prevails. As the remedy against destruction God bestows gifts through which man can slowly be restored. Recovery will not be complete, Luther repeatedly says, before our death and resurrection. "All things are forgiven through grace, but all things are not yet corrected by that gift."[98] Faith, remarkably enough, belongs to that gift. The sphere where the long battle must be fought little by little is called *internum,* whereas the relation to God is called

[96] *WA* 19, 205f (*Exposition of Jonah,* 1526): "Where law cannot exist, there can be neither sin nor injustice." Clearer still is p. 248.
[97] *WA* 8, 106f (1521).
[98] *WA* 8, 107.

externum. This is directly opposite to Luther's usual mode of expression.

Even while man contends on earth with a specific outer sin which is hard for him to master, that sin is forgiven in heaven, before God. The battle lies outside of the conscience and leaves faith undisturbed, since it rests secure in God's promise. Sin is resisted in such a way that man is not cast into despair; the outcome is certain, through God's word about eternal life after death. If a man cannot believe that the sin with which he struggles is forgiven, the law has risen up in the conscience (that is, in heaven) and faith gives way to works before God. Then eternal life does not depend on God's promise but on man's progress in the battle against his sin. That is desperation.

This desperation increases the earnestness of the battle against sin, and prepares man to see the great miracle in the gospel when at length it comes back and makes the conscience free and calm. God wills the agony of the Christian which enters into the crucifixion of the old man, for crucifixion is fellowship with Christ, and Christ endured the agony of despair on the cross. In his earlier writings Luther exhorts us to seek the cross and hardships. In his *Treatise on Good Works,* in 1520, Luther still divides the death of the old man into two parts: that which we bring upon ourselves and that to which we are subject by reason of the connection our lives have with the lives of others.[99] This is a remnant of Luther's pre-Reformation thought. We miss the attack on a self-chosen and self-imposed cross found in his later and more detailed expositions of the Christian's cross. The fanatics excelled at putting on a furrowed countenance. With Luther's perception of this new

[99] *WA* 6, 244f.

monastic spirit in evangelical circles came the end of his commendation of self-chosen crosses. The cross is not to be chosen by us; it is laid upon us by God, i.e. the cross comes to us uninvoked in our vocation.[1]

Otto Ritschl, in using the term *theologia crucis* to characterize Luther's pre-Reformation theology, makes the concept of the cross the criterion in distinguishing between the pre-Reformation and the mature Luther. He says the mature Luther makes vocation central in place of the cross. In keeping with this Ritschl presents it as something new and peculiar to Melanchthon that the cross should appear in vocation and be coupled with it. Against this interpretation it must be affirmed that from the beginning vocation was viewed as a means of making the cross real in the life of the Christian. This view was already in Luther's basic utterances on vocation about 1520.[2] Apparently Ritschl had observed this himself, though he chose not to regard it as significant in his systematic exposition. He used the term "theology of the cross" only in reference to the pre-Reformation period, during which Luther had also spoken positively about self-chosen suffering.

Since Ritschl wrote in 1912, Luther research has completely reversed itself on this point. Walther von Löwenich, for example, uses *theologia crucis* as the descriptive title for Luther's whole outlook. Other scholars have also seen the cross as the center of Luther's theology, men like Erich Vogelsang, Erich Seeberg, and Eduard Ellwein. Unfortunately this shift seems to involve an overemphasis on the

[1] *WA* 27, 466-467 (*Sermons*, 1528; Rörer), and *WA* 34^I, 355f (*Sermons*, 1531; Rörer); also *WA* 40^{II}, 72 (*Commentary on Galatians*, 1535).
[2] We do not deny that this idea is found even oftener in Melanchthon.

53

young Luther. In modern literature about Luther, hardly a word appears about the strong stress the mature Luther places on vocation as the place where God himself lets the cross take form.

This coincides with a deficiency common in later Luther research. Faith is discussed thoroughly without simultaneously considering *love;* relation with God is discussed without at the same time considering relations with our *fellow-man.* Faith and love move in different directions. God and one's neighbor are two different focal points. But the Christian lives at once in relation with God and with his neighbor, in heaven and on earth. We cannot isolate man's relationship with God, speaking only of faith and overlooking man's relationship with his neighbor.

When Luther declares that works fulfil a role, not before God, but only before men, this is another side of the fact that the Christian's cross effects nothing in his relationship with God, but is relevant to his relationship with his neighbor, to vocation. Before God, a self-imposed cross belongs in the category of works. Its motivation is not the need of one's neighbor, but one's own desire to attain holiness. The cross does not disappear from Luther's maturing theology any more than do works, but the cross, works, and office are confined to earth and one's neighbor, and excluded from heaven.

Luther insists that Christ commands us to do such works "as concern people here below who are in need, not those that concern God or angels. Therefore the Christian life does not consist of that which such men as monks invent; it does not drive people into the wilderness or cloister. It is Satan who commands you to forsake men. On the contrary, the Christian life sends you to people, to those that need your works."[3]

This side of Luther's "theology of the cross" cannot come into its full right as long as relationship with God is viewed as it now is in much of the newer German literature in this field. The nature of the cross for the Christian is thought to consist more of distress of thought, a perpetual bankruptcy of reason, than of concrete and tangible hardships which arise in vocation and purely earthly matters.

A good exposition of what is meant by the old and the new man is found in the concluding discussion about baptism in Luther's *Large Catechism* (1529). The old man is characterized by wrath, envy, greed, laziness, pride, unbelief, and such obvious sins, which manifestly constitute an encumbrance on vocation and one's neighbor. When the demand of vocation and of neighbor is laid upon the old man, he is made amenable. These sins are repressed and give place to a gentle and patient new man, who receives his life from God's hand. In daily activity baptism is realized as a daily repentance.[4] Thus the Christian is both old and new man, not only in relation to God's judgment, God's forgiveness, but also in his encounter with vocation and neighbor. He is still the old man, insofar as the encounter irritates him, and new man when the encounter takes place with inner calm and joy. Since the neighbor is not just one person but many at any given time, and since

[3] *WA* 29, 403 (*Sermons*, 1529; Rörer). In his *Fastenpostille*, he denies any merit in our cross-bearing and our suffering, i.e. the cross counts for nothing before God; there it is one with faith. The cross has its place in love. In relation to his neighbor, the Christian travels "on the way of love and of the cross." *WA* 17[II], 173, 175 (1525). Cf. *WA* 39[I], 93f: "Before God faith is in place, not works; before men works and love are in place." (*Disputatio de iustificatione*, 1536).

[4] *WA* 30[I], 220-222. Compare the answer to the question in the Small Catechism, "What does such baptizing with water signify?"

vocation has many ramifications, the complete interplay of life's changing situations is tied into relationship with God. In this is the real meaning of the expression *simul iustus et peccator* (righteous and sinner at the same time).

In his treatise *Wider die himmlischen Propheten*, Luther, contrary to his usual practice, sums up his entire outlook on these six points: the second use of the law; the gospel; the judgment (the work of the old man unto death); love of neighbor; the first use of the law (worldly government); Christian freedom.[5] The slaying of the old man, the cross, holds a central place in the evangelical instruction of the people. In describing how the old man ought to be stifled and subdued, Luther uses all the details of the crucifixion of Christ. The irritable and proud nature in us ought to be bound, scorned, cursed, scoffed, crowned with thorns, etc., and finally die. This last takes place in bodily death.[6] If a person is in earnest in acknowledging his sinfulness, he does not begin to complain of sickness, slander, and the like. All this he accepts from the hand of God.[7] The same attitude is to be taken toward poor rulers: a person cannot usually have a worse ruler than he deserves.[8] Thus different aspects of external circumstances serve their function in the crucifixion of the old man. "These are true morti-

[5] *WA* 18, 65-66 (1525). The entire discussion is directed against Carlstadt and the enthusiasts, who teach error about mortification of the flesh: "These false prophets do not deal in the right way even with these mortifications; for they do not accept what God inflicts upon them, but what they choose themselves—they wear grey coats, try to appear as peasants, and do many other foolish things." (65f.)

[6] *WA* 1, 337 (*Sermo I de passione Christi*, 1518).

[7] *WA* 56, 231-233 (*Commentary on Romans*, 1515-16). It is very unusual for one to be in earnest when he confesses his sin. In the *Commentary on Romans* the ecclesiastical prelate or the superior in the cloister acts as the bearer of discipline, which is later accorded to social and political order. See, e.g., *WA* 56, 251-252.

[8] *WA* 19, 637 (*Whether Soldiers Too Can Be Saved*, 1526).

fications, not in deserted places apart from the company of people, but right in the social and political order."[9]

It is in the external and earthly that the slaying of the flesh is to be effected; the crucifixion of Christ was certainly not something inward and refined. Fellowship with Christ is realized in something apparently very unspiritual, just as Word and sacrament, which are the risen life of Christ to us, appear unspiritual and external.

So man is slain through cross and suffering, and raised through the gospel or, through the church, born a new creature. The cross of Christ is grouped with the law, the old man, vocation, the earth. But the resurrection of Christ belongs with the gospel, the new man, the church, heaven. The old man is to be crucified and slain by the law, which in earthly life has taken form through worldly government. We are disciplined in vocation, in labor, and in the demands of social life. Vocation is earthly, just as shockingly earthly as the humanity of Christ, apparently so void of all divinity. In the crucifixion of Christ the divine nature was only hidden, not absent; it was present in the lowly form of love for robbers and soldiers.

Similarly God conceals his work of love to men in cross-marked vocation which is really of benefit to the neighbor. In Christ's victory on the cross, which looks so poor—love's victory in lowliness—God is hidden; therefore the resurrection takes place on the third day. Now Christ's victory is proffered through the gospel to sorely tried man, who in the labors of his vocation undergoes the crucifixion of his

[9] *WA* 43, 214 (*Commentary on Genesis,* 1535-45). Cf. the entire treatise *Vom ehelichen Leben,* 1522, where *mortificatio* within the social order is described (*WA* 10^{II}, 267f); also the burdens of a ruling prince, in the *Treatise on Secular Authority,* 1523, where the worldly regime is described (*WA* 11, 229f, especially 278f): "The cross will soon rest on the neck of such ventures."

old nature. Through faith in the gospel I arise as a new
man, born of the church, in hope possessing heaven and
eternal life beyond bodily death.[10]

From the roughness of earthly life there opens up a vista
of life and freedom in the coming kingdom, and only one
way leads to it—subjection to the cross here. Through the
cross Jesus came to Easter, and only in him are life and
resurrection to be found. So Luther can connect the
commonplace hardships of marriage, for example, with our
certainty of eternal life after death.[11] Since the body is to
be raised, we live in our vocation, in which, by bearing
the cross, the body is carried forward on the way whose
end is the resurrection. Since man is at the same time both
old nature and new, both crucifixion and resurrection are
already on the way to realization. Man is embraced in the
process which makes of him two beings, even while he is
psychologically one and entire. If a person is convalescing
from an illness, he is not divided into two psychic subjects,
one sick and the other well. He is a single individual, embraced in a process which leads out of one condition into
another, out of sickness into health.[12] To begin with, he is
simply sick; later sickness and health contend; and finally
he becomes well. Similarly man is at first simply sinner.
Through the work of Christ he enters into a life in which
he is *simul iustus et peccator*. Finally comes full recovery
in the death of the body, when man's crucified body is
raised in the resurrection as wholly righteous. Then the
time of earth is over, and heaven is reached. The age of
the law is ended. Vocation, office, orders, the cross are

[10] *WA* 40[I], 443-445, Cf. 662f and 40[II], 170-173 (*Commentary on
Galatians, 1535*).

[11] *WA* 12, 93 (*Exposition of I Corinthians 7, 1523*).

[12] *WA* 56, 343 and 350-351 (*Commentary on Romans, 1515-16*).

past. The old man is taken up in the new man, who is now new and holy even in body and not just in conscience, as was the case during the earthly struggle. Living the purely earthly life, as man does, means to faith a life with eschatological reference. Man's ordinary life is, in its very ordinariness, a life that reaches out beyond earth when the church's message of heaven is proclaimed through the labor of vocation.

As has been said several times, the law or works have no role to fill in conscience or before God. It was pointed out in this section that desperation and doubt arise when the law intrudes into conscience; that God wills this, because he wills the crucifixion of the old man. This peculiar paradox needs further discussion, and it fits well in this discussion of the second use of the law.

The old man cannot be crucified except through the dread which the law lays upon the conscience. It is Passion Week and Good Friday; but "now we come to Easter and the resurrection of Christ," through which all sin is overcome. If we cast our sins upon him who arose, we can, in simple faith freed from responsibility, "make the conscience free."[13] The conscience is set free through the gospel.

Runestam, in his doctoral dissertation, pointed out the noteworthy character of Luther's doctrine of the political use *(usus politicus)* of the law. "Here we come to the ultimate point in Luther's doctrine of the freedom of conscience from the law, and to the point where contradictions appear to pile up. He—Luther—says that Christ has banished the law from the conscience or already removed the wrath of God from it, just as he denies the law any right to oppress the conscience, however much it may rule over

[13] *WA* 2, 139-140 (*Sermon von der Betrachtung des heiligen Leidens Christi,* 1519).

the body and the flesh. And yet it is in the conscience that the law is to fulfil its most important role, its *usus Theologicus seu Spiritualis* (theological or spiritual use), the awakening of sin. It is in the conscience after all that the law is to operate—and thereby effect a good work—in the conscience where it is the uninvited guest."

The two uses of the law are set forth most fully in Luther's *Large Commentary on Galatians*.[14] Its first function is to hold coarse and dangerous people in check. Here the law appears as earthly government. When the body of a Christian is said to stand under the law, this also implies the civil or political use of the law. There the combat against sin goes on all the time, below the level of conscience; and neither fear nor trembling holds sway. The second use of the law is to cause anguish and to increase the sense of sin in the conscience, to crush all security. Then man cannot see it otherwise than that his eternal life after death depends on his works on earth. In that way the law rules both in heaven and on earth. Works count not only on earth and with one's neighbor; they have claimed position before God, and there obliterate faith and trust. This is the spiritual or theological use of the law, the terror of conscience which is not an end in itself but a preparation for the entry of the gospel into the conscience, and the retreat of the law to the body.[15] Grace would not be grace without prior terror of conscience.

[14] *WA* 40I, 429f, 479f, 528f (1535).

[15] Furthermore the terror of conscience deepens man's earnestness in the battle against sin. Hence it is not final in the same sense as faith is. In the conscience (faith) the law is to depart, after contrition has been awakened, giving room to the gospel. In the body, the law is to continue its combat with sin. The deepening of earnestness in the struggle against sin is thus a function of this spiritual anxiety, beyond the ordinary use of the law.

Man is not able to let his civil righteousness, in all modesty, be something which God has effected on earth through man's vocation. Inwardly he exalts himself above others because of it. That is letting good works lift themselves up to heaven; so man feels no need of forgiveness of sins. God must, by means of the law, establish the right order; and that can take place only through the awakening of dread (that is, the sense of need for forgiveness) in the conscience.[16]

Hereby Christ comes to man in the gospel, just as he came to earth, when he became man and suffered and arose. Again and again Luther stresses the fact that what happened historically through Christ now happens daily to every Christian in a spiritual way. "What is done in history and according to the time when Christ came, whereby the law was abolished and liberty and eternal life brought to light, is done spiritually every day in every Christian, in whom is found alternately, now the time of the law, and now the time of grace."[17]

Given through the law and the gospel is that salvation which Christ gained through his cross and resurrection. In this way, according to Luther, the law is God's "strange" work, which holds the gospel in prospect; and the gospel is God's "proper" work (opus proprium), his "own" work. The function of the law is thus twofold, civil and spiritual. The first is the ordinary function of the law (on earth, ruling the body), while the second is the entry of the law into an area other than its own (before God, in the conscience). Peculiarly enough it is the second which is the

[16] Cf. WA 40^I, 224-225 (Commentary on Galatians, 1531; Rörer).

[17] WA 40^I, 523-524 (Commentary on Galatians, 1535). See also 492f and 550-551.

61

law's "right" and "proper" task.[18] Here we note again the eschatological foundation of Luther's thought. The function of the law in promoting order on earth is subordinate and unimportant in comparison with its work of disturbing and driving man to the gospel in prayer, of leading us forward on the way from earth to heaven.

Through pride in his works on earth man had blotted out the gospel from his conscience, since he had no need for the forgiveness of sins. Now the law, driving him to terror, prepares anew a place for the gospel in his heart. Now the gospel, faith, and the Spirit, and the new man are living, since the old man and his pride are broken. Man humbly bows down under his vocation. He performs his work in keeping with his vocation, a poor and lowly work, but pleasing to God when done "in faith, in joy of heart, in obedience and gratitude to God."[19] We refer in this connection to what we said in the preceding section about faith and love, about the new man's joy and release from compulsion.

There we tried to show that the works of the new man, directed toward the earth and set free from the law, break through the boundary between heaven and earth. The freedom of the gospel in the conscience also confers freedom on the actions which love, by the Spirit, does in the realm which otherwise is under the rule of the law, the earthly kingdom, the realm of neighbor and vocation. Here we

[18] *WA* 40[I], 482: "the peculiar and absolute use of the law." Cf. 499 and 512: "if you have perceived the true and proper use of the law"; 520: "This is the true and particular use of the law"; 534: "The civil use of the law is good and necessary, but the theological use is the peculiar and the highest use," cf. 612 (*Commentary on Galatians*, 1535). That even one is brought onward toward heaven is more important than order and peace for all others on earth; cf. *ibid.*, 40[I], 644-645. See also *WA* 19, 247 (*Exposition of Jonah*, 1526).

[19] *WA* 40[I], 573-574 (*Commentary on Galatians*, 1535).

have attempted to show that the second use of the law includes a breakthrough heavenward of the boundary between the two kingdoms.[20] In the desperation of doubt, there is nothing but law in heaven and earth; conscience suffers under the law, whose task is properly to rule the body. God wills it so. The *usus spiritualis* of the law is, as the term implies, the work of the Holy Spirit. This is the law's loftiest and noblest task. In this way, in his opposition to the devil, God refashions that which he himself instituted. For man himself, without faith and without need for forgiveness of sins (man in the hands of the *devil*), by sheer pride in his own works removed the gospel from its throne. Therefore God must give the law permission to overstep its boundary and "with lightning inflame and destroy the wild beast."[21] The dualism of God and Satan comes to the fore both in Christ's redemptive work and in man's battle of faith.

6. *Relationship with God, and Vocation*

In the conclusion of *Vom Abendmahl Christi* (1528), Luther sums up his doctrine in an impressive confession. There vocation is accorded its place in the profession of three "holy orders and true institutions, established by God": the office of the ministry, marriage, and earthly government.[22] If there were only these three "hierarchies" and nothing more, vocations would stay fixed and unchanging within the walls of the three. But above these three "foundations and orders" there is an inclusive establishment into

---

[20] Here we use improperly the expressions first and second uses of the law. Luther himself does not say "first" and "second," but civil or political use and spiritual or theological use. Any use of the law beyond these two Luther does not recognize.

[21] *WA* 40I, 482 (*Commentary on Galatians, 1535*).

[22] *WA* 26, 504f.

which the three institutions are incorporated. This is Christian love, in which man serves all who are needy, forgives his enemies, prays for all, and willingly suffers wrong.[23] Love is the inner willingness to do and bear all that is required by vocation, but does it gladly and without resistance. Indeed it willingly exceeds what is called for; and this gives to love the right to pronounce judgment on all laws.

There is nothing in all this which saves man, neither work done in one's vocation nor the exercise of love, set above all stations in life. All this, both works and love, belongs to earth. "So all these are called simply good and holy works. Nevertheless none of these orders is a way to salvation. There is only one way, which is above all these, namely faith in Jesus Christ."[24] He does not mean that faith stands above the church, i.e. above the gospel, but it does stand above "the priestly office." That is the term which Luther uses here, to embrace all work in the church. See p. 504. Faith stands above all vocations of service to the church.

Above the three hierarchies, and above love, faith reaches up to heaven. The regenerating work of the Spirit takes place only in faith. Through the love born of the Spirit through faith, the freedom of faith is active in the three hierarchies.

In 1523 Luther says that I Corinthians 7:20 speaks of the call of the gospel which comes to man in his definite vocation in society.[25] Man is not to give up his *Stand* when the *ruff des Evangelii* (call of the gospel) comes to him. He is to remain in his office, *im Beruf,* as Luther says. But when the call of the gospel comes, it is a call to member-

[23] *WA* 26, 505.
[24] *WA* 26, 505 (*Vom Abendmahl Christi Bekenntnis,* 1528).
[25] *WA* 12, 132 (*Exposition of I Corinthians 7*).

ship in a kingdom above all stations and offices. One is called to "faith and love." Faith and love are above all stations. Faith and love are necessary, while stations are optional in that one person can occupy one position, and another a different one.[26] But faith and love all Christians have.

It looks as if the freedom of faith carries with it a relaxing of all definite outer standards in vocation. The faith and love of the new man are at their fullest before both God and man.

As soon as I think of my neighbor, all vocations no longer stand on a common plane, but a certain vocation comes to the fore as mine. One important fact in God's providence is that I have the neighbor I have. So there is not only a connection between God's love and his providence, but between law and his providence.[27]

The hard, legalistic character of vocation, the cross, appears to be only in relation to the old man. For him the same external relations, free and neutral for faith, are filled with constraint, bearers of the law, laden with the wrath of God. The various thoughts of Luther here seem connected in an entirely mechanical manner. Interpreters of Luther have often fallen for the temptation of making obedience to command and spontaneous love for neigh-

[26] *WA* 12, 132. The monk rests his salvation on one certain, fixed status. Cf. *WA* 10I, 2, 176: only faith and love are commanded, all else is free (*Adventspostille*, 1522); and *WA* 11, 272-273: if the prince is to know how to discharge rightly his vocation, he must live in prayer before God, "only to cling to God, to cry in his ears, and to implore," as well as to give constant attention to what is best for his subjects, i.e. to live in faith and in love. See *WA* 34II, 313f, where love to God and love to others, as one special "status," is placed above all other offices, and is asserted to be the only thing required in them (*Sermons*, 1531; Rörer).

[27] Concerning man's neighbor see *WA* 12, 132f: "Here you cannot sin against God, but against your neighbor" (*Exposition of I Corinthians 7*, 1523).

bor opposite views, to be ascribed to different periods of
Luther's authorship. That is what Eger did in his work
about Luther's view of vocation, in 1900. Ernst Troeltsch,
who does not build his exposition of Luther on his own
study of the sources, but on writings of others which he
read, takes his stand with Eger. All such divisions, untrue
to the materials themselves, assume that the question deals
only with ideas, and not with real actions of God. But
in Luther's faith everything falls into singleness and con-
sistency.

When God, through the orders he has established, deals
with man, he aims to save man in heaven, and he wants
man to serve his neighbor. In the law which speaks in the
vocations of men God compels man without the assent of
his heart to serve others. Thereby the old man is crucified,
the neighbor is helped, and, through his cross, man himself is advanced on the way toward heaven and salvation,
all by one concrete action of God. In the gospel the gate
of heaven is opened, and a miracle takes place. He who
enters heaven immediately descends in love, in "free bondage." He gives himself to the care of his neighbor, concerned about his well-being. Thus God carries forward his
double work in new concrete action, not now without the
assent of man's heart, but with the heart through the Word
and the Spirit.[28] The freedom of faith does not dissolve
vocation. On the contrary, it sustains it and gives it new life.

In differentiating between office and its holder in that
man has no office before God, but holds his office before
men, Luther indicates a clear difference between the two
kingdoms, a juxtaposition of earth and heaven. A person
just as a person has commandment laid upon him, such

[28] Cf. *WA* 56, 458 (*Commentary on Romans*, 1515-16).

as the Sermon on the Mount, as an ethical mandate which belongs to the relationship he has with his neighbor.[29] In that obedience to God which rises from the heart's will to act in harmony with divine commandment, something new enters which goes beyond naked or "raw" order or office.

In the matter of vocation God's work is primarily ethical. He changes the character of it when the person who occupies the office, from having been "flesh," has become "spirit." Before God man is either flesh or spirit. What he is he is as a whole, and his relation to his neighbor changes with the change of his relation with God. The person who wills to obey God, for that reason receives more crosses and suffering in his vocation than does a man who, before God, is cold though honest. These sufferings, rather than being self-imposed, are imposed by God; not that God brings them upon him merely from without, through divine direction of affairs and dispensations. They are brought upon him from within, through God's direction of his heart.[30] It is believable that this counsel about fasts and vigils, etc. Luther would later have condemned as the imposition of a self-chosen cross. Nevertheless in 1525, in *Wider den himmlischen Propheten,* where the attack on the fanatics' contrived suffering is in full swing, Luther recognizes the cross willingly taken up for the sake of one's neighbor and direct measures in the interest of self-discipline (*WA* 18, 65-66).

Since man is at the same time both old and new, so both works of God, the law and the gospel, proceed at the same time. In the activity of daily living, it is impossible

[29] *WA* 32, 382 (*The Sermon on the Mount,* 1532).
[30] It is possible so to interpret what is said in *WA* 6, 244f (*Treatise on Good Works,* 1520).

to distinguish what are respectively the actions of the old man and of the new. Unwillingness and joy, antagonism and love are so intertwined that God alone sees which is which. Hence his judgments are always surprising to men. To be both old man and new means to be one who is sick, in whom illness and health contend. One cannot mechanically identify which is which in the actions of a convalescent. When God approaches man, both law and gospel are in action. Man's outward life is filled with demands, and the many responsibilities are frightening. But at the same time faith lifts him up in freedom above neighbor and vocation; and in this very freedom from law he finds joy in stooping down to serve his neighbor. The Christian knows both fear and joy at the same time.

"Although these two are radically different, nevertheless they are most closely connected in the same heart. Nothing is joined together more nearly than fear and trust, law and gospel, sin and grace. They are so joined together that the one is swallowed up by the other. Wherefore there is no mathematical conjunction like this."[31]

God is both wrath and love; and all of this deep interplay of contradictory feelings and thoughts gives expression to the fact that the God who is at the same time both love and wrath has come near to man.

In view of this action of God, it is improper to raise the question whether vocation derives from the Fourth Commandment ("Honor thy father and thy mother"), from "Christian morality," or whether vocation rests on "natural law," independent of Christian faith. This is a false alternative. Since God does act in earthly government, through the Fourth Commandment, he bids those faithful to him

[31] *WA* 40I, 527 (*Commentary on Galatians*, 1535). Cf. p. 523.

to heed parents and masters. The obedience which faith accords this commandment is of course something quite different from the reluctant subjection of the natural man to those in authority over him. Yet God does actually function through the ruler, even though there be no one who, as a Christian, gives obedience willingly. These two activities exist side by side: God's constraint through external orders, without renewal of the heart of man, and God's renewal of man's heart, out of which flows free and abounding fulfilment of the divine order. Thereby the order is itself changed in significance: it loses its character of force and its power to accuse.

It is hardly possible to agree with the judgment of Einar Billing that there is a continuing remnant of medieval dualism in Luther's treatment of the "earthly" and the "religious." We certainly do not find in Luther Billing's view of vocation as "our own little history," from which we have to hammer out the hidden gold, the message of grace, just as Israel's prophets found the actions and word of God in the history of his chosen people. According to Luther, the forgiveness of sins is proffered to us, in the clear Word of the gospel, and not in vocation which rather discloses to us our responsibilities to earth and our neighbor. The two kingdoms are sharply differentiated by Luther.

Eschatology is brought into history by Billing as a divine border on the fabric of human life; he conceives of forgiveness as being within our vocation and brought to us through it. In this way vocation is viewed as a peculiarly double-sided approach to the church. For Luther it is the church which through Word and sacrament proffers us the forgiveness of sins, the gospel. Vocation is primarily law. But, as we saw in the two preceding sections, the barrier between the two kingdoms is breached in both directions. Thereby all of man's relations with man and affairs are involved in his relation with God.

In the second use of the law it is the bodily law which mounts up into conscience. We cannot differentiate between civil righteousness, righteousness in vocation, and the righteousness which is bestowed on us, the forgiveness of sins. We are beset with the temptation to view the righteousness of our works as the condition for salvation. All our external tribulations, in public and domestic areas, contribute to this temptation.[32] But when faith arises, when Christ comes (which is the same thing), the gospel takes the place of the law in the conscience. And then the new man stoops down into his vocation, where everything testifies to God's satisfaction, and nothing now terrifies or appalls. To him who believes, all things are helpful and none injurious; but for him who does not believe, all things are harmful, and none beneficial. In its civil use the law applies to the flesh; but when faith is absent the entire person is flesh and not spirit before God; so the law concerns the whole person. Then the two uses of the law coincide.[33]

When faith leads to action in outward affairs, that which takes place is *spiritual* in the midst of the carnal. "Everything that our bodies do, the external and carnal, is and is called spiritual behavior, if God's Word is added to it and it is done in faith. There is therefore nothing which is so bodily, carnal, and external that it does not become spiritual when it is done in the Word of God and faith."[34] It is only in faith and the Spirit that what God wills is

[32] *WA* 32, 490 (*The Sermon on the Mount*, 1532).
[33] *WA* 2, 723f (*Treatise on the Sacrament of Penance*, 1519).
[34] *WA* 23, 189 (*Dass diese Wort ... fest stehen*, 1527); cf. *WA* 12, 105-108 (*Exposition of I Corinthians 7*, 1523). When all is spirit, the law does not apply at all. The works of the new man are spirit.

effected. Thus it is only in faith that vocation is fulfilled as God wants—with willingness of heart.[35] Only he who is secure in faith has the ability to obey God's command without ulterior motives.

Such a faith, on which peace and assurance in vocation can rest, is belief not only in the forgiveness of sins (the heavenly kingdom), but also in God's providence, protection, and direction in material matters (the earthly kingdom). In answer to the anxious question as to whether the vocation I find myself in is the one God willed for me, Luther refers to the saying of Christ that not even a sparrow falls to the ground without the will of our heavenly Father, and that all the hairs of our head are numbered.[36] All the external, daily events which form the course of a man's life are guided by God and proceed from his will. In the *Exposition of Psalm 127*, which Luther sent in 1524 to "the Christians in Riga in Livonia," the main theme is God's providence; this is taken up again and again. For the poor and young who do not have the courage to marry, Luther especially wishes to affirm the fact that God cares for all who believe in him and will heed him.[37] God's love finds expression in God's direction in external matters. "God has set the forgiveness of sins in all his creatures."

Though this divine care discloses glimpses of the same love of God as is clearly declared in the gospel, God also introduces his law and wrath into life's events. If a person becomes our enemy and opponent, that is a test of our patience and an opportunity for Christian obedience to the commandment of love.[38] Such bitter experiences reveal how

[35] *WA* 46, 614-619 (*Exposition of John 1 and 2*, 1537-38, edited by Aurifaber).
[36] *WA* 10[I], 1, 316-317 (*Kirchenpostille*, 1522).
[37] *WA* 15, 364f.
[38] *WA* 6, 266-267 (*Treatise on Good Works*, 1520).

strongly the old man still lives in us, and impel us to stifle him.

The incomparably clearest sign in God's providence is the fact that we have the neighbor we actually have. In that fact lies the law, an evidence of a definite vocation. Uncertainty as to whether one is called is often due to regarding oneself as an isolated individual, whose "call" must come in some inward manner. But in reality we are always bound up in relations with other people; and these relations with our neighbors actually effect our vocation, since these external ties are made by God's hands. A craftsman's workshop is like a Bible, in which is written how he is to conduct himself toward his neighbor. Tools and food, needle and thimble—not even excepting "your beer-vat"—call aloud, "Use us for the well-being of your neighbor!" Things are the vehicle of the Word of God to us.

"To use a rough example: If you are a craftsman you will find the Bible placed in your workshop, in your hands, in your heart; it teaches and preaches how you ought to treat your neighbor. Only look at your tools, your needle, your thimble, your beer barrel, your articles of trade, your scales, your measures, and you will find this saying written on them. You will not be able to look anywhere where it does not strike your eyes. None of the things with which you deal daily are too trifling to tell you this incessantly, if you are but willing to hear it; and there is no lack of such preaching, for you have as many preachers as there are transactions, commodities, tools, and other implements in your house and estate; and they shout this to your face, 'My dear, use me toward your neighbor as you would want him to act toward you with that which is his.' "[39]

[39] *WA* 32, 495-496 (*The Sermon on the Mount,* 1532).

Thus a Christian finds himself called to drab and lowly tasks, which seem less remarkable than monastic life, mortifications, and other distractions from our vocations. For him who heeds his vocation, sanctification is hidden in offensively ordinary tasks, with the result that it is hardly noticed at all that he is a Christian.[40] But faith looks on simple duties as tasks to which vocation summons the man; and by the Spirit he becomes aware that all those "poor, dull, and despised works" are adorned with the favor of God "as with costliest gold and precious stones."[41] The monk is always uncertain about his works; but in work which really contributes to the neighbor's well-being and is commanded by God, peace and certainty are found. The works of one's vocation are liberating, as are also the works of the gospel. The insight the gospel gives, that no work is to be done before God for the purpose of conciliating him, can also be mediated to us through the command to work for the sake of our neighbor, that is, through the command of our vocation. The works of our vocation are so puny that certainty of God's favor, even without those works, is implied in heedfulness to those commands. The command of one's vocation can become the bearer of the gospel.

He who inquires effectively into his neighbor's real welfare already has faith, and he is a child of God. This is precisely what is commanded, to inquire about one's neighbor. The gospel (faith in God) and the command (service to the neighbor) are in line with each other. Both are parts of a single reality. Psychologically one or the other may be the first to emerge in consciousness. It may, for example,

[40] WA 10^{I}, 1, 138 (*Kirchenpostille*, 1522).
[41] WA 10^{II}, 295-296 (*Vom ehelichen Leben*, 1522). The duty he has referred to is, for instance, to rock the baby's cradle or to wash its garments. Luther here discusses the parental vocation.

73

be the command. Note the role of the First Commandment in awakening repentance.

Faith in God and willingness to serve one's neighbor constitute an organic unity. Psychologically the first can be a simple willingness to receive earnestly the command to serve one's neighbor. Faith is concealed under obedience to commandment, but it is active and effects obedience. This spiritual unity, faith and love, marks the living Christ or the Spirit taking possession of man. Heeding the commandment without knowing yet that one has faith is the same as the concealment of the deity of Christ in his humanity.

Even if the gospel can garb itself in the form of commandment, we do not have the right to say that commandment and gospel are identical. Vocation is a summons to work for the neighbor's sake; it is not the gospel. A peculiar view of vocation, following Billing's book of 1909, was common in Swedish theology (it played a certain part for Gustav Ljunggren and a large, perhaps a fateful role for Arvid Runestam). It was that vocation is supposed to be the forgiveness of sins, which is not a correct presentation of Luther's standpoint.

Of course, no one claimed that it was. The book *Vår kallelse (Our Vocation)* was not presented as an exposition of Luther, but as an independent study expressing the author's own reflections on vocation. That the thoughts which Billing presented are not Luther's can be seen from the fact that he presented vocation as positively containing the gospel and the forgiveness of sins. The same author, in his doctoral dissertation nine years earlier, in his only reference to Luther's social ethics, points out in two different passages that from the religious point of view, the

74

work of one's vocation has only a "negative" role for Luther. In his work of 1909, Billing corrects the defect which, in 1900, he found in Luther. Vocation, which according to Luther belongs to earth and neighbors and commands works, has become the gospel which bestows forgiveness of sins. What was two kingdoms for Luther has become one for Billing. What for Luther was eschatology is woven into history by Billing, and vocation for Billing is history for the individual, a history which to prophetic insight comprehends God's message of grace. Billing gives us Luther with the removal of the eschatological, and the addition of a romantic view of man's civil vocation. Earthly vocation is presented in brighter colors than Luther gives it, for it gives us heaven.

Even though Billing did not offer his concept of vocation as Luther's view, but as something of a dissent from him, his concept has nevertheless often been construed as Luther's. As a result Luther's own view has been brushed aside, and only Billing's attractive but vulnerable view of vocation has been heard. Runestam seeks to find a gospel in vocation: one detects an altogether too optimistic view of vocation as the background for his declaration of war against a petrified concept of vocation, as he says in *Kärlek, tro, efterföljd* (1931). Runestam looks for the gospel, but really finds the law, the quality in vocation that stifles personality. This quality Luther knows very well. He called it "the crucifixion of the old man," but he does not believe that vocation is to be given up on account of the dark side it shows. To Luther the meaning of life is eschatological. Light lies beyond death. For Runestam too it appears that Luther's two kingdoms have become one. Yet one is always to demand of the law that it shall give us the gospel, that what is in itself without solace shall give us solace. For Luther the stronghold is the gospel, Christ, the church, not the law, or works, or vocation. That commandment or vocation can, in a concrete situation, be bearer of the gospel, is no contradiction. The stronghold is heaven, not earth.

Luther himself has differentiated between the certainty that comes from the awareness of the work to which we are called by our vocation and that which the gospel gives. Conscience does not find peace through any work. Here it is only the gospel which is fully effective. In addition it is also necessary to know that one's works are those God has commanded.[42] Vocation gives steadiness and strength before men, because righteousness in vocation, according to earthly rules, is a real righteousness, which before men we are not to despise or label as sin. But before God, on the other hand, even the most righteous work is serious sin, which stands in need of forgiveness, since it proceeds from an evil heart. Against such an evil heart other men have no right to complain, if behavior is honest and not mastered by the evil of that heart. But God passes judgment on the inner, resisted, invisible evil. Only the gospel, not one's vocation, can remove that judgment against the sinful heart and gives peace to the conscience. A. D. Müller has made a distinction between *Berufseros* and *Berufsagape*. *Berufseros* seeks its power in the vocation itself; out of the vocation it looks for something for itself, and in so doing commits itself to an idol which destroys its devotees. *Berufsagape* seeks its strength from God, does not expect deliverance through vocation, and holds itself radically apart from the vocation at the very time when, in inner

[42] *WA* 40[II], 154 (*Commentary on Galatians, 1535*). The special vocation which Luther here discusses is that of the office of the ministry.

76

freedom, it stoops down to its vocation. Müller's definition of *Berufsagape* agrees very well with Luther's position. This basic view of the Christian's relation to God, on one hand, and to his work responsibilities, on the other, can serve well here to summarize this section in which we have been discussing relation to God and vocation. The soul is to be "open and free" while the body works. The inner man is to be without confidence in the work of his hands, receptively lifted up to God and praying. "While the outer man labors, the heart of the new man makes his entreaties, as his cares press upon him. He says, 'Lord, I follow Thy calling; therefore I do all things in Thy name. Do Thou rule, etc.' "[43]

God's love certainly clothes itself in external things and insistent commands, but faith clings not to these things, but to the gospel or to God himself. To be sure, faith cannot sustain its independence of vocation in the time of temptation to doubt, when earthly and heavenly righteousness are not kept differentiated. But the purpose of the temptation is to strengthen faith's dependence on the gospel alone. Conscience cannot be made secure through any work, not even through that which belongs undeniably to man's vocation. Conscience is the bride of Christ, and none but the Bridegroom has the right to bind the bride to him.[44]

[43] *WA* 40[III], 234 (*Exposition of Psalm 127*, 1532-33). Cf. 253: The devout one "sleeps" all through life; his heart is calm and peaceful in the midst of his responsibilities. This calm is the product of trust in God and deep distrust of his own works, which can nevertheless for that very reason be done thoughtfully and thoroughly. Cf. *WA* 15, 732: "To watch and to fulfil what is our office, with a free and true faith, neither to worry when we are badly off nor to boast when we are well off—that only a believing heart can do" (*Exposition of Psalm 127*, 1524).

[44] *WA* 40[I], 595f (*Commentary on Galatians*, 1530; Rörer). "One ought not to trouble his conscience. The body must suffer these things; but the conscience ought to be his bride and at liberty with the Bridegroom in the realm of this relationship."

_____God and the Devil

1. *The Concept of Governments*

The concept of "a people" or *Volkstum* embodying a
norm has been especially prevalent in German theology.
The norm of politics "consists in the genuine life necessity
of a special *Volk* in the midst of others." According to that
view it is the responsibility of government to give expression to something which inheres in a people and which, so
to speak, sets the governmental norm from below. *Volkstum*
is the collective counterpart of what the immortal spark
of the divine meant to an earlier, individualistic mode of
thought. It is not something that must be ruled; on the contrary it is to rule and to conquer. Under both such views
lies the common presupposition about human nature that
man or the character of the people is not sinful.

It follows from Luther's view of sin that he stands in
opposition to both these types of humanity religion. The
man who seeks to reject the Word of God and follow his
own heart does not become a free man, but one in subjection to the devil. There are only two alternatives: subjection
to God and subjection to the devil. "Between these two
man stands, like an animal to be ridden. If God be the
rider, the creature goes where God wills. . . . If Satan be
the rider, he goes where Satan directs. Man cannot freely
choose to leap to the side of one or the other of these riders,

or to seek one out. It is the riders themselves who contend to win and possess man."[1] The aggregation of people, whom government is to rule, is not different from single individuals or better than they. A people too is subject to a rider. A good government, which fulfils its duty of office, rules the people in opposition to a contrary power which would control. The authority of the government is not derived from the fact that it gives expression to a people's genius, but from the fact that God has ordained it to thwart the devil. Government is of God, created by him. Of course, like all other people, those whose vocation is government are also exposed to attack and perversion by the devil. They themselves are under the rule of a higher government. But over all governments, the highest and the lowest, the Word of God must rule. As the law it exposes sin and impels man to battle against it; as the gospel it takes away sin, preparing for the coming of the eternal kingdom.

Such a concept of government, by its very nature, implies belief in the existence of the devil. If God directed his action toward a world whose inhabitants were only ignorant of him, but not hostile to him, divine action would not have the character of government but of gentle intellectual enlightenment. But instead, God deals with the world through stern, worldly government, through the sword and law, and through a tangible church where the Word is preached and the sacraments administered. The law uses coercion against the flesh, in which the devil operates, and the gospel works with all the power of the Spirit against the accusations of conscience, in which the devil is also at work. The law and the gospel are not uttered to a passive and unresist-

[1] *WA* 18, 635 (*The Bondage of the Will*, 1525).

79

ing neutrality. Both law and gospel advance against a steady and persistent blast.

It is for man that the struggle between God and the devil goes on, for every single individual. God wishes man to be saved from the power of sin, and the devil wants man kept in it. Out of that invisible combat, which goes on even when man does not think of it, come all the agony and anxiety that enter into human life. A creature must know suffering when two powers lay hold of it, struggling to "win and possess it." It is in the very nature of such a struggle that, in any particular case, man cannot say which of the two contenders laid a particular tribulation on him. Both are pulling at man at the same time. Therefore Luther says that man's cross and despair come both from God and the devil. In his *Commentary on Romans,* in 1515-16, Luther says emphatically that our hardships are God's discipline. Two years later, in his *Commentary on Hebrews,* he considered sufferings to be due to the fact that the Christian life is God's action and our passion *operatio Dei* and *passio nostra.* "No one is purified unless by hardships and disturbances. The more the suffering and oppressions, the better the Christian. The whole life of a Christian is in faith, i.e. in cross and sufferings."[2]

In his *Treatise on Good Works,* in 1520, Luther says expressly that it is God who sends offense, suffering, ignominy, troubles, and death. This is all God's "strange work," done in order "that he may come to his proper work."[3] But in the *Exposition of the Sermon on the Mount,* in 1532, Luther affirms again and again that all trials come from

[2] *WA* 57, 61f.

[3] *WA* 6, 248; cf. 266f. God's "proper work" is the gospel which establishes peace and gives joy.

the devil, who makes his hardest attacks on the children of God. The devil does not concern himself about coarse sinners, since they are already in his grasp without much effort.[4] And in 1540 Luther said, for example, that the devil will certainly always find a piece of wood from which to make a cross for us; it is he who sends the cross on us.[5]

Investigation would probably show that, from the time Luther rejects the idea of self-inflicted crosses, declarations that the cross comes from the devil are commoner. To a certain degree, his earlier writings show the dominance of the view that the cross comes from God, so there is no impropriety in man's seeking of the cross. Yet we are not sure that scrutiny of the sources would show this. Ragnar Bring has shown clearly the inner connection between the devil's work and God's law and wrath in Luther's Reformation theology. It is clearly no problem to Luther how despair can come simultaneously from God and Satan. In his *Commentary on Hebrews* Luther presents the statement that God's "strange" work is the work of the devil, whereby the devil thinks he makes his work effective against God while he is really helping to overthrow his own efforts.

"For thus God advances his purpose through his strange work, and with marvelous wisdom he knows that through death the devil can effect nothing else than life, so that while he does his utmost against the action of God, he is by his characteristic effort actually working for the divine cause against his own."[6]

Of course there is no problem in saying that the distress

---

[4] *WA* 32, 335f and 502f. Concerning spiritual trial in vocation, see 519. The sovereignty of God over the devil and his attacks is always clear to Luther: cf. 520.

[5] *WA* 51, 412 (*An die Pfarrherrn wider den Wucher zu predigen*).

[6] *WA* 57, 128 (1517-18). See also sec. 3 (Confusion), note 79 below.

of the Christian life comes both from God and from the power of evil. This is the distress which results when God snatches one from the hand of the devil. It is through pain that one is freed from Satan's grip ("the cross from God"). Except for the devil the pain would not be ("the cross from the devil"). The love of God is love in one who is to deliver from the peril of death. One must take firm hold, and that can hurt.

Luther's *Vermahnung zum Gebet wider den Türken,* in 1541, sheds special light on belief about the devil. Those who are threatened by the Turks and the devil acknowledge that they have sinned against God and deserve to be punished. But they have not offended against the devil, for they have not lived a blameless Christian life. So it is not of the devil but of God that they deserve punishment. When the Turks attack the Christians, it is God's punishment which befalls them, a punishment which God lets his adversary execute. "But Thou knowest, O Almighty God and Father, that we have in no way sinned against the devil, the pope, or the Turks; and they have neither the right nor the power to punish us. But Thou canst and mayest use them as Thy grim lash against us, who have sinned against Thee and deserve all misfortune."[7]

But then the Christians, beset by Turk and devil, confess the name of the Triune God. In their peril they believe in him and pray to him. That is to "sin" against the devil. By prayer, penitence, and confession they step over to God's side. Now they stand for God and against the devil; and Luther is certain that they would be left in peace if they desisted from their confession and denied their faith.[8] We

[7] *WA* 51, 608.
[8] *WA* 51, 609f.

shall presently deal more fully with this view of prayer as an objective change in the whole relationship between God and man. To pray is to depart from the devil's power, in which man stands over against God, and to enter into the power of God, in which man stands over against the devil.

The devil is clearly no longer the instrument of divine punishment but the enemy of God. Therefore the peril approaching in the Turks is no longer God's punishment, with the devil as God's agent; it is the devil's own attack against the Christians, and thereby against God himself. "Look upon us, O Thou who art a merciful Father to us and a stern Judge of our foes, for they are Thy foes more than ours. When they persecute us and strike us down, they persecute and strike Thee down; for the Word which we preach, believe and confess is Thine and not ours, entirely the work of Thy Holy Spirit in us. This the devil would not allow, for he would be our God in Thy stead."[9] Thus he who prays seeks to persuade God that the devil is God's foe, and ought not to be accepted as a servant of God.

The prayer is a prayer for God's fresh, strong action against the Turk and the devil. "Awake, O God, hallow Thy name which they dishonor. Strengthen Thy kingdom. Fulfil Thy will, which they would stifle in us. Let them not trample Thee underfoot, because our sin has to be punished; for the Turks and the devil are not unwilling that we sin against Thee. What they would bring to naught is Thy work in us, O God!"[10] If they who are beset by the Turks pray thus and turn to God, their misfortune will yield amendment: the devil opposes God, but succeeds only in driving God's faithful ones to prayer, making them the chil-

[9] *WA* 51, 609-610.
[10] *WA* 51, 610.

dren of God.[11] The final outcome is thus God's supremacy over the devil.

Sometimes Luther seems to play with his thought about the devil, his presentation is so variable. Sometimes he mixes a certain gaiety with his seriousness, but not in his writings on the Turks. Prayer is a human action through which man's entire situation is changed. When man was far from God, God gave the devil permission to work harm to man. But then man prays, in his desperation repents, and comes close to God again. Then the devil loses his right, and stands as the enemy of God and man alike. The relationship of God and the devil, in their mutual combat for the individual, is reversed and changed when man prays. In Chapter III we shall consider again the question of prayer, for it has great significance in the question of vocation. Prayer is a door through which God enters into vocation in transforming action against the devil. But for the present we must return to the general juxtaposition of God and the devil.

The realms of church and social order are governments, because in a special way these two are involved in resistance to sin. They are two governments, not one, because they contend with sin in fundamentally different ways. Worldly government compels an outward righteousness on earth, without being able to remove evil from the heart. It only checks sin and keeps it within reasonable external limits. The spiritual government points to heaven, promising both the complete elimination of sin after death and, on earth, its removal from the conscience, even while the law slowly contends with the body, and confronts us in

[11] This appears more clearly in another of Luther's writings about the Turks (*On War Against the Turks*, 1529), *WA* 30[II], 116. Cf. also *WA* 30[II], 176-177 (*Heerpredigt wider den Türken*, 1529).

the form of earthly orders as vocation. "The fixed cosmos of vocation, in Luther's thought, is set in a dynamic process of tremendous dimensions which embrace heaven and hell. It is the metaphysical conflict between God and the devil which surges upon the cosmos of vocation and rushes through it."

At times Luther says that these two wielders of power, God and the devil, rule each over his own kingdom *(regnum)*. "I say that Christians know there are two kingdoms *(regna)* in the world, engaged in fierce mutual combat. One of these Satan rules. . . . In the other, which always opposes and battles with Satan's kingdom, Christ rules."[12] It is clear that *regnum* is used here with a different meaning from that intended when earth *(terra)* and heaven *(coelum)* are spoken of as two kingdoms. The spiritual and the earthly governments constitute two kingdoms, but both of these are God's. They are not in opposition to one another, but, side by side, both contend against the devil, one guided by the gospel, and the other by the law. The kingdoms of God and Satan cut across all orders of being. Against the devil, God uses both of his governments as weapons, and the devil seeks to destroy these weapons of his enemy. The devil corrupts the spiritual government through popes and masses, and the worldly government by peasant revolt, fanatics, and cloisters.

The combat between God and Satan is fought over persons. Offices are on God's side, but persons who occupy offices can belong to God or to the devil, which makes an enormous difference in the way the duties of office are met. "The offices, both of rulers and officials, are godly and right. But those who occupy and practice them are usually

[12] *WA* 18, 782-783 *(The Bondage of the Will,* 1525).

of the devil."[13] Evil officeholders want to make themselves God, rather than servants of God; they want to rule and not to serve, ascribing to themselves the power and the righteousness which belong to the office, to God, not man.

The order is and continues good and divine, just as the sun is still God's pure creation, even if some use the light of day to commit murder and other crimes. Who could commit a crime if the sun gave him no light, if the earth did not support and sustain him, and the air did not let him breathe—that is, if God did not care for him? Creation is available for man's use or misuse.[14] But misuse never derives from anything in itself evil; it has its root in the corrupted human heart. Evil is the devil's work through the heart of man. The combat between God and the devil for all vocations and orders takes place within every single human being. If God is victor, then that part of external existence which lies within man's reach is made to serve God. If Satan wins, God's creation is used in the opposite way. But an office is good, even when it is misused, even as the spear that pierced Christ's side did not for that reason cease to be God's good creation.

"For it does not follow that because the kingdoms of the world fight against the kingdom of Christ, they are bad in themselves; even as it does not follow that the spear, with which the side of the Lord was laid open on the cross, was not a good creation. We ought to differentiate between a creature or thing and the abuse of it. The creature is good, even if it be abused. The abuse does not spring from the

13 *WA* 51, 254 (*Exposition of Psalm 101*, 1534-35).

14 *WA* 30[II], 572-573 (*Sermon on Keeping Children in School*, 1530). About the office of the soldier, he says, "Although some of them abuse this office, destroy and slay without necessity, in sheer wantonness, that is not the fault of the office but of the person," *WA* 19, 627 (*Whether Soldiers Too Can Be Saved*, 1526).

thing, but from the depraved mind. Even so civil righteousness, laws, trades, and human efforts are things which are by nature good; but it is abuse that is bad, because the world misuses these gifts against God. . . . Abuse does not inhere in the substance. That thing is good in which the devil activates abuse."[15] The devil is the active force behind the misuse. Abuse involves an action directly opposed to the work of God. The greedy, for instance, interrupt God's outpouring of gifts and conceal God's care for him who has the misfortune of being the neighbor of the greedy.

The only exception to the thesis that the office is clean in itself is the kingdom of the Turks. Persecution of Christians has arisen in many earthly kingdoms, under one ruler or another here or there, but their governments had not been instituted for the purpose of dishonoring God. They may do so through misuse; but government is to be of God. But Mohammed's sword and kingdom are the devil's own government, "directed outright against Christ."[16] In this case the office itself is evil, and the devil's position is pushed forward exceptionally.

Otherwise, the devil's onslaughts consist of temptations to misuse a good and divine office, to mismanage one's vocation. A Christian always lives in such temptations. Satan's attack on life's external order is, as Franz Lau expresses it, "real for the first time in misgiving about my office." I lose my certainty that God speaks to me through my superior and wills to work through me "in the exercise of my office to those under me." In his *Kirchenpostille*

[15] *WA* 40[II], 203 (*Exposition of Psalm 2*, 1546).

[16] *WA* 30[II], 172 (*Heerpredigt wider den Türken*, 1529). Cf. 116f: "He is God's rod, and servant of the devil; of that there is no doubt" (*Vom Kriege wider den Türken*, 1529). The sovereignty of God is affirmed; note "God's rod."

Luther ardently develops this theme. The evil spirit makes vocation very irksome for all the faithful. But if the enemy can bring man so far "that he forgets his vocation and deserts it, he no longer besets man so severely," for he has thereby led his victim off the main highway. Thereafter he finds it easy to lead man astray, to lead him into an especially fine and religious effort. From there man keeps moving on without taking alarm, and every step carries him further from God's command.[17] Later in the same sermon, Luther declares that doubt and despair in vocation are direct evidence that one is indeed in his proper position, in which faith is to be confirmed and the battle against darkness continued. "Take it as a sure sign that you are in a right station which is pleasing to God, if you feel disgust and dislike for it. God is certainly at hand. He permits the evil spirit to attack and tempt you, to see whether you are fickle or steadfast, or not; and he provides an opportunity for your faith to fight and grow stronger."[18]

Luther himself had felt again and again that kind of indecision in his office of preacher. "The wicked devil makes everyone's vocation so hard and so confuses understanding that people are unable to recognize the office and work which God lays on them."[19]

Behind man's deviation from the path of his vocation

[17] WA 10¹, 1, 309-310 (1522).

[18] WA 10¹, 317. Cf. WA 12, 11: "You have to be prepared and to consider confidently that everything you do, if it is done under God, will be tempted seriously, for the accursed devil will not rest or be idle" (Ordnung eines gemeinen Kasten, 1523).

[19] WA 32, 519 (The Sermon on the Mount, 1530-32). Cf. WA 34¹¹, 313 (Sermons, 1531; Rörer): "Reason is the devil's bride, which plans some particular course because it does not know what may please God, but thinks, 'If I elect a work which pleases me, it will also please God.' . . . The best and highest station in life is to love God and one's neighbor. Indeed that station is filled by the ordinary manservant or maidservant who cleans the meanest pot."

the devil is always present as the impelling force. Particularly serious are the consequences of treachery against God's command, if this treachery and inability to stand against temptation is found in either of the two governments, political rule or the office of the ministry. In the area of earthly government, corruption takes place through the rise of tyranny and the spread of anarchy in society. The former means that in his pride and lust for power, the ruler spreads his power over areas where he has no right to do so. The latter means the ruler's indecision in his responsibility of maintaining order, so that transgressions of law are not sternly punished, and his power is not used. Tyranny is the ruler's presumption; anarchy is his despair.[20]

Of disturbance in the spiritual realm, the papacy and the fanatics are examples. Monks and fanatics travel the same way; for all who consider themselves above regular vocations and higher than faith are and remain monks, even if they do not all act alike in the observance of hours. The earlier cloistered monks of the papacy were actually easier to understand. The newer monks are more difficult to keep off the conscience. "They do not wear cowls, but put on other special demeanor, pretend great devotion and sanctity by solemn faces, grey garb and hardness of life."[21]

Against such hypocrisy there is no weapon except God's command and the gospel, which give us certainty that before God works are unnecessary, and therefore helping the neighbor is their only objective. If one's station is correctly used, and not misused, one's neighbor will be served just by faithfulness in one's vocation. To be sure, such faithfulness always involves fellowship with evil people, whom we

[20] *WA* 40[III], 211-213 (*Exposition of Psalm 127*, 1532-33).
[21] *WA* 32, 514 (*The Sermon on the Mount*, 1530-32).

encounter in all positions, "misusers" of their stations. But this gives us no right to forsake our *Stand*, which maintains its divine character through all misuse. "If you have Christ through faith, then be obedient and subject to the authorities, and practice love among yourselves in all stations. . . . Against this there arises that divisive spirit saying, 'Oh, that is a common thing, and there are many bad people in all walks of life. All this is merely secular. Ah, we must look for something better.' So he goes and brings forth something special and strange. However, if you are possessed by God's Word, you will be able to judge quickly and say, When did God order the establishing of such special stations over against the common walks of life which he ordained? I know very well there are many villains, as well as devout people, in all walks. But what is it to me that others misuse them? I stand by the Word which teaches me that these stations are good, even though there are bad people in them."[22]

To cut oneself off from other people, regarding them as inferior in sanctity, is something which Luther, in his *Commentary on Romans,* rejects as satanic perversion.[23] When this is taught as sanctity and true Christian living, the exercise of the office of the ministry has gone wrong and the spiritual government is corrupted, even as earthly government can be distorted by a tyrannical prince.

The devil makes especially severe attacks on him who fills the office of the ministry according to God's Word. For through correct preaching the devil is unmasked, so that people understand that what is called holy is the work of the devil, and what is called earthly is God's work by which

[22] *WA* 32, 516 (*The Sermon on the Mount,* 1530-32).
[23] *WA* 56, 266 (1515-16).

90

evil is checked. Therefore he who preaches God's Word faithfully threatens to bring to naught the very center of the devil's activity, religious works. For this reason the devil makes a powerful attack on such a spokesman for the truth. As soon as he preaches the truth, dissension and strife arise around him; but as soon as he forsakes his responsibility and preaches falsehood that pleases men, a quiet and pleasant calm is present among his hearers. If he remains faithful to the Word of God, the result is discord, but if he yields to the devil, the result is peace. God appears in the garb of the devil, while the devil presents the garb of God. Faith recognizes both God and the devil, despite the fact that both are masked. That is faith's positive achievement.

"In this way Paul holds it to be a most certain sign that it is not the gospel if it is preached in undisturbed peace. On the other hand, the world takes it as a certain sign that the gospel is a heretical and seditious doctrine because it sees that the preaching of it is followed by great tumults, disturbances, scandals, divisions, etc. Thus God appears in the mask of the devil, and the devil wears the mask of God; and God wishes to be perceived behind the devil's mask, and he wishes the devil, wearing God's mask, to be spurned." [24]

In an earlier section, we sought to establish the connection between relation to God and vocation. Man's office gives tangible direction about works, but "faith and love" modify the work done in the office. Apart from relation with God, man has an office, established by God, but not a vocation.

The comments about "misuse" of one's office fit into our familiar statement of this problem. Office constitutes a fixed

[24] *WA* 40[II], 54 (*Commentary on Galatians,* 1535).

reality. Right use or misuse of office constitutes a tangible reality. Use and misuse vary with change in our relation to God, with sin or opposition to sin: that is, the devil and God are involved in the concrete picture of the exercise of office. Vocation is a focal point of decision in the combat between God and the devil. In this combat the Word is God's weapon. The spiritual government modifies the shape of vocation under earthly government.

Rulers are held in check by still higher rulers. But the sovereign ruler, who has no higher ruler above him, has over him only the Word of God, not some other power armed with force. Under a tyrannical sovereign a Christian can only suffer; revolt is sin. Within God's order there is no power which may legitimately punish a tyrannical sovereign ruler. Here God himself stands guard and reaches in from outside the order.

There would be a gap here in the system which Luther conceives to be erected for the checking of evil, if he meant that the sovereign is checked only by his own thoughts. But God himself is at work in the world of tangible fact: "If the ruler is evil, well then, God is also on hand! He has fire, water, iron, stone and countless ways to bring death. How suddenly he can take the tyrant's life!"[25]

Furthermore God can foster a revolt, using that which is clearly sin on the part of men to punish the sin of the ruler, and he can arouse a foreign ruler to make war against the tyrant.[26] Here comes into view an incalculable and revolutionary reality which lies directly in the hand of God, and which he does not surrender to any order. This fact points to the thought, typical for Luther, of supermen *(viri*

[25] *WA* 19, 637 (*Whether Soldiers Too Can Be Saved*, 1526).
[26] *WA* 19, 638.

heroici) who, with violent force, impelled by God, change an entire world.

2. *The Concept of Freedom*

Earlier we touched on the question of freedom in connection with our discussion of the two kingdoms, the heavenly and the earthly. Man does not have freedom in that which is "above" him, in the heavenly kingdom, before God. There he is to proffer no works; he only accepts that which God accomplishes, he is passive before God. Facing upward, man can only believe and pray. There the bound will obtains. But in those things which are "below" man, man is free, for before man he is not to be merely passive or enduring, but active and working. Toward what is below him, he is to effect works, for earth is the arena of his vocation. In heaven the gospel rules; hence the bound will. On earth law rules; hence freedom of will.[27]

Apparently quite a contrary line of thought is presented by the statements of Luther on the inner man (conscience) as set over against the external man (the body). In them conscience expresses relation to God, and body expresses relation to earthly station, vocation, neighbor, the world. Luther has said elsewhere that man is bound before God, in those things which are "above," and free before the external, in those things which are "below." Now he says that, on the contrary, the conscience is free through the gospel, and the body bound by the law.

"The law abides outside of heaven, that is, outside of heart or conscience. On the other hand, gospel freedom remains beyond the earthly, that is, outside of the body and

[27] See Chapter I, sec. 2, above.

its members. Therefore just as soon as law and sin enter heaven, that is, the conscience, they must be ejected thence forthwith. For there is nothing which conscience needs to learn from the law, but so much from Christ. In turn, when grace, freedom, etc. come into the earthly, that is, into the body, let it be said: You ought not to be occupied in the pig-sty and the uncleannesses of bodily life. You belong high up in heaven, etc."[28]

In heaven (in the conscience) the gospel rules; hence freedom. But on earth the law rules; hence bondage. "For baptism frees not life and goods, but the soul."[29]

Nevertheless these different expressions can be coupled. Freedom in conscience or in faith means freedom from the law, freedom from the demand for works. The gospel is something which man hears and receives, not something which he does. But this hearing and receiving, this "freedom," is identical with helplessness before God, identical with the bound will. Man has freedom in outward matters, for there he must effect something, there lies his station in life with multitudinous works. But as soon as that station confronts him, his "freedom in externals" is changed into bondage to the law, he is free to obey the law. The freedom of the conscience is freedom from the law, into the empty hands of faith, unto bondage before God. Freedom in externals is freedom to the law, to the full hands of the work of one's vocation, unto bondage before one's neighbor.

Luther's view of freedom grows somewhat more complicated when he introduces the idea of "freedom to do or

[28] *WA* 40¹, 208 (*Commentary on Galatians,* 1535). Notice the constant identification of conscience and heaven on the one hand, and of body and earth on the other.
[29] *WA* 18, 359 (*Against the Robbing and Murdering Hordes of Peasants,* 1525).

not to do." To the Jews Paul was a Jew according to the law; to the Gentiles a Gentile without the law. In both cases he was motivated by faith and love, which confer the right to formulate entirely new decalogues according to the situation and need of others. "Only faith and love are necessary. In everything else one is free to omit or to do."

Luther's point of departure is I Corinthians 9:20-22: Paul "ate, drank, and lived with the Jews according to the law, even though it was not necessary for him. With the Gentiles he ate, drank, and lived without the law, as they did. For only two things are necessary: faith and love. Everything else you are free to do or to leave undone. Therefore you may do everything for the sake of one, and for the sake of another refrain from everything, and in that way treat all impartially. If a blind and opinionated person were to appear, insisting that some certain thing must or must not be done, as was the case with some of the Jews, that matters must be as he demands, that others must heed him while he has to heed no one, that would be violating both equality and Christian liberty, and distorting faith. To such a person one ought not to yield, as St. Paul also did not, for freedom and truth must be maintained."[30]

One cannot bind oneself to a fixed external action without at the same time destroying faith and "Christian liberty," i.e. the freedom of conscience which consists of the repose of faith in the gospel apart from the bondage of works. So "freedom to do or not to do" is an integral part of "Christian liberty"; more accurately, it is the most conspicuous part of "Christian liberty."

Runestam has sometimes said that this "freedom to do and to omit" is an unnecessary insertion into Luther's view.

[30] *WA* 10¹, 2, 175 (*Adventspostille*, 1522).

But at the same time it is striking that Runestam himself has a sharply critical eye for a dead and stiff quality in vocation. Peculiarly enough, it may be that if vocation is not frozen and lifeless for Luther, it is just because "the freedom to do and to leave undone" must function. There is freedom to do, if love to another requires it, and freedom not to do, if that is what love to one's neighbor requires. Through such freedom of action faith and relationship to God have real significance for the shaping of vocation. Life according to vocation never becomes fixed or rigid. Again and again we find in Luther concepts which keep his system open for new action, doors through which God creatively enters into the orders of creation. "Freedom to do or not to do" is one of these concepts.

The same door which opens these orders to God also opens them to the devil. In an unchanging vocation only a robot could function. In fact the use made of the office plays a vital role, for through its proper use vocation is transformed through faith and love in the fellowship of God. God makes new.

Deriving from the concept of use is the concept of abuse, a satanic transformation, the entry of the devil into the world of orders. We must reckon with the fact that the "freedom to do or to leave undone" will be used by the old man for his own satisfaction and convenience, or by the devil who produces just this sin in the heart. We should expect that in certain concrete situations Luther will deny the freedom to do or to omit regarding sin, or misuse of that freedom by human slackness. And that is exactly what Luther does do.

In his *Kirchenpostille,* he advises the abandonment of the cloister, if the conscience is bound by the monastic vow, for the conscience must be free from that vow. Here Christian liberty, the royal freedom of the conscience, finds outward expression when the monastic vow is broken and the door of the cloister thrown open. But in the same breath he warns each one to take care that it is not the old Adam which impels one to leave the cloister for the sake of "free life" out in the world. It is to make conscience free that one may break the monastic vow, not to free the flesh to follow its desires. It is as the child of God, not as the child of the devil, that one has liberty to break the monastic vow. In the latter case freedom is the same as sin. In the former it is the same as faith and love. "Take care that it is not a rogue within you that is looking out, so that you leave such an order because of a false motive. For the old Adam likes to dress himself up, and where a finger is offered to him he takes a whole hand. You may be able to deceive people, but you will not deceive God. If you leave your station on this account, that you may escape from the order and live as you like, and not that conscience may be liberated, you have not followed me and I have not counseled you. That you must know! You may well stay in your order and yet have a free conscience, according to this doctrine. But if you are so weak that you are unable to keep your conscience free, then it is better to flee from that station."[31]

In *On War Against the Turk* (1529) Luther consequently directs severe attacks against rulers that look upon defense against the Turk as something one may give or withhold as one chooses. It is obligatory to help the emperor in this struggle with both life and possessions. To fail here

[31] *WA* 10^I, 1, 494 (*Kirchenpostille,* 1522). We might also compare two passages in *De votis monasticis: WA* 8, 615-616 (against the liberty to do or to leave undone) with 664-665 (love rises above all laws) (1521).

is to resist the command of God. Here one does not have "freedom to do or not to do."

"The princes do not care, nor do they realize, that before God it is their high duty and obligation to advise and help the emperor in this matter, even with life and possessions. Each one lets things go as they may, as if they did not concern him or he had neither law nor necessity to constrain him, as if it were up to his discretion whether to act or not."[32] Over against this indifference about the welfare of their subjects (the welfare of their "neighbor") Luther affirms that God's command makes it imperative for the prince to act for the sake of his subjects; the responsibility is involved in the prince's vocation.

This is just one illustration, in a given situation, of the principle that the old man is under the law, and does not have liberty to do as he may like. Such loose reins only the children of God may have. They do not misuse their liberty, for from the heart they aim to serve others and rejoice in doing so. It is not that the new man is required to serve his neighbor, any more than that a tree is required to bloom, or 3 plus 7 are required to equal 10, or the sun required to shine.[33] If a man is really greedy, we need not tell him of ways to get hold of money; he himself will find a thousand different ways to pile up his capital. Likewise one may trust the children of God with liberty. The result will be service to others. But limits are necessary for the man in the grip of evil.

"Freedom to do and to omit" is an attribute of Christian liberty in relation to the law on earth. As we have already said repeatedly, the law takes form in outward order, morals,

[32] *WA* 30[II], 132f.
[33] *WA Tischreden*[VI], 153.

and demands in man's immediate environment, "vocation" in its widest sense.

"Although the gospel may not subject us to the decisions of Moses, nevertheless it does not free us completely from obedience to all laws of society; rather in this bodily life it subjects us to the laws of the regime in which we live."[34]

Christian liberty of conscience, indissolubly united with love for others, means that in external matters one must "do" according to the law, follow the accustomed course, or "leave," break away from the accustomed course. Christian love would break away because something else would be better for others, for love lives in the heart of him who "leaves" the accustomed course, and love impels to a new action in preference to the old practice. Thus the changeable element in vocation is represented in love born of faith (liberty of conscience). This love acts quite as it pleases, as it discerns God's will.[35] The unchanging element in vocation lies in the office itself, which reaches out as a barrier against the old man, inasmuch as the old man is not free to "do and to omit"; he is simply bound to obey. For if the old man deviates from the requirements and substitutes something new, the new will be worse and more injurious to others than the accustomed. He who wants to follow his own course must ask permission, and be examined as to whether or not he has love for others, whether it is the old man or the new who motivates him. Permission (i.e. freedom to do or to omit) is granted to the new man, but not

[34] *WA* 40[I], 673 (*Commentary on Galatians*, 1535).

[35] For concrete examples of freedom in relation to parents and to the law, see *WA* 30[III], 239-247 (*Von Ehesachen*, 1530). Even natural reason and fairness may transcend written law. We shall have more to say about this later, in the section on "The New Creation."

to the old. For him who has an unaffected love for his neighbor and his work, vocation becomes flexible and adaptable. For him who in truth loves only himself, vocation becomes rigid, unyielding, and coercive.[36]

Though the old man does not have permission to do as he wishes, he does so none the less. That God is a hidden God means, among other things, that man can oppose God, that he can set himself up against God, or, in other words, that the devil can exist. He who is in Satan's power brings Satan into God's order, and carries on a work which is diametrically opposed to God. Work hostile to God can take the form of negligence in vocation, indifference, and idleness, all of which are barriers in the way of God's ongoing creation and care for human beings, that divine care which aims to attain its purpose through the proper use of every office.

Above all the devil makes use of religion as he spreads the false idea of salvation by works rather than through the gospel. Such a belief, like that represented by the pope and his slaves of the law, is Satan's main onslaught against God's order both in heaven and on earth. Misled by this perverted religion, man turns freedom and bondage upside down. He thinks himself bound where he is free, and considers himself free where he is bound. We must examine some passages in which Luther considers this.

Christ makes conscience free from works before God, where it is the gospel that rules, not the law, not bondage to a special outward behavior. In direct contradiction to the work of Christ, the monastic life binds conscience to a

[36] This rigidity in vocation is not at all an absence of God's will, but an expression of it. Selfishness is to be kept under control by the pressure of the law, and the old man is to be crucified by the compulsion to be faithful in vocation and service to others.

fixed, outward form of life. The monastic life is law and works before God. At the same time the cloister removes man from his earthly vocation, in which by the will of God he is bound by the law to serve his neighbor. The monk does not serve his neighbor, the work which God has given him, but makes himself free to forsake it. So the cloister binds man to works "before God," where he should be free, and makes him free from works and love "before man," where he should be bound.

"From this you may learn once more that monasticism and clericalism are wrong for our time. For they bind themselves before God in external matters concerning which God leaves them free; thus they resist the freedom of faith and the order of God. On the other hand, where they should be bound, namely before men, to serve everybody through love, they make themselves free. They neither serve, nor are they of use to any except themselves. Thus they set themselves against love. Therefore they are a perverted people that perverts all the laws of God. They want to be free where they should be bound and bound where they should be free. Yet they hope for higher thrones in heaven than common Christians will receive. No, in the abyss of hell they will sit, they who pervert heavenly freedom into such an infernal prison and loving servitude into a hostile freedom."[37]

So Luther expresses himself in his *Exposition of I Corinthians 7* (1523). In his *Large Commentary on Galatians* (1535) he says that "reason and human nature" turn freedom and bondage upside down much as monastic religion distorts the truth. It is difficult to let grace illuminate the conscience while law disciplines the body. Man, he says,

[37] *WA* 12, 133.

101

would rather "be free in the body and bound in the conscience." "Wherefore let the burdened conscience think nothing, know nothing, and meet the wrath and judgment of God with nothing but the Word of Christ, which is the Word of grace, the remission of sins, salvation, and eternal life. But to hold to this is an arduous and most difficult thing. For reason and human nature do not cling to Christ in firm embrace, but forthwith slide back into thoughts about the law and sin. Thus they ever seek to be free in the flesh, but bound and captive in conscience."[38]

Man wishes to liberate himself from bondage toward his neighbor, to free himself from the law, or from love, and escape the works which are only to help others. He prefers to do works which God will reward, works which satisfy his own need to regard himself as fine and holy and religious.[39] These works wipe out faith before God, rob man of childlike freedom before all natural and earthly life and give him the anxious and cowardly conscience of the slave of the law.

We recall that Luther used the words "free" and "bound" in a way that seemed to be a contradiction. Instead of "free before God" and "bound in relation to one's neighbor," Luther can say "bound before God" and "free in outward matters."[40] Since man is not to proffer works to God, but only believe and receive, he is bound "upward" towards

---

[38] *WA* 40^I, 214.

[39] In the treatise *On the Freedom of the Christian Man* (1520), Luther says often that a person is free through faith and bound through love; in his *Commentary on Galatians* of 1535, he says that a person is bound in external matters by the law, in spite of his inner freedom. The relation between the two, love and law, is expressed in the sentence which appears several times, that love willingly submits to laws and takes burdens upon itself for the sake of others. It enters in this way into a "voluntary captivity." This final point is a basic idea in the *Treatise on Secular Authority*. See, for instance, *WA* 11, 253f.

[40] See the beginning of this section.

102

THE CONCEPT OF FREEDOM

God. And since on earth he is to do works for his neighbor, he is free "downward" toward outward action, i.e. free toward law or love. The perverted, satanic religion turns freedom and bondage upside down in one of these meanings. In place of bondage to one's neighbor, reason and monasticism substitute a loveless freedom which violates natural society. In place of freedom of conscience in faith before God, they substitute bondage to certain fixed, self-imposed works. Here, when rigorously construed, it is implied that reason and monasticism, the two primal forms of satanic religion, turn freedom and bondage upside down in the second sense too. In place of freedom in outer matters, there is substitution of legalistic bondage to precise rules or slavery to idolatrous things, and in place of bondage of the will before God, "upward" freedom of the will is substituted, in the fact that man does not believe in God and receive from God, but comes before him with works. Separated from God, man does works which have God as their focus, not one's neighbor. They are pointed toward heaven, not earth. That false religion changes and inverts freedom and bondage in this second sense is just what Luther specifically says in his treatise against Erasmus.

In one place in *The Bondage of the Will*, Luther sets the gospel on one side, and Moses and the pope against it on the other. The gospel leaves man bound in those things which are "above him," and at the same time gives him freedom in external relations to created things. On the contrary, Moses and the pope deprive man of freedom in outward matters, and make him bound in relation to created things. "The gospel leaves us to our own counsel, that we may decide and act in matters as we would. But Moses and the pope have not left us to that counsel; they have

103

coerced us by laws and subjected us rather to their will."[41] Thereby he becomes a slave to the law and a slave to sin, i.e., in bondage to the powers of evil. This implies that before God he has free will which is evil, and must of inner necessity be of evil.

Bring has directed attention to the peculiar dualism in *The Bondage of the Will*. On the one hand, Luther denies absolutely that man has any freedom of will; but on the other hand, he speaks of free will before God as a positive reality, evil in character. Free will thus represents hostility to God, "the devil," as Runestam expresses it in his summation of Luther's course of development up to 1525. Free will does effect something before God, but what it effects is sheer evil. To the law activity always answers; and since man under the sway of an evil free will lets the law determine his relation, he is really, and not merely apparently, active against God. For according to the will of God the law is to be operative not in relation to God, in heaven, but only on earth. In the conscience, or before God, the law is a tyrant and the work of the devil, which must be reduced to its proper place, the body and earth, by the gospel of Christ.[42] In the conscience, law and free will are evil in their activity; all of it is the devil's activity against God.[43]

[41] *WA* 18, 672 (1525). The context speaks of the two kingdoms, the heavenly and the earthly.

[42] The other side of the matter, however, still remains true. In the second use of the law it can be said that God himself forces the law into the conscience. The cross and the spiritual turmoil can be represented as coming from God as well as from the devil. God's purpose in a deviation from his own order such as the second use of the law, is victory over the devil, the salvation of man from the power of evil.

[43] Among the places in which Luther speaks of free will as evil and actively opposed to God, the following may be mentioned: *WA* 18, 670, 750, 751, 759, and 760.

The dualism between God and the devil can be the element in Luther's thought which makes meaningful the terminological duality which Bring has pointed out. On the one hand, when man is bound by God in faith, he has no free will before God. He has only freedom in outer matters to do good on earth against the devil. On the other hand, when in false belief man is bound by the devil, he abandons his freedom in outer matters and, a slave to the law there, turns his free will upward before God, making his freedom of will evil, a tool in the hand of the devil, against God. Man is set between God and the devil. When he is bound by God, he is free against the devil. When he is bound by the devil, he is free against God. In the former case free will operates in outward matters, in vocation, directed downward, bound by God; it is good. In the latter case free will operates before God, in heaven, directed upward, bound by the devil, and therefore evil. One or the other of these positions man must take.

But how can such real freedom of the will be reconciled with the concept of that bondage of the will which Luther demonstrated in his writing against Erasmus? To that question two complementary answers can be given.

Before God man can be free only as evil. He cannot be separated from God and independent of God without being captive to God's adversary and foe, a slave of the devil. Just as he can be free in outward matters at no price lower than that of entrusting himself to the power of God, so he can have freedom over against God only by the subjection of his will to the devil. Thus man's will is bound, either in relation to God or in relation to the devil. Such double significance in the term "the bound will" is not a mere device to make Luther intelligible; it corresponds with

Luther's own definition in the introduction to *The Bondage of the Will,* where he makes use of the picture of the mount and the rider; either God "rides" the will or the devil does. In both cases man's will is bound. Man would be free from the bondage of the will only if the will were free and unengaged, with the ability to choose its rider or to pursue existence with no rider at all. But it is impossible, for God and the devil are not remote from the will, but close to it, and there is never a pause in their struggle, their changing grip on the will, the beast of burden.[44]

So much for the first answer. Up to this point the two contestants, God and the devil, appear to be on even footing. But when Luther considers the point in the struggle when God triumphs over the devil and wins the will to his side, he affirms that here too, just as when the will was in Satan's grasp, men are "slaves and captives" to God; but, he observes, "this is nevertheless a royal freedom."[45] Nothing like this is said in picturing the will's captivity to Satan. On the contrary, Satan is called a tyrant. When God subdues the will to him in faith, he frees it from the tyrant's power. In God's power man's entire status is called freedom; in the devil's power it is called thralldom. This is the broadest possible use of the concept of freedom and bondage. And here the two contestants no longer seem to be on even footing. God created man, and man is intended for God. When man becomes God's, he becomes that for which he was created. Therefore it is freedom to be constrained by him, to escape this alien, evil power, who has usurped that which is God's. It is liberation to become that for which man was created. The two contestants are not

[44] *WA* 18, 634-635.
[45] *WA* 18, 635.

identically situated. But since God is Lord and Creator, it involves absolute guilt before him if man with willing heart strives against his will, and that is just what he does in Satan's hands. When he turns his evil freedom of will upward toward God, he stands inevitably under God's judgment, without the possibility of evading it. This is the second answer. In faith he is bound by God's love. In unbelief he is bound by God's wrath. So in both cases his will is bound in its relation to God, i.e., he has no choice. He has to take God as he is and suffer him.

3. *The Confusion of the Kingdoms*

We must give further attention to the recently mentioned confusion of the right place for freedom and the right place for bondage. Instead of enforcing freedom of conscience and bondage of the body, as God's order intended it, Satan misleads man, on the one hand to bondage of the law in the conscience (the pope), and on the other hand to freedom from the law in bodily matters (e.g. the peasant uprising). Both of these forms of confusion, which seem so different, do violence to one and the same divine order of the two kingdoms, with the gospel in one and the law in the other. In the spiritual kingdom the gospel is to rule, which is against the pope's tyranny over consciences. In the worldly kingdom the law is to rule, with its demand for obedience; and this is against the peasant uprising. Observing more closely these two forms of confusion, we have occasion to interpose here what was said in the preceding section about the concept of vocation.

The law is intended to rule in society and show men the requirements of their vocations on earth. The pope takes this and places it in heaven as the way in which obedience to the law leads man to heaven and salvation. In so doing the pope destroys the gospel, even if the law, set up for entry into heaven, were God's own good law, commanding true fulfilment of one's vocation.

"Even if the servant fulfil his office, obey his master, serve with utmost diligence; if he that is free, exercise authority and govern the realm or rule his family praiseworthily; if the man does whatever belongs to him as a man, in marrying a wife, in governing the affairs of his family, in obeying the magistrate, in acting honestly and decently towards all; if the woman live chastely, be subject to her husband, care diligently for her home, bring up her children well (which are indeed lofty gifts and distinguished works); nevertheless all these things mean nothing as righteousness before God."[46]

Then Luther charges that the pope also changes the content of the law. He preaches ceremonies and the like, which lead men away from their vocation on earth. "But the pope has not only mixed the law with the gospel, but of the gospel he has made mere laws, and only ceremonial laws at that. He has commingled the political and the ecclesiastical, which is indeed a satanic and infernal confusion."[47]

The two distortions of shifting the law from earth to heaven, and corrupting its content, belong together, as Luther sets forth in his exegesis of the text about the ten lepers.[48]

When man believes, there is no law in the conscience but Christ. Therefore works do not aim at supporting faith

[46] *WA* 40[I], 543 (*Commentary on Galatians, 1535*).
[47] *WA* 40[I], 209 (*Commentary on Galatians, 1535*).
[48] *WA* 8, 362-363 (1521).

or the religious life. Faith is already complete and needs no support from any Christian living, for Christ is perfect. Works have an utterly different significance. One's neighbor does not possess all he needs; he is in need of one thing and another, of counsel and strength. There is a task for good works, a reaching down to the earthly situation. The neighbor is the object sought, and beyond that there is nothing, just as a road leads to an insignificant little house and goes no further. This work is according to God's command.

But the pope and blind leaders make works a power for salvation and a stronghold for faith. Thereby man loses his unmixed and purehearted concern for his neighbor. Everything is aimed at man's own salvation, to profit himself; it is twisted up toward God and heaven.

Material things are to be given to one's neighbors, not to God. "But in this most tragic time insistence is laid upon them, just as if these things were necessary (to salvation) and they alone relate to the worship of God, though they are given for the comfort of men; and though it is not God but men who have need of them, they are not given to men but to God through an amazing blindness. There are some who say, 'We know that God does not need them'; but they do not answer if you ask them, 'Why do you give these things to God who does not desire them, and take them away from your needy brother, contrary to the will of God?' "[49]

This is a morality which always sees behind the neighbor something besides the neighbor himself. Unable to let anything be purely earthly and human, it must let its falsi-

[49] *WA* 1, 460, in which Matthew 15:5 is exposited (*Decem praecepta,* 1518).

fied religion drip down over everything. For this morality
the content of works necessarily becomes something different, "more Christian" than that which God has commanded. Here the sick and clouded conscience must set
church buildings, wordy prayers and fasts in place of unaffected love to one's neighbor.

"Turning the works from itself, faith directs them in love
to others. But those blind masters snatch them from their
neighbors and transfer them to themselves, thus suffocating
and extinguishing both love and faith. They lead man only
to love himself, and to strive only for his own salvation,
and to rely on his own works. The consequence of this
must be a terribly disturbed conscience, resulting in much
anxiety about one's own salvation, the building of churches,
many prayers, fasting for saints, and such works, which
are of use to no one. All kinds of misery and misfortune are
bound to follow, even as can now be seen in monasteries,
nunneries and universities."[50]

It is from the works of vocation that this churchly morality pulls man away.[51] When works are made the condition
for salvation, they easily become something other than those
of vocation. When the law becomes the way of salvation,
it goes against God's commandment and order.

Peculiarly enough the other form of confusion, the peasants' revolt, from the viewpoint of vocation, has the same
result, despite the fact that this confusion moves in the
opposite direction. Freedom of conscience from all law was
effected by Christ and is possessed in faith until it is fully

---

[50] WA 8, 363 (*Exposition of the Pericope about the Ten Lepers,* 1521).
See also 362.

[51] The Smalcald Articles and WA 6, 448 (*Address to the Christian
Nobility,* 1520). A characteristic line of attack against pilgrimages: one
leaves home, church and neighbor behind.

realized in heaven after death. This freedom the peasants change into a freedom in outer matters here on earth, shake off the power of their rulers, seize their weapons, and loose bloody revolt.

A serf can have Christian liberty, freedom of conscience, Luther holds, and yet remain a serf. A prisoner or an invalid does not cease to have the inward freedom of a child of God simply because he is confined to prison or to bed. To insist that differences in external position must be abolished would be to transform into a worldly kingdom the spiritual kingdom of Christ, in which rulers and serfs indubitably stand on the same level. That is both impossible and contrary to God's will. For worldly government cannot be sustained without these differences, i.e. without authority and obedience.[52]

We must differentiate between earth and heaven, law and gospel, life here and life that is to come in the resurrection. In existence on earth the law must hold sway. That means, among other things, that we must expect cross, tribulations, and heavy burdens. "The gospel does not take worldly matters into account, and makes the external life consist only in suffering, wrong, cross, patience, and contempt for temporal wealth and life."[53]

Taking matters into our own hands and rejecting the yoke, refusing to obey and to suffer, means leaving the fellowship of Christ; for when Christ was on earth he was subject to the law and crucified. Because of this he ascends to heaven, and he promises eternal life in heaven to each

[52] Cf. *WA* 18, 326-327, with reference to I Corinthians 7:20f. This is the point of departure for Luther's use of the term vocation (*Admonition to Peace: a Reply to the Twelve Articles of the Peasants in Swabia*, 1525).
[53] *WA* 18, 321.

and every one who believes and bears Christ's cross on earth.

A man cannot, as a Christian, attack his ruler, even if the ruler be unjust. As a Christian he must accept the situation and prepare to suffer injustice. If he insists on attacking, so be it; but then he must surrender the name of Christian.[54] The sword has no place in the spiritual realm. Even a necessary and just war, like the war against the Turk, is, according to Luther, an earthly necessity. It is something in which one participates as a subject, not as a Christian.[55] It was more perverse, then, that the peasant uprising was carried on in the name of the gospel. The war against the Turk was faithfulness to one's earthly vocation, but the peasant uprising was a violation of one's vocation and a surrender of vocation.

We recall Luther's exhortation to prayer, when danger from the Turk drew near.[56] For the oppressed peasants the exhortation is just as proper. The only thing for them to do is to pray, to call on God to give his hand to the support of the order he himself has instituted on earth.

"You have heard above that the gospel teaches that Christians ought to endure and suffer wrong, and pray to God in all their necessities, yet you are not willing to suffer, but like heathen, force the rulers to conform to your impatient will. You adduce the children of Israel as an example, saying that God heard their cry and delivered them. Why then do you not follow the example that you bring forward? Call upon God and wait until he sends a Moses, who will prove by signs and wonders that he is sent from

[54] *WA* 18, 322.
[55] There is no kind of war which Luther would regard as a "crusade," a word which in itself implies a confusing of the two kingdoms.
[56] See sec. 1 of this chapter.

God. The children of Israel did not riot against Pharaoh, or help themselves as you propose to do. This illustration, therefore, is dead against you and condemns you. You boast of it, and yet you do the opposite."[57]

Prayer is a positive action through which new and revolutionary ways are opened, for it brings into the earthly situation the God who is free from all external orders. The end of persevering prayer is to call in God, who turns the world upside down.[58] To this important aspect of Luther's view we shall devote a special section later in our study. Just now we must concern ourselves with the type of confusion we have observed.

The confusion of the two kingdoms, earth and heaven, or of the two realms, the earthly and the spiritual, is the outcome of confusing freedom and bondage, in the two forms we have noted (by the pope and by the peasants). These perversions of God's world are the work of the devil, *opus diaboli,* a hostile action against God, through the evil in men's hearts.[59]

Luther uses strong language to describe how men are taken captive by Satan and led to treachery to vocation, disobedience, and violence. As for the revolting peasants, he says that the devil has left hell and taken up his abode in the peasants.[60] It is the devil who leads the pope and the Anabaptists to substitute the sword, entrusted to earthly rulers, for the weapon of the spiritual realm, i.e. the Word.

[57] *WA* 18, 320f.

[58] The overthrow can occur through the sending of a miracle-man, a *vir heroicus,* who breaks through the established order, and with great power beings in new circumstances. In the illustration which Luther uses here Moses steps forward as such a *vir heroicus* (see quote above preceding note).

[59] Such confounding is a misuse, responsibility for which lies with man.

[60] *WA* 18, 359 (*Against the Robbing and Murdering Hordes of Peasants,* 1525).

But he immediately adds that it is also the devil who
leads worldly authorities (princes, kings, nobles, and
judges) to intervene in the exercise of "the oral sword,"
the office of preaching. When earthly rulers want to tell the
ministers of the Word how to preach, they are guilty of
leaving their vocation and overstepping the limits of earthly
government. To such action the preacher of God's Word
ought to say, "You fool, you ungodly simpleton, look to
your own vocation; don't you take to preaching, but let your
pastor do that."[61]

It is vital for each to limit himself to his own vocation
and remain in it. He must not forsake it, as do both revolting subjects and tyrannical princes. Even those who are
mightiest on earth must, according to the will of God, stop
before the Word.

For his part, a churchman must abstain from all earthly
weapons, from all coercion and lust for worldly power; for
the Word is to use no outward force. The preacher who
goes forward, simply trusting in the inner, invisible power
of the preached Word, is thus one who is faithful to his
vocation. "Therefore we have to distinguish between these
two rods or swords, so that neither one interferes with the
office of the other. They are all reaching for the sword.
The Anabaptists, Müntzer, the pope, and all the bishops
want to have the mastery and rule, even though it does not
belong to their vocation. It is the accursed devil."[62] The
church, or the gospel, is Christ, and Christ did not have
worldly power. He was defenseless against those who crucified him.

[61] *WA* 46, 735f (*Exposition of John 1 and 2*, 1538); Cf. 734 and 735;
"the devil is the author of all this, who does not rest until he confuses these
two swords. It is nothing new that the devil mixes up everything."
[62] *WA* 46, 735 (*Exposition of John 1 and 2*, 1538).

In general, the devil mixes the two kingdoms through people's deviation from vocation and violation of vocation, i.e. through misuse of their proper offices. Satan tempts men to do this. It is vocation, the right care for office, which is betrayed when confusion takes over. Against this, against *opus diaboli,* God presses his opposition both as gospel and as law. The gospel is to hold sway in the kingdom of heaven, and the law in the earthly kingdom.

In this double form the Word of God again places the two kingdoms in proper relation and undoes the devil's confusion of them. For the law says that men are to be subject to the earthly orders. At the same time the gospel says that this obedience on earth, obedience to vocation, avails nothing before God, nor does it need to, for in heaven it is freely given mercy that holds sway. Thereby both forms of confusion are eliminated, the pope's confusion, in which the law is set up in heaven; and the peasants' confusion in which the gospel is viewed as law in earthly matters.

In the law's spiritual use God himself lets the law act on the conscience. The anxiety which God awakens is the law's upreach to heaven.[63] For another thing, in the new man's love God himself lets the gospel bestow an outward freedom from earthly law, since love rises above all laws.[64] Could it be, then, that God himself mixes the two kingdoms and wipes out the boundaries between them? This is true in a certain sense, even though Luther never speaks of this action of God as confusion or mixture of the kingdoms. But the struggle between God and the devil is seen to be a real struggle in the very fact that the actions of the two contestants are so much alike and the positions of both are so mobile and changeable.

[63] See Chapter I, sec. 5 and 6.
[64] See Chapter I, sec. 4 and 6, Chapter II, sec. 2.

115

In regard to man's desperation and Christian love as sovereign over the law on earth, we recognize that vocation plays a prominent role in both. We have just declared that, in the satanic confusion, both forms (the pope's and the peasants') rise from a forsaking of vocation. In God's breaching of the boundary between the two kingdoms, the two forms of the breach (both turmoil of conscience and love in the new man) appear in man's faithful continuance in vocation. It is vocation itself that overcomes man, and it is as he endures that he is troubled. The free, new man does not drift in his action; apart from law he gives himself with inner joy to his vocation, transforming it in harmony with God's creative will of love, which lives in the new man through Christ. His aim is to serve his neighbor.

We look first at man's desperation. In his exposition of Jonah 2:4 Luther lays special stress on the statement that it was God, not merely the boat's crew, who cast the prophet into the sea; that it was not simply the waves of the sea, but God's waves, that encompassed him.[65] For so the troubled conscience looks upon everything about him— nature, things, and all creatures. They are all instruments with which the wrath of God terrifies the conscience. To Jonah, who took it into his own hands to escape from God and his will, the crew, the storm and the waves were a divine expression, God's action and instruments in the troubling of the conscience.

"Then he forgets the people who have thrown him into the ocean, and says God has done it. 'Thou,' he says, 'Thou hast thrown me' etc. For so it seems to the conscience, that

---

[65] The verse is included in the psalm which Jonah 2 puts into the mouth of the prophet, "Thou didst cast me into the deep . . . all thy waves and thy billows passed over me." Luther's exposition is found in *WA* 19, 226-227 (1526).

every misfortune that befalls us is God's wrath; and all created things seem to us to be God himself and the wrath of God, be it even no more than a rustling leaf. . . . So he does not say, 'The waves and billows of the sea passed over me,' but 'All thy waves and thy billows passed over me,' because he feels in his conscience how the sea with its waves and billows serves God and his wrath which punishes sin. He says, 'All waves and billows passed over me,' for it feels to him as if all the waters in heaven and on earth had passed over him, as if no one other than he was oppressed by the wrath of God, and as if all created things were with God and against him."[66]

Here it is implied that the external things and relationships in which man lives represent God to him; they are God's "masks," *larvae Dei*. This aspect of Luther's view of existence is of utmost importance. We soon will give thoroughgoing attention to it. God does not come to man in thoughts and feelings which well up in him when he isolates himself from the world, but rather in what happens to man in the external and tangible events which take place about him.

In the light of this we can understand an important development of thought in the *Treatise on Good Works* (1520), where it is explained how faith can be the whole content of the life of a Christian, so that beyond faith, there is no peculiar action called for at all. Luther explains it this way: Life is never inactive. Every moment man is doing something or avoiding something, enduring something or fleeing from something. If a man makes up his mind that every minute of his life is to pass in undoubting trust in God and certainty of God's grace, "he will find how much there is

[66] *WA* 19, 226-227.

for him to do and that everything is rooted in faith, so that he may never be idle except as idleness itself contributes to the exercise and work of faith." [67]

His viewpoint is not that works flow forth from faith, but that works pour in on man from the outside, through the very movement of life. Faith demands that every moment and action be accepted in faith and borne in faith; the works are to be done in faith. Faith is severely tested when in outer circumstances God brings us suffering and troubles, such as hatred and slander by our enemies, sickness, and other bitter misfortunes. [68] Sometimes it is impossible to accept trustfully whatever happens, and desperation comes. Then God's discipline comes upon us with force. God lays the cross on the old man, whom he would slay and raise from the dead. In such times of cross and desperation man must pray and cry out. Through prayer and praise faith grows "and comes to itself," so that in strength it can go forth again in new works.

"As soon as the evil spirit encounters such faith, honor and service to God, he rages and begins his persecution. He attacks our body, goods, honor and life. He brings upon us sickness, poverty, shame and death, which God inflicts upon us and ordains for us in this way. Thus faith is tried severely, like gold in the fire. It is a great thing to keep so firm a trust in God as to look upon him as the most gracious Father, though he appears in so terrible a semblance of wrath, as he inflicts upon us death, shame, ill health, and poverty. . . . Then suffering urges faith to call upon God's name and to praise him in such suffering. . . . Faith grows precisely by such prayer and praise to God,

[67] *WA* 6, 212-213.
[68] *WA* 6, 266-267 (*Treatise on Good Works*, 1520).

118

and thereby recovers and strengthens itself. Thus faith flows forth in works, and returns to itself through works, as the sun rises and sets, and again returns to its rising."[69]

Here is the idea, typical of Luther, that prayer is a turning point in which the suffering laid upon us ceases to be a heavy cross and becomes easy to bear, because in prayer God himself comes to man and helps him to live and act.

For a Christian desperation and inner freedom alternate, and between them stands prayer which changes everything, because in it God is creatively present. Cross and despair come together in vocation, and drive man to prayer. Faith, strengthened and born anew in prayer, by God, enables man to "descend from heaven as a rain that fructifies the earth"; for man "fulfils his vocation with sincere joy" and submits to unjust laws.[70] The struggle between the old man and the new is indeed prayer. It is the old man who endures the cross of vocation; it is the new man who rejoices in vocation, and from within gives it new character, just as a man changes and adorns a prison in which he lives willingly, and flourishes. Between the night of despair and the peaceful day of labor hangs faith, praying and struggling.

Continuing the long quotation given just above from the *Treatise on Good Works,* Luther states, "Therefore in the Scriptures the day is associated with peaceful life in one's work, and the night with life's suffering and adversities. Faith lives and is active in both, going in and out in them, as Christ says in John 9."[71] With this we are already touching on the second point, love in the new man. In this love live joy and freedom, for if one gladly helps others and

[69] *WA* 6, 249.

[70] *WA* 40[I], 51 (*Commentary on Galatians,* 1535). Cf. *WA* 34[I], 511 (*Sermons,* 1531; Rörer).

[71] *WA* 6, 249.

with willing heart accepts the day's tasks, one is inwardly released and set free from the law. What is done in freedom from the law is in line with the law as the divine imperative; and it goes beyond all obedience enforced by law.[72] What promotes the well-being of others and brings them peace cannot be laid down in advance as fixed rules.

"What love is must show itself in relation to time and place."[73] Love aims at what is good for others, and therefore rises above all laws (whose very aim is to exact something that is good for others). And since vocation involves my relation with others, love for others is *eo ipso* the fulfilment of my vocation. It is the vocabulary of vocation itself, the terms "station" and "office," which Luther uses when he speaks of spontaneous love toward others. "If you find yourself in a work by which you accomplish something good for God, or the holy, or yourself, but not for your neighbor alone, then you should know that that work is not a good work. For each one ought to live, speak, act, hear, suffer, and die in love and service for another, even for one's enemies, a husband for his wife and children, a wife for her husband, children for their parents, servants for their masters, masters for their servants, rulers for their subjects and subjects for their rulers, so that one's hand, mouth, eye, foot, heart and desire is for others; these are Christian works, good in nature."[74]

Even in the simplest duty in the home, for example,

[72] *WA* 10[I], 2, 178 (*Adventspostille,* 1522), *WA* 17[II], 95 (*Fastenpostille,* 1525); cf. Chapter II, sec. 2, above.

[73] *WA* 56, 511 (*Commentary on Romans,* 1515-16).

[74] *WA* 10[I], 2, 41 (*Adventspostille,* 1522). Here this labor of love in vocation is set in contrast with "the work of the papists" which does not regard others but is directed toward God and the worker's own salvation. For instance, various liturgical actions, pilgrimages and fasts are named. But if man neglects his neighbor, he forsakes his vocation. Conversely, if man flees from his vocation, he flees from his neighbor.

marriage shows itself as a spiritual status, full of faith and love, while so-called spiritual orders are worldly, lacking faith and love, because they separate man from his neighbor and daily work, hence from life's despair, hence from fellowship with God. In the cloister one is removed both from the anxieties of vocation and from the transformation of vocation.[75] God's "commingling" of the two kingdoms, against the devil, takes place out in the world, in natural life as God made it. God becomes real, both as wrath and as love, for him who maintains unbroken contact with his vocation and holds himself to it. Real confusion and intermingling of the two kingdoms, apart from vocation, is the devil's mixing of the kingdoms.

The strife between God and the devil surges back and forth through the whole world and through every heart. Where victorious faith holds sway, all is gospel and freedom, and nothing brings despair or weighs down. Where there is not faith, everything in heaven and earth is law and terrifying darkness, which feeds our desperation. Both belief and unbelief transform all things. Both God and the devil transform all things, each making use of everything in the struggle against the other. Temptation in vocation is the devil's attempt to get man out of his vocation. If he succeeds, the temptation has been a good tool for the devil and has brought him victory. But if faith stands the test, the temptation has only served to strengthen God's hold on man; as a good tool it has confirmed God's mastery over satanic power.

According to Luther, one must speak not only of the

[75] *WA* 12, 105-108 (*Exposition of I Corinthians 7*, 1523). Luther stresses both the fact that the work of the household takes place in faith and therefore in the Spirit, and that all troubles that arise to burden every family drive people to anxious prayer.

living God, but also of the living devil. God is present everywhere, and so is the devil.[76] Therefore man's struggle must go on constantly, and he must pray without ceasing. "Who is master of his heart? Who can resist the devil and the flesh? It is impossible for us to defend ourselves even against the smallest sin. The Scriptures say that we are prisoners of the devil, our prince and god. We are forced to do what he wants and prompts us to do. . . . But should such a condition therefore be unpunished and right? By no means! We are to call upon God to help and resist sin and what is wrong." Certainty of the active presence of the devil drives us to prayer.[77]

God is in all things, "in the stone, in the fire, in the water, and in the rope," but he wants us to seek him only in the Word, which is clear and plain.[78] The devil conceals himself behind all things that he may ensnare man, but the Word unveils the devil in all his disguises and unmasks him. "Only the Word uncovers him, so that he cannot hide himself."[79]

Thus the Word, together with vocation, stands out as

[76] We have already spoken of the will as a mount for which two riders, God and the devil, are contending: *WA* 18, 635 (*The Bondage of the Will*, 1525). Neither of the contenders is remote from the will. Both are immediately with it, like two men beside a horse which they are both attempting to mount.

[77] *WA* 18, 395 (*An Open Letter Concerning the Hard Book Against the Peasants*, 1525).

[78] *WA* 19, 492 (*Sermon von dem Sakrament*, 1526).

[79] *WA* 32, 36 (*Sermon von Leiden und Kreuz*, 1530). Here we find a basic discussion of the question whether cross and suffering come from God or from the devil. In the first place he says that suffering comes from God: "he wants to transform us into the likeness of his dear Son, Christ, that we may be like him in suffering in this life and in glory and honor in the next life." Even if God did not intend to burden and trouble us (this is the second answer) the devil would still do so on account of evil. Cf. 36f, even though this treatise is of somewhat uncertain trustworthiness.

man's firm support, placed as he is between God the Creator and the devil the usurper.

The gospel and one's station are placed side by side as constituting together a sure defense against all doubt, come what may.

"As long as he (e.g. a shoemaker or a blacksmith) clings to these two, to the Word of faith toward God by which the heart is made clean, and to the word of understanding which teaches him how to act toward his neighbor in his station in life, everything is clean to him, even if with his hands and his whole body he deals with nothing but dirt."[80]

Since the Word or the gospel is the peculiar mark of the church, this position side by side can also be expressed as follows: A Christian lives in vocation and in the church. Vocation is the concrete form of the law, and the church is the concrete form of the gospel.[81]

When heaven and earth are differentiated as two kingdoms, one might get the impression of two static worlds, a world of idea and a material world. But when the boundary between these realms is blurred in the struggle between God and Satan, it is clear that such a division into "above" and "below" is not a complete description of Luther's view of the world, despite the fact that Luther himself ceaselessly uses these terms and others like them. God is over everything, both as wrath and as love, in law and in gospel. God dwells in heaven, but he lives and works on earth. In his work on earth he wants men as his fellow-workers.

4. Co-operation

The concept of man as a fellow-worker with God implies that man is an independent ethical subject with a certain

[80] *WA* 32, 326.
[81] See, above, Chapter I, sec. 5; also sec. 3.

amount of free and unshackled activity. Yet the fact is that the idea of co-operation grows up directly and simultaneously out of Luther's belief in the bondage of the will before God. To understand Luther here, let us consider an earthly master in relation to a serf. The serf is free, for example, to move his hands and feet; the master does not decide their movements in detail. But this freedom of his members the serf has to use in the service of his master. That the slave is free to work only intensifies his bondage to his master. Because this property of his, this slave, has the ability to move, the master can make much more effective use of him than of a lifeless thing. When the slave, using all the strength and understanding he has, does what he is commanded in field and meadow, he is his master's "fellow-worker." This is about the way Luther conceives of man as a "fellow-worker" with God.

Co-operation takes place in vocation, which belongs on earth, not in heaven; it is pointed toward one's neighbor, not toward God. Man's deeds and work have a real function to fill in civil and social relationships, despite the fact that works done by man cannot lift from man the condemnation that rests on him before God. Only the action and work of Christ, not that of man, are effective with God.[82] The forgiveness of sins is the only righteousness which man can present before God, or in which he can die.

"The law shall not have power up there. . . . This is what ought to be preached: The law is no more. In place of the law, of obedience, of labor, sits Christ, King of grace and of the forgiveness of sins, who does nothing but give, help and comfort. It is nothing that I have done, not my works that I will contemplate. I have the upward look, seeing what

[82] *WA* 40ᴵ, 392-395, 411, and 542 (*Commentary on Galatians*, 1535).

124

Another has done, how he has lived. It is with his works that I am concerned."[83]

But while life on earth continues, and we live among men, our righteousness consists of our works; and our station or office, i.e. our vocation, is simply our mandate concerning the works man ought to do here in God's earthly realm, while he awaits death. God has so constituted this vocation that, quite apart from man's devoutness and love, others are served by vocation when it is fulfilled.[84] "The married person must, in external (bodily) relations, serve another besides himself, and an earthly ruler must somehow be of service to his subjects. Boys, girls and all servants must benefit and serve others."[85]

That monasticism is a sheer invention by men and not instituted by God is betrayed by the fact, among others, that the monk does not give his body to serve the well-being of others, but has severed his relations with others that he might busy himself about his own soul and spiritual things. By this course none of the vocations instituted by God are fulfilled. A "station" instituted by God is a channel for God's love to the world and his care of human beings.

Luther's way of using spatial terms when he speaks of the work of vocation is striking. To do one's work "in vocation" is to perform works "below," "down here." If one

[83] *WA* 34[II], 27 (*Sermons*, 1531; Rörer). Cf. also *WA* 19, 661 (*Whether Soldiers Too Can Be Saved*, 1526). The forgiveness of sins is the only righteousness that can stand in the judgment, to which man goes when he dies.

[84] *WA* 27, 514: When the work of vocation is carried out, the neighbor is profited. See, for example, the idea of the cross as immediately coupled with the idea of vocation, 515, 3: "the holy cross which is there" (*Sermons*, 1528; Rörer). See also *WA* 32, 459: he who is concerned about his faithfulness in vocation is also concerned about his neighbor; cf. 472 (*The Sermon on the Mount*, 1532).

[85] *WA* 10[I], 1, 656 (*Kirchenpostille*, 1522).

hears the gospel with faith and is true to his vocation, "he is pure through and through, both inwardly in his heart before God and outwardly toward all that is below him on earth."[86] In his *Commentary on Romans*, analyzing Romans 12:8 ("He that ruleth, with diligence"), he says to "mount up" is to become a ruler, to receive office; but to serve with diligence is to "descend." "For to ascend makes one exalted; but to descend makes one a lover";[87] as the angels in Jacob's dream of the ladder ascended only to descend, so a Christian is placed in an eminent position only that he may be the servant of servants (Gen. 28:12).

It is clear that to "descend" is the same as to serve or love one's neighbor.

In his *Kirchenpostille* we find the concept of a Christian as a conduit or channel, which receives from above, from God, through faith, "and then gives forth below" to others, through love. Luther makes it clear that God's own love reaches out to others through Christians as channels. God is present on earth with his goodness when a Christian directs his service downward to others. God dwells in heaven, but now he is near and working on earth with man as his co-operator. In *The Large Catechism* it is said that all creatures ("parents and all in authority" are specially mentioned) are God's hands, channels and means through which he gives us all things.[88] The whole idea of man as a channel is brought into close relation with the doctrine

[86] *WA* 32, 326 (*The Sermon on the Mount*, 1532).

[87] *WA* 56, 458 (1515-16).

[88] *WA* 30I, 136 (1529). If I thus receive God's gifts through the faithfulness of others in their vocations, the same is true about my vocation in relation to others. "The same relationship with God must express itself in my office." Cf. also *WA* 28, 618 (*Sermons on Deuteronomy*, 1529; Rörer).

of vocation. Characteristically enough, a warning is added against turning away from God's mandate and created order. Very true to Luther's thought is his constant affirmation that the prince, just because he has so many people under him, is the servant of all. Again we see the downward-reaching character of work in vocation which leaves the officeholder no room for pretensions, even if his office is the highest, yet which is most significant as an opportunity for serving.[89] God is actually present in the prince's exercise of his office, since God is active in the direction of all things. "He who is in the seat of authority is, as it were, an incarnate God."[90]

The statement that works are directed downward is in harmony with Luther's terminology concerning bondage and freedom, in his treatise in opposition to Erasmus, in 1525. A person is bound with regard to what is "above" him, but free in what is "below" him. In *The Bondage of the Will*, as we pointed out earlier, the terms "superior" and "inferior" refer to the heavenly and earthly realms respectively.[91] Therefore vocation's direction downward means that *cooperatio* takes place in the earthly realm, where we are free to direct our works toward others, as God has commanded. Among men, in the area of *libertas in externis*,

[89] *WA* 11, 273 (*Treatise on Secular Authority*, 1523).

[90] *WA* 43, 514 (*Commentary on Genesis*, 1535-45). It is very important that, precisely because of the divine nature of the prince's office, Luther holds that the prince must be one who prays as he fulfils his vocation. "It is most certain that without prayer you will effect nothing at any time, because government is a power of certain divine character." They who rush in to church, government, or business without prayer, shut God out of the orders he himself has established; for they do not seek his direction in prayer (514, 9-19). In a later section we shall present statements about prayer when we present the idea of "co-operation" with God. For the present, we pass them by.

[91] See above, Chapter I, sec. 2.

127

man is a fellow-worker with God. But before God man is only passive and receptive; for there bondage of the will obtains, and there Christ rules alone with his grace and gospel, without law, i.e. without works on man's part. Ascending faith receives what God does; *operatio Dei* and *passio nostra;* it is not co-operation. Thus we see the role of co-operation in relation to the two kingdoms: co-operation is barred from heaven, and relevant to earth.

Wanting to be exalted instead of serving, regarding office as a possibility for selfish power instead of for service, is offense against vocation. Through this offense man falls away from co-operation with God, and comes, on the contrary, to work against God. Then one becomes a hindrance and an enemy in the path of the Creator's self-giving love. This self-exalting ambition, loveless and greedy for power, is pride, *superbia;* it is self-commitment to the power of sin and the devil. "The fact is that we have a true and Christian knowledge of the mind of Christ; and the grace of God has made me a preacher thereof. I am commanded not to be proud because of that gift. In the course of my journey I should both serve my neighbor and serve him. Princes, nobles, the learned, the scholars and the noblemen are generally guilty in this respect, even as burghers and farmers are also puffed up. I should rather think like this: 'You have the gift of God and you are a teacher. If you are puffed up, then the villager in the hamlet, who is not your equal, is better. So he goes to heaven, but I go to hell. If princes, noblemen, farmers and burghers want to exalt themselves, remember this: God did not create only princes, nobles, men. Why are you proud?' "[92]

The common rule is: "God gives you office that you may

[92] *WA* 49, 606-607 (*Sermons*, 1544; Rörer).

serve."[93] God's action is determined by his self-proffering love, which seeks the lost and the fallen. For to Luther God himself, when he is described as Creator, becomes utterly like a human being faithful to his vocation, who gives himself to the lowly. God creates out of nothing, i.e. he gives heed to the despised and helpless who are at the point of death.[94] In the crucifixion of Christ on Golgotha, he who was despised by the world showed himself a true Creator, one who makes his costliest work out of that which is nothing. A Christian is therefore also a person who is ever in desperation, need, and weakness, since he is that *nihil* out of which God creates.[95]

The natural man is always aspiring to rise out of lowliness to the heights; he follows his evil bent to get away from serving. Through the very action of striving upward toward honor and self-complacent splendor, he separates himself from the living God, who in sacrificial love bows down to created things and stands close to all who are in the depths. This man forsakes his neighbor, so he lives not with God but with the devil who leads him away from the path of his vocation.

"Daily we experience how everybody tries to rise above his own level and strives for honor, power, wealth, art, comfortable living and for everything which is big and lofty. Wherever one finds these people, there everybody clings to them, follows them, serves them eagerly. Everybody likes to be there to share in their high standing. On

[93] *WA* 49, 610 (*Sermons,* 1544). Pride in one's station in life and unwillingness to serve are looked upon as expressions of satanic perversion: "O nobleman, do you set yourself up, exalting yourself? That is of the devil."

[94] *WA* 7, 547-548 (*The Magnificat,* 1521).

[95] *WA* 56, 303 (*Commentary on Romans,* 1515-16).

the other hand, nobody likes to look down where poverty, shame, need, misery and fear dwell. Everybody averts the eyes from them. Wherever you find such people, everybody runs away, flees, shies away from them, leaves them. Nobody thinks of helping them and standing by them, to help them to become somebody. . . . There is no creator among men who would make something out of nothing, although St. Paul, in Romans 12, teaches and says, 'Dear brethren, regard not the lofty things, but give yourselves to the lowly.' "[96]

Creation, the work of God, is carried out through the person who, being faithful to his vocation, is a coworker against the devil. He resists temptation and lives humbly in downward-reaching and unobtrusive common toil, through which God sustains his earthly realm against all onslaughts of evil. Vocation and the man who fulfils it are used as tools and means for God's continuing creation, which occurs "out of nothing," i.e. under vocation's cross. When the cross of any vocation is borne, that vocation appears lowly. "No one is poor among Christians. If you do not have as much as the burgomaster, do you not rather have God the Creator of heaven and earth, Christ, and prayer? Yea, the emperor does not have more. Remain in your station in life, be it high or low, and continue in your vocation. Beware of overreaching. . . . Rather say, 'O God, heavenly Father, defend me against haughtiness.' "[97]

Viewed from without, some offices seem to be surrounded by a pleasing luster. But seen from within, it is evident

[96] WA 7, 547 (The Magnificat, 1521).
[97] WA 49, 609 (Sermons, 1544; Rörer). Cf. WA 10[I], 1, 313-315 (Kirchenpostille, 1522). Through the concluding sentences in this reference there is brought in the concept of man's co-operation in the dualism between God and Satan.

that those offices too demand sacrificial, downward-reaching service, which is a cross for the old man. If a person yields himself to this demand to serve, even though he is unaware of it, he is God's fellow-worker. God continues his creative work on earth where man's vocation lies.

In *The Bondage of the Will* Luther distinguishes between the free will's "own power and efficacy" and its "co-operation." The former is denied, and the latter affirmed.

Man has no ability of his own, independent of God, with which he can act before God. This power would be from the devil; it would not mean freedom. On the other hand, Paul co-operates with God when he instructs the Corinthians or speaks in the Spirit of God.[98] Even the ungodly co-operate with God, for God alone has made all things and set all in motion. But when God works through the ungodly, he works without his Spirit.[99]

The righteous are moved by the Spirit of God and co-operate with God, because through them he lets the fruit of the Spirit grow. "By the Spirit of grace he acts in those whom he has justified, i.e. in his kingdom; he so acts in them that they are new creatures. They follow him and co-operate, or rather, as Paul says, they are impelled."[100]

In a Latin sermon of 1519, he says that our own righteousness, co-operating with a righteousness not our own but given to us by God without works of ours, consists of three things: the putting to death of the flesh, love to others, and humility before God.[1] Here God is not working outside

[98] *WA* 18, 753 (1525).

[99] *WA* 18, 753f: "without the grace of the Spirit." Cf. *WA* 30III, 213f: "without his Word" (*Von Ehesachen*, 1530). In *The Bondage of the Will* the term "co-operation" is expressly used in this general context: "Thus even all things evil co-operate with Him" (753f).

[100] *WA* 18, 753.

[1] *WA* 2, 146 (*Sermo de duplici iustitia*). The reference is to Gal. 5:22f.

of us, for a regeneration has taken place "that he may work in us and we work together with him; through us he preaches, has pity on the poor, and comforts the faint-hearted."[2]

Luther often affirms that God gives us good gifts even through evil people.[3] In *The Babylonian Captivity* (1520) this point is discussed in an incisive way which is extremely instructive in our discussion of co-operation. In the passage referred to here Luther attacks the sacrifice of the Mass and explains that the sacrament comes from God through the priest to the communicant. It is not offered to God; it "comes down" *(descendit)*, as he expresses it.[4] The sacrament is the same gift whether it is presented to us through a good or an evil minister. But prayer "rises up" *(ascendit);* it is addressed to God, and God does not heed an ungodly minister who does not believe. When one who is unworthy is sent to pray, i.e. when the sacrifice of the Mass is offered, the judge, God, is only stirred to greater wrath. The difference between that which "rises up" and that which "comes down" is affirmed by Luther as something which is self-evident.

"We must not confuse the two, the Mass and prayer, sacrament and work, testament and sacrifice; for the former comes from God through the ministration of the priest, and demands our faith, but the latter proceeds from our faith to God through the priest, and calls for his answer. The former comes down, the latter ascends. The former

---

[2] *WA* 18, 754 (*The Bondage of the Will*, 1525). Cf. *WA* 56, 398-399: God so directs man's will that he becomes the instrument of God (*Commentary on Romans*, 1515-16).

[3] See, for example, *WA* 10¹, 1, 617 (*Kirchenpostille*, 1522). To refuse to receive good from evil persons is to tempt God.

[4] *WA* 6, 526. Cf. *WA* 18, 775 (*The Bondage of the Will*, 1525).

does not necessarily require a worthy and devout minister, but the latter really does, because God does not hear sinners. He knows how to bestow blessings through evil men, but he does not accept the work of any evildoer, as he showed with Cain, and as Proverbs 15 says, 'The sacrifices of the wicked are an abomination to the Lord,' and Romans 14 says, 'Whatever is not of faith is sin.' "[5]

Luther's thought about the gift coming down from God to men, regardless of whether it is given through a good or evil man, is not restricted to the sacrament. It is true of all human functions through which God effects something good, whether temporal or spiritual. As for co-operation in office, we need not decide to what extent the fellow-worker God uses is or is not made new in heart by the Spirit. Co-operation is limited to the earthly realm, where outward rectitude counts. The matter of the heart's purity or impurity is relevant to heaven, and its solution lies with Christ, with the forgiveness of sins through grace alone. On earth the prime consideration is that our works do good to others, whether they come from willing or unwilling hearts.

This clear juxtaposition of the two realms is probably not maintained when the term "polarity" is used to characterize co-operation. Man hears the gospel; but he does works according to the law. He is passive and receptive before God or in heaven, and active in love on earth. This is not thought of as a paradox or something which is hard to conceive in fact. It can be illustrated by a housewife who sits quietly in church and listens, whereas at home she is active and does her work (passive in the spiritual realm and active in the earthly). The serf is silent and receptive

[5] *WA* 6, 526 (*The Babylonian Captivity*, 1520).

before his master, but imperative and active toward the livestock. In this very action of the slave, moving out from the master and toward the cattle, the master's care for his cattle is effected through the slave. In like manner God cares for people through other people as co-operators.

"The father is the instrument of procreation, but God is the fountain and author of life. So too the magistrate is just such an instrument, through whom God preserves peace and law. In the home husband and wife are instruments, through whom the Lord increases the human race."[6]

The goodness or wickedness of the one who co-operates is a lesser consideration because of the relative independence of the office from its incumbent. God works through the station, the office, which, as his creation, is good under all circumstances, regardless of the character of the incumbent.

For that reason, implicit in what is said about co-operation is a constant demand for humility and an aid to our understanding of man's littleness before God and God's great creative work. "This psalm (Ps. 127) appears, as it were, to be a compendium and comment on that book [Ecclesiastes] where it teaches both what is the efficient cause, in state and society, in public or domestic economy, and to what end government ought to be kept. Certainly we may to such an extent be God's instruments and co-workers. Yet we may not be the efficient cause, but only the instrumental cause through which God acts and effects such things—even as Ecclesiastes says, 'It is through me that kings reign.' "[7] The words from Ecclesiastes just referred to are those that speak about the vanity of every-

[6] WA 40III, 210-211 (*Exposition of Psalm 127*, 1532-33). See above, Chapter I, sec. 1.
[7] WA 40III, 210.

thing under the sun, i.e. on earth (4:7), and about the modest joy man ought to feel in the presence of the outward gifts God bestows (5:18). Man's constant mistake is that he thinks he is doing something by himself.[8]

Co-operation takes place when we make use of created things. "Even though we are certain of God's providence and care for us, we must know that the things and means which God has placed in our hands are to be used, that we do not tempt God *(ne tentemus Deum)*." He who turns to God in prayer for help from above, without doing all he can with the help of the outward gifts God has given, is putting God to the test and cannot expect his prayer to be heard. When work does not avail, when one's strength no longer suffices, the time for prayer has come. Then by prayer one brings in a new power where the ordinary powers within creation do not suffice.[9] God's special participation as answer to prayer is, in such a moment, absolutely certain. When the need is genuine, it is impossible to put God to the test.[10] In need, faith and prayer are simply the more pleasing to God, the bolder they are and the more hopeless matters look from the world's point of view. Man can never know what God does in answer to prayer in the hour of need; but it is certain that he does enter in a tangible way and concretely effect something new on earth. Being in need means that all creation's possibilities have been tried

[8] Cf. *WA* 51, 254 (*Exposition of Psalm 101,* 1534-35); and *WA* 47, 857 (*Sermons,* 1539; Rörer).

[9] *WA* 44, 648 (*Commentary on Genesis,* 1535-45).

[10] *WA* 44, 648: "When we have done those things which are possible to us, let us leave the rest to God, casting our care on the Lord, for he will take action." Cf. *WA* 10^I, 1, 616: "From this it is clear that when man is in need, he cannot tempt God; for all his words and promises apply to the time of need, when no man is able to help by himself" (*Kirchenpostille,* 1522). Luther refers to Psalm 50:15.

and found incapable of helping. At that point God descends and complements his creation. The door by which God enters to effect the new is often the prayer of a person in need.[11]

Man's work with external things as tools in various vocations and stations is in truth his co-operation with God. In the church, man uses the Word and the sacraments.[12] In government he uses the sword and other weapons. In the economic field, children are fed and nurtured through outward means. Such created goods, intended to serve life, are reason, the mind, the senses, and all the powers of body and soul. When there is something to be done, whatever it be, man is to make use of all these powers, just as he uses ax and saw to cut down a tree, and does not try to bring the tree down with his nose or a straw.[13] Turning to God in prayer for help, without using the external means which God has given, is tempting God; it is *praesumptio,* superciliousness. But not to turn to God in prayer for help in vocation, when all outward available possibilities are exhausted, is to blaspheme God and treat his promises as lies. It is *desperatio,* unbelief. Faith moves between the two, between presumption and desperation; the hands labor, but

[11] *Cooperatio* involves the same double quality of the fixed and the modifiable which we meet everywhere in Luther's view. The usual co-operation occurs in daily work, when matters move on in due course. But when God uses as a coworker a person who is in need and cries to him in prayer, then the unexpected and marvelous takes place. Prayer is a truth of revolutionary power in society, home, and church.

[12] *WA* 44, 648 (*Commentary on Genesis,* 1535-45): "Thus Paul calls the apostles coworkers with God. It is God himself who alone does the work and yet through them."

[13] *WA* 44, 648: "[It is] as if he were to say, 'Now I will make them free through your co-operation.' Thus it is in all actions in the common life. I should not cut down a tree with someone's nose; I should take an ax or a saw. A tree is not to be laid low with a straw or a stalk, but with an ax. On this account God gave reason to men, and senses and faculties. Therefore use these as the means and gifts of God."

the heart is passive and rests in God. "These things ought always to be striven for and carried on in the church of God, that we may walk in the royal way and turn aside neither to the right nor the left. We should neither doubt his promise nor tempt God by lightly esteeming or neglecting the means which God has ordained."[14]

In this way prayer and work belong together. He who does his work thoroughly can pray with power, for then he has a good conscience. If, for instance, in the matter of preparedness against the Turks, one lets matters go haphazardly, one will find that it will not suffice to call loudly upon God, for the external resources have not been put to full use. So Luther says he does not know whether, in such a situation, prayer will be heard.[15] Here we see how man's ordinary works and God's extraordinary, new works are interwoven.

The concepts of co-operation and masks of God belong together. Natural occurrences such as storms and thunder, or sun, or rich harvests are also God's masks, behind which his wrath and his love are hid. But for our concern it is more important to note that, in co-operation in vocation, man becomes God's mask on earth wherever man acts. A mask of God is therefore found only in the earthly realm where man labors and does his work for others. In his toil he is a tool in God's hand, bound before God, i.e. receiving and passive before God, but active outwardly, so that God reveals himself to others through man's actions.

"All our work in the field, in the garden, in the city, in the home, in struggle, in government—to what does it all amount before God except child's play, by means of which

---

[14] *WA* 44, 649 (*Commentary on Genesis*, 1535-45). Also cf. *WA* 40[III], 234 (*Exposition of Psalm 127*, 1532-33).

[15] *WA* 30[II], 146-47 (*Vom Kriege wider den Türken*, 1529).

God is pleased to give his gifts in the field, at home, and everywhere? These are the masks of our Lord God, behind which he wants to be hidden and to do all things. . . . God bestows all that is good on us, but you must stretch out your hands and lay hold of the horns of the bull, i.e. you must work and lend yourself as a means and a mask to God."[16]

Instead of coming in uncovered majesty when he gives a gift to man, God places a mask before his face. He clothes himself in the form of an ordinary man who performs his work on earth. Human beings are to work, "everyone according to his vocation and office"; through this they serve as masks for God, behind which he can conceal himself when he would scatter his gifts.[17] God would be able to create children without making use of human beings, but it pleases him to conceal himself in marriage, in which he lets men and women think that they bring the children into the world, "but it is he who does so, hidden behind these masks."[18]

Therefore man must beware lest he place his faith and reliance in external things, which are only a garb for God, and not God himself. Our equipment is only a "costume" for God, behind which he hides to help us; but he expects us to give our hearts to him, not to his "costume"; we must not pray to that.[19] All creation is good, but it becomes evil if it is worshiped and substituted for God. Faith in God

[16] *WA* 31^I, 436 (*Exposition of Psalm 147,* 1532).

[17] Cf. *WA* 30^I, 205-206 (*Large Catechism*) where gifts which God bestows through people of all stations are presented as our "daily bread," which the devil would take away from us; also *WA* 31^I, 437 (*Exposition of Psalm 147,* 1532).

[18] *WA* 31^I, 436.

[19] *WA* 15, 373 (*Exposition of Psalm 127,* 1524). Cf. *WA* 16, 263: "Thus the Lord is at work in all things. Man must plow, reap, sow; but he is God's mask" (*Sermons on Exodus,* 1525; Rörer).

as the Creator of everything good has the very function of making known that man can make no claims before God.[20]

It is only in relation to my neighbor that I can consider anything mine, given to me that with it I may serve my neighbor, thereby being to him a mask of the goodness of God. In the view of the "mask" we again come upon the basic aspect of Luther's thought which we have already encountered in our analysis of station and office, cross and suffering, works and co-operation. All these were instituted by God, and are relevant on earth in our relation to others; but they are excluded from heaven and must not present themselves before God, where man is naked, empty-handed and praying, i.e. where he has only his faith.

Before God all are equal, for before God we have no offices occupied in relation to our neighbors on earth and the basis of distinction and difference there.[21] The work of our offices are directed downward upon earth and are for that very reason the bearers of God's own creative action. Therefore office or station has no function to fulfil upward toward God unless it be the work given to it by Satan to wipe out faith, to take away our receptivity, and to make us reject our bondage before God in which co-operation is to reach down to others.[22]

God gives all offices and stations that they may reach downward, but he abolishes all of them before him. Man

[20] *WA* 7, 573 (*The Magnificat*, 1521). Here Luther's belief about creation borders on the idea of justification: righteousness is of God, for it is given by him; therefore no claim before God can be built on it. Righteousness is the forgiveness of sins.

[21] *WA* 51, 240 (*Exposition of Psalm 101*, 1534-35), *WA* 41, 484-485. Here Luther affirms that all differences of station cease before death and before the babe in its crib, i.e. before God (*Exposition of Matthew 18-24*, 1537-40; Aurifaber).

[22] The office is abolished before God; see *WA* 19, 652-653 (*Whether Soldiers Too Can Be Saved*, 1526). But the devil can upset God's order.

139

in his vocation is a mask of God on earth, but in heaven the mask is abolished and removed; for there the word of the gospel holds sway, as it discloses God's attitude. That in the true sense is "revelation," i.e. the disclosure of God and the end of all concealment.[23]

One who does not have the gospel cannot differentiate between God and his mask.

"This the man of this world, in his natural state, cannot see. Only the spiritual distinguishes the Person by the Word, the mask of God from God himself and from the work of God. Now we meet the veiled God, for in this life it is not possible for us to deal with God face to face. Here every creature is the face and mask of God. But wisdom is necessary to distinguish God from his mask. This wisdom the world does not have; so it is not able to distinguish God from his mask."[24]

He who does not have faith and, through faith, access to the heavenly kingdom, knows only different masks. He knows only the earth, where God appears solely as hidden behind his many masks: parents, rulers, neighbors, wives, children, etc. Without faith, a man cannot distinguish between God and his masks. To some who fill certain offices he accords a glory of their own, independent of God, as if the mask were not a mask, or veil, but God himself. He cannot see, in their proper relations, princes, relatives, and the like; he makes idols of them.[25] Similarly he cannot see his own relative position as a helpless tool in a stronger

[23] Through co-operation the existing order, i.e. society, can become an expression of the law. Through his masks, God meets us with his demands in outward relationships. The concept of the law always necessarily carries with it the concept of hiddenness (the veiled God). As God *revelatus* God presents himself in Scripture, or in Christ. The verb "reveal" always retains something of its original and pregnant meaning to uncover.

[24] *WA* 40[I], 173-174 (*Commentary on Galatians*, 1535).

[25] Cf. *WA* 30[I], 181 (*Large Catechism*, 1529).

hand. He inevitably has excessively lofty ideas about himself and thinks himself the efficient cause when he is only the instrumental cause.[26]

Not being able to differentiate between God and his mask is the same as not being able to distinguish between the two kingdoms of earth and heaven. The stations and offices which are excluded from the heavenly kingdom remain inescapably in the earthly kingdom. Faithfulness in them benefits one's neighbor, who is the objective of the works required of man on earth. But it is toward God that faith is directed; faith turns away from earth toward heaven.[27]

A Christian despises nothing; he maintains a proper perspective in respect to all earthly glory by putting everything in its right place. In his affirmative response to his vocation he affirms a world whose totally relative character before God he has already recognized. As he looks upon the context of his earthly vocation, his thought is that this is not a world in which man can place his trust, but one in which he can serve.

Here it becomes clear that co-operation, directed downward to the lowly, belongs with the fact that God is engaged in combat with Satan and vocation has its place in an evil world. Its work is fraught with distress and temptation. To Luther world-affirming joy in culture is utterly strange. For a man, to enter upon vocation is to enter upon cross and suffering, to give his strength to something whose meaning he cannot discern.

When Billing concludes that vocation has only "a negative significance for the religious life" and rejects the un-

[26] See the illuminating passage in *WA* 40III, 236-237 (*Exposition of Psalm 127*, 1532-33).

[27] See *WA* 40I, 175-179 (*Commentary on Galatians*, 1535). In this place Luther uses the term "person" as equivalent of office or mask.

balanced view of life held by Luther, we may ask if he is not really reacting against Luther's statements about "the lost love." Luther really means that love and faithfulness to vocation are lost things, things which, according to the world's view, are thrown away. Here his life-view breaks down, disrupted by his belief in a real devil who holds sway here in the darkness. That disruption is not surmounted in the setting of the earthly kingdom. Eschatology is the first field to restore harmony and meaning to what happens in earthly life. For that reason faith yearns for death and heaven.

The cross of Christ on Golgotha would have no meaning if there were no resurrection, but resurrection is a transition from earth to heaven. Within the earthly kingdom the love of God, the love of Christ, and the love of Christ's disciples are all rejected, despised, and crucified.[28] The power of evil still holds sway here and retains its power as long as earth lasts; but in heaven the power of the devil is broken.

This dualistic quality in Luther's view is very closely tied up with the eschatological.[29] On earth vocation implies

[28] Of course faith in Christ is also faith in that which is poor—the babe in the manger, the man on the cross. . . . To believe in Christ in his humiliation and to lose oneself in one's vocation both involve the same kind of difficulty for the natural man. As in Christ God bows himself under the cross, so, through the faith and love of men, God also bows himself under the drabness of human vocations. In both cases God creates "out of nothing"; he shows himself "in the depths," in the despised. Creation, incarnation, and vocation are in line with each other. Cf. also *WA* 7, 546-549, and 575 (*The Magnificat*, 1521).

[29] Service to others, which in the final judgment will be regarded above all else, is despised on earth because of the power of evil. Both heavy labors and simple pursuits are esteemed lowly on earth but in heaven they are highly regarded. *WA* 34[II], 313 (*Sermons*, 1531; Rörer) and *WA* 14, 171 (*Sermons on Genesis*, 1523-24; Rörer): "Now you see how the world may be: that which is of the devil is extolled, but that which is of God is considered mean."

the cross as a consequence of the ceaseless enmity of evil against every work of God, but the cross points to another kingdom after death, a kingdom without Satan. On earth one's powers are to be spent in service to others, an unlovely prospect from which the devil would turn us away, but in heaven it is made evident that the poor neighbor whom we served was Christ, the King (Matt. 25:31-46).

5. *Regeneration*

To Luther the law is not a fixed magnitude that is codified, either in the Bible or in any other book. When a person in authority exercises his office as a fellow-worker with God, through him requirement is made of those who are subject to him. Each of God's masks is just such an embodied law: parents, neighbors, etc. The law is a sum of living points. Accordingly the law constantly requires something new and unexpected. One is never through with it. It always has a character that tries man.

When the love of the new man reaches down into the world of the law, it reaches down into a world already characterized by openness, a world in which there is already place for personal initiative. It is the world of the law, but it is not on that account the haunt of the meticulous and bureaucratic, who have to look something up in a book before they venture anything. On the contrary, it is a world in which the law gets its form from effective people who proceed under the guidance of their discrimination, impelled by their native endowment and force. Of course the written law and fixed orders are necessary, since the good things given by creation, talents and ability, are so susceptible to use for evil ends. But concerning life on earth, God can

143

use the reason of the natural man as a means to care for human beings, just as well as he can use the love of the Christian. It is not only God's demand that presents itself ceaselessly in new form, but also his gifts. The goodness of God comes to us, among other ways, through other people, who are "God's masks" whether or not they have faith.

In this section we will now discuss the flexible and changing character of external life, as Luther sees it, and consider it in connection with God's new creation that goes on here on earth without cessation. Therefore it is of utmost importance to make clear at once that no distinction is made here between the natural man and the Christian. The primary thing that must be said about a Christian is that through the gospel's promise he lives in heaven, and that life is the same as the reception of grace; he embraces another kingdom than the earth.

This life in heaven has its effects on earth too, but one does not find in Luther the modern fad for defining the ethical advance of the Christian and in that way setting him apart from others as better qualified to solve all earthly issues. It is hard to avoid the suspicion that the present enormous interest in the good moral and social consequences of Christian faith arose simultaneously with the loss of the simple belief in actual life after death.

Luther takes it as a matter of fact that to be a Christian implies the renewing of the earthly realm, where the Christian is. But the same is true of every able and intelligent person who is faithful to his position. Luther does not compare the Christian and the non-Christian in their works on earth, or contentedly affirm that the Christian is foremost. That would be a blow at Christianity's character as pure grace, and an infraction of the spontaneous gladness of the

144

child of God. Luther recognizes two kingdoms, not just one. There is in him no apologetic tendency to argue for Christianity on the claim that its "contributions" to earthly matters are indispensable.

So here we consider together, without basic differentiation, the love of the new man, the work of the ordinary man and of the giant, Christian love and natural justice. The unity of such different variable factors is found in God, who is at work in all of them. Accordingly the unity does not lie in any psychologically observable human goodness, held to be common to both natural man and Christian, and to supply the basis for a unified view of man in general. God works both through the Christian and through an Alexander the Great; they are both instruments of his, and in this is their only unity. For that reason "Regeneration" is the proper title for this section. We are dealing with different forms of God's activity as Creator.

Because God is unfathomable, the centering of unity in God manifestly implies the incompetency of man to see through the workings of God in the world. When we confront a concrete change on earth, something new and revolutionary could well be the work of the devil, rather than God's work. Man must bear the risk of taking a position concerning all such events.

Demanding a clarity of principle from Luther in this, so that we could differentiate in advance between good and evil in various conceivable changes, would be the same as demanding the removal from his view of such aspects as his conviction about the hiddenness of God and the inevitability of desperation. Man does not control God and the devil; he stands between them, exposed to the strife. He cannot lift himself out of the present moment. He must have the courage to venture, in prayer and faith, to take a decisive position, despite the fact that he is bound to the limits of "the hour" and unable to survey anything completely.

As for the Christian, his action as a new man rises from the presence of the Spirit within him, and no rules can be written for the works of the Spirit.[30] His action is not of necessity, for in the Spirit the love of God abides in man. Hence what law and rules would effect is already freely present; it flows to us from God and continues on to others. Every difference among works has come to an end, all the commandments are annulled, there is no more compulsion or coercion, but only sheer joyous will and zeal for doing good, be the work petty or costly, small or great, short or long.[31]

Actions that are carried on in external relationships vary widely in different situations.[32] The moment the law ceases to be the guiding principle for the action of the new man, any Christian uniformity is also made impossible. Olsson has emphasized this naive and vital quality of Luther's social ethics. He has contrasted Luther's view with Lutheran orthodoxy's theory about the third use of the law, according to which the conduct of the Christian can be defined and schematized in a way that is entirely different from Luther's view. It is conceivable that political conservatism was the result of the view of orthodoxy, whereas one must

[30] *WA* 56, 363 and 511 (*Commentary on Romans*, 1515-16), *WA* 23, 189 (*Dass diese Wort*, 1527), *WA Tischreden*[VI], 153 (No. 6728, from 1536).

[31] *WA* 10[I], 1, 102 (*Kirchenpostille*, 1522). Cf. *WA* 10[I], 2, 41, and 178 (*Adventspostille*, 1522).

[32] *WA* 57, 87 (*Commentary on Hebrews*, 1517-18), *WA* 8, 588 (*De votis monasticis*, 1521), and *WA* 31[II], 543-544 (*Lectures on Isaiah*, 1527-30; Lauterbach).

see that Luther cannot possibly be penned up in any political category.

In explanation of the flexibility in vocation which becomes possible through the faith and love of the new man, Luther's words that love "rises above all law" are naturally useful. Typical is his statement in his Lenten postil of 1525:

"So this commandment of love is a short commandment and a long commandment, a single commandment and many commandments. It is no commandment and all commandments. In itself it is short and one, and easy to grasp with the understanding. But in its fulfilment it is a long commandment and many commandments; for it comprehends and rises above all commandments. If one regards works, it is no commandment at all. It has no special works of its own which can be named. Yet it is all the commandments, because the works of all the different commandments are its works and must be so. So the love commandment both removes all commandments and affirms all. All this is to let us know and understand that we are not to keep or regard any commandment or work which love does not require. As we are living on earth we cannot and may not be without works. Therefore we need manifold commandments to set the works right. However it should be done in such way that love does not lose its power and sovereignty through such rules. Love bids us to do or to leave undone, as its purpose may be best served, and no work will be done but for love's incentive."[33]

Sovereignty of love before the law involves a creative factor whose expression it is impossible to foresee, since it can steadily open up fresh and unsuspected perspectives for life's activity. In this connection we must recall Luther's

[33] *WA* 17^{II}, 95 (*Fastenpostille*, 1525).

frequent statement about the freedom of the Christian "to do and to omit."[34] Through this freedom faith and relation to God attain real significance for vocation, and vocation is shaped solely according to the need of others. I can "do," if love for some definite person should demand it, and "omit" if another would be better served by refraining from what is customarily done. The living persons in my environment, who one by one become my neighbors in the providence of God, through the variety of their needs have the function of serving as unforeseen moderators of my actions, as long as I actually love them and care about what they need.

The concept of the "use of office" is similar in position and related positively to the concept of "freedom to do and to leave undone." Everyone who occupies a good office, instituted by God, finds himself in the power of God or of the devil. On his part the office is thus subject to a proper use or to a false and selfish misuse. In that way God's work is modified through the office. Luther, in dealing with autonomous and egoistic lovers of freedom, denies "freedom to do or to leave undone" and simply insists on the obligation to do. In discussing the "use of office," he makes corresponding statements.[35]

When Luther turns from station and office "in itself" (i.e. station as a good creation independent of the person who fills it) to "the person and use of the station," he points out first of all that affirmations of a proper use must not be too definite and detailed.[36] Possibilities for new beginnings in vocation open up because its "use" is not rigidly fixed. But on the next page he writes that man, when such a possibility

[34] E.g., WA 10I, 2, 175-176 (Adventspostille, 1522).
[35] See, above, Chapter II, sec. 2.
[36] WA 19, 630-631 (Whether Soldiers Too Can Be Saved, 1526).

confronts him, strives toward only one end, namely, to effect his own purpose, without inquiring into neighbor or the right.[37]

That the "use" must have a certain freedom of action, and not be too closely regulated, is often expressed by saying that offices must be served with "equity" and not according to "stern law"; but Luther sees clearly that this "equity" can open the door, not only to a better solution of a confronting situation, but also to selfish desire.

"One of the vices which dwell within us human beings is called *fraus*, i.e. cunning or guile. If the cunning soul learns that fairness is above justice, as has been said, then it is an enemy of justice. It searches and ponders day and night how to enter the market under the name and semblance of fairness." Satan is ready, by way of such fairness, to supplant God. Against this, the responsibilities of office must be fixed by rigorous laws.[38]

Just as God can enter in and through good works, so the devil can enter in and through evil works. We face not only the possibility of a divine transformation of the world, but a satanic transformation as well.

In the face of these corruptions of office "stern law" or "written law" has its value. "The common law of the book" is definite in comparison with the undefined creative law which decides each case by itself and which permits various arbitrary actions. Against corruptions of office there always stands that which is fixed, vocation as law against the freedom demanded by evil. "The justice and wisdom of our secular government has to be studied and mastered. It would be a fine thing if an emperor, prince, or lord were wise by

[37] *WA* 19, 632-633.
[38] *WA* 19, 633.

nature and able to judge the right by heart. . . . But because such birds are rare, and their example dangerous, as well as for the sake of those who are unable to do these things by nature, it is better if government stick to the common laws that are written down, so that it may have the greater esteem and respect, and need neither miracles nor special gifts." [39]

The variable element is love, which can freely go its way, since it is God. The love of the new man, which shapes his "use" of his office, is a form of God's new creation in the world.

From what has preceded we are already acquainted with Luther's view of the works of the Christian which, as "the fruit of the Spirit," are in a peculiar sense "masks" of God and the result of love's "co-operation" with God, through which God enters day by day into life on earth with changing countenance. But through other people who have not accepted the gospel, God works without his Spirit. They have, for example, the offices which are created by God.

The earthly activity of the natural man also involves a variable factor and serves as an organ of God's new and unexpected action. Outside of every given order, God can call forth revolt or attack against a tyrannical government which he wants to punish; i.e. he uses sin as punishment for other sin. [40]

All in all God has at his command possibilities of action of which the Word of God, by which we are bound, but not he, tells us nothing. Through his activity in the natural world God can also enter in new ways and change the situation in which a human being stands. In his view of

[39] *WA* 30[II], 558 (*Sermon on Keeping Children in School,* 1530).

[40] The thought that God uses sin to punish sin is very common with Luther. See *WA* 19, 637-638 (*Whether Soldiers Too Can Be Saved,* 1526).

divine directions of the world, Luther is notably eager to stress constantly the aspects that keep the door open for God's new beginnings and give actual content to his repeated affirmation of "God's freedom." God is free and not subject to any law or confined within any limits. God's new creation on earth can also be effected through the natural man.

Here we must bring in Luther's concept of "equity." It is of course uncertain whether the term is applied only to the ethics of the natural man. Holl always sought support for his thesis that Luther never recognizes a natural law in any form, that all expressions seeming to imply anything of the kind must be construed as referring to "Christian morality." Holl accordingly held that for Luther the real content of "equity" is a "feeling nurtured by the thought of Christian love."

Franz Lau is opposed to this. According to him "equity" belongs to the role of reason, and applies to the administration of civil affairs, to issues within the earthly realm. Luther's position that laws and offices must be conducted with "equity" is relevant on the natural and purely rational plane.

As a matter of fact it is impossible to draw a sharp line of distinction. Equity is something that God demands, to which room must be given in life on earth, but God demands it of Christians and non-Christians alike, for on earth there is no decisive difference between Christians and non-Christians. All are to tell the truth. All are to obey civil law. All are to show fairness and consideration. Where works and external behavior are concerned it is not merely difficult to make a sharp demarcation between Christians and non-Christians; it is erroneous.

In his Advent postil Luther exposits the statement in Philippians 4:5, "Let your moderation [leniency, gentleness in judgment] be known unto all."[41] Luther translates this, "Let your mildness be known to all men"; and in his interpretation he introduces a distinction between "stern and mild justice."[42] Moderate judgment is not blind and abstract, but is concerned with the particular situation and acts in the concrete case. In connection with this line of thought, Luther demands moderation or fairness because in all our action we have to deal with others in their particular situations. The living and ever changing character of the situation in the light of which behavior has to be judged moderates all law. The straits of our fellow-men change, and the people themselves change; our neighbor is one person at one time, a different person at another, and often several persons at once.[43]

This type of judgment, of special importance for those in authority, Luther considers an art, for which certain natural leadership talents are competent. The art is to unite firmness with the ability to make exception where exception is really called for. Reason is to rule over all justice and all

[41] The term *epieikeia,* which Luther often uses, is directly related to the New Testament. Philippians 4:5 says "Let your mildness be known to all men."

[42] *WA* 10ᴵ, 2, 174 (1521): "This is the meaning of the word which the Apostle uses here—*epieikeia, clementia, comoditas*—which I cannot translate into German otherwise than by the word *gelindickeyt.* . . . The law distinguishes for the same reason between stern and mild justice; that which is too harsh is softened. That is 'equity,' 'moderation,' 'clemency of justice.' "

[43] *WA* 10ᴵ, 2, 175-190. In conclusion this mildness and reasonableness is presented as "the fruit of the Spirit," i.e. as something which is Christian (180). We have encountered this thought, that the neighbor is the basis for variation in the administration of justice, when the same passage in Luther was discussed in connection with freedom to do or to leave undone. (See page 149 above.)

laws.[44] When this natural reason is not sufficient, there is no other help than prayer. "What shall a prince do if he is not wise enough himself and has to let himself be ruled by lawyers and law books? Answer: For this reason I said that the station of a prince is a dangerous one. . . . (Therefore Solomon asked God for a wise heart.) . . . A sovereign ought to follow this example . . . to cling only to God, to cry in his ears and pray for insight to rule wisely, which goes beyond all books and masters."[45]

What is possible through reason in persons of great talent, and what is possible through prayer when all human resources fail, natural justice and Christian love are equal in value in regard to earthly labor that deals with worldly matters below; for there the judgment of a man before God is irrelevant. (In heaven, before God all depends on whether or not faith is present.) In the fair administration of the law, Christian love *(die liebe)* and natural justice *(naturlich recht)* are forthrightly placed side by side in Luther's view.[46] God the Creator acts through both the talent given in natural birth and the love of the new man given by new birth in the Word.

An example of fairness is in Luther's *Von Ehesachen,* where he cites the popular expression, as he often does: "Greatest justice is the greatest injustice." He has neither regard nor respect for a moralistic exactness bound to the letter, requiring fulfilment of the law in every jot and tittle. This moral preciseness is not concerned with realities, for it is concerned, not with one's neighbor, but only with a counterfeit irreproachableness which is counterfeit because there is no life without sin, and it ought not to be set up as

[44] *WA* 11, 272 (*Treatise on Secular Authority,* 1523).
[45] *WA* 11, 272-273 *(ibid).*
[46] *WA* 11, 279 *(ibid).*

the standard.[47] The goal of action must be this: In the midst of a sinful world in which we inescapably participate, we must live to help our fellow-men and further their well-being. This is impossible by any other course than by taking our place between God and our neighbor and doing "whatever comes to hand." In our actual relation with God, one action is called for in one hour, another when the external setting has changed.

A rigid law is without regard for times and the complexities of human situations. Fairness adjusts the law to particular circumstances. The administration called for by fairness is modifiable according to "time" and "hour."[48] The way Luther, in *Von Ehesachen*, deals with questions of betrothal against parental wishes, betrothal under compulsion, divorce, etc., is marked throughout with this feeling for the "equitable," interest in the concrete, and scepticism about lifeless principles; i.e. with "mildness" or "moderation."[49]

For Luther actual justice is not simply to be found in the law book, in a static, written sum fixed before particular occasions arise. Genuine justice is the joint product of the co-operation of the law book and the judge in the setting of the ongoing legal procedure, where justice is being administered.[50] And it is not only a judge who gives form to the

[47] *WA* 30III, 222-223 (1530). Cf. the advice given to merchants with sensitive conscience, in *WA* 15, 297 (*Von Kaufsshandlung und Wucher*, 1524): No matter how careful one is, one always fails at some point. "Let this enter into your Lord's Prayer, wherein you pray, 'Forgive us our trespasses.' For nobody's life is without sin."

[48] *WA* 51, 372-373 (*An die Pfarrherrn wider den Wucher zu predigen*, 1540). The concept *epieikeia* is discussed. The final statement is characteristic, "You cannot set everything down on paper."

[49] *WA* 30III, 236-248 (1530).

[50] See *WA* 19, 632 (*Whether Soldiers Too Can Be Saved*, 1526) for definition of "fairness." The passage enters into consideration of what is meant by the "use" of an office, as differentiated from the office itself.

law this way and brings it into operation from case to case, from day to day. The head of a household, in dealing with its members, also has his commission to dispense, and to adapt whenever necessary. In his household, the master is "the living law," in Luther's expression. "Thus he (the head of the household) takes his position: 'I am the living law in my home, and in my hand I have the *epieikeia*, the right of moderating and mitigating the law.' There mildness breaks through the law, because the act was sudden and unplanned."[51]

Of God's supermen in earthly government, i.e. real statesmen, he says likewise that they "produce the laws themselves," indeed that "such people are masters and the law itself." An emperor is "the living law on earth."[52] Therefore we can properly speak of a personification of the law that applies in outward relationships, according to Luther's view. To some extent the law is individualized when judges, heads of households, or princes exercise their vocations, when the law concerns and is rightly applied to people within the orbit of each officeholder's vocation. But vocation is manifestly also an individualization of the law for officeholders. They are to act in fairness. Vocation demands of them something which gives particular quality to their action; they cannot simply follow old patterns mechanically. Every vocation has its setting in a particular place and deals with particular people at a definite time. The problems arising in one frame of reference are somewhat different from those occurring in any other vocation. Fairness, which requires consideration of particular situations, makes my vocation mine alone.

51 *WA* 44, 704 (*Commentary on Genesis*, 1535-45).
52 *WA* 51, 212 (*Exposition of Psalm 101*, 1534-35).

In his great decisions a man stands alone, without pattern, without prototype.[53]

Thus we introduce the concept of the "heroic man" *(vir heroicus)* in its place in Luther's view of faith. Such a "heroic man" embodies the law and natural reason at a given time. Empirically it is evident that the majority of the people are incapable of discerning what natural reason demands.[54] The ability to apply natural justice in a particular situation is given to a few creative leaders, who might be said to incarnate natural right in their action. "That precious jewel called natural justice and reason is a very rare thing among the children of men."[55]

We have here another variable in Luther's view of society, which keeps the system open for new starts and accentuates God's freedom in his creative work on earth. It is impossible for anyone to know in advance when such a talent will appear. The different distribution of talents among all people is an evidence of the fact that God "wills to be free and unbound, as is fitting for God; he will not be subject to his creation, even though creation is beautiful and fine."[56] God has placed princes, nobles, citizens, etc., in a graduated scale from above downward; and that order pleases him. But when he bestows talent and character, he can give a citizen just as much as six nobles, and a noble just as much as three

[53] Vocation stands in contrast with imitation which copies certain saints as models and a sort of patent solution. We shall return to this point in our section on "Vocation-Imitation." In his solitariness man stands in prayer and is to proceed and to act according to the law's requirement.

[54] *WA* 51, 361-362 (*An die Pfarrherrn wider den Wucher zu predigen,* 1540).

[55] *WA* 51, 212 (*Exposition of Psalm 101,* 1534-35).

[56] *WA* 51, 255-256 (*ibid.*). Cf. *WA* 30[II], 575-576 (*Sermon on Keeping Children in School,* 1530). When out of a simple man's son God makes a significant officeholder in either the worldly or the spiritual realm, he creates "out of nothing."

156

princes; for as Lord of his created order God is "free and unbound." Even more difficult to calculate than such unexpected common talents is the sudden cropping up of a *vir heroicus.*

Such a superman may do what others do not. Or rather, he does it. In the case of a "heroic man," we cannot say what he may or may not do. İnstruction for all must proceed on the assumption that there are no exceptional persons. But if there is a "heroic man" anywhere, he blazes his own trail, and must make his own way forward, without help and guidance, because otherwise he is no "heroic man." A real superman is instructed by God himself, who drives certain thoughts into his mind. "Everything they touch succeeds and even if the whole world were against it, it will nevertheless move on unimpeded. For the same God who has planted these plans in their hearts, who stimulates their minds and their courage, also guides their hands to bring it about and effect it."[57]

Thus Moses put his hand to a work of liberation from Pharaoh, which looked very much like revolt, and which is not to be taken as a pattern for average people. The revolting peasants can pray to God for such a superman to restore good social conditions, and endure till such a person arises.[58] When incorrigible conditions prevail, God sends his man. The task of the "heroic man" is exactly that of making the right and reasonable regnant. This simple task calls for a hero and is so hard to effect because the world is in Satan's power. Apart from this dualistic background, the struggle between God and the devil, Luther's thoughts about "heroic men" are incomprehensible.

[57] *WA* 51, 207 (*Exposition of Psalm 101,* 1534-35): Illustrations: Samson, Cyrus, Themistocles, Alexander the Great, etc.

[58] *WA* 18, 321 (*Admonition to Peace,* 1525).

Two subordinate points must be noted in connection with the opposition between God and the devil. The first is that the devil also has his "supermen," who try to counterfeit divinely favored revolutionaries, but whom God has not sent. Consequently it is difficult to discern a "heroic man." It may possibly be a diabolical person whom we face.[59] When a flexible factor appears in Luther's view of society, as we have seen, the door is open to both divine and satanic transformation. For that reason faith must always strive against uncertainty and always remain faith, which cannot pass over into knowledge and full clarity before the time comes when we shall see in the resurrection world. Since this heaven comes after earth, we cannot distinguish between the divine and the satanic by asking whether or not an accomplished transformation produces suffering at the present. Pain is, so to speak, normal in this world, the world of the cross.

The second point is, that even God's own heroic men generally bring destruction upon themselves in the end. Because they move forward "without God's Word," they do not understand that their work is really God's work through them, and accordingly do not give God the honor. "Before you teach them how to do it, they have already done it, without having any need for God's Word to teach them to attribute such fortune and great deeds to God and give him the honor, rather than to praise and exalt themselves. This they cannot know without the Word of God, so they usually come to a bad end, as history shows."[60]

As a result, for many of them, the time comes when God "withdraws his hand" from them and they fall to earth. "When the hour has come that God draws back his hand

[59] *WA* 51, 212 (*Exposition of Psalm 101*, 1534-35).
[60] *WA* 51, 207-208.

from them because of their presumption and ingratitude, they will fall, and no advice or reason will avail. They are bound to perish, even as Hannibal did."[61] Even in the hearts of God's supermen surge the struggles between God and Satan, and either result of that struggle is possible. Both fairness in daily life and "heroic men" are points where God's creative love breaks through into life. Fairness opens a rift in the law and lets mercy trickle in. Fairness is expressly said to be "a portion of grace" which is to have a place in the earthly realm.[62] Luther himself brings in the idea of *viri heroici* in this connection. It is these exceptional persons who rise above the law and serve God's love by the very fact that they exercise moderation of the law, as circumstances have changed. "There let love be queen and mistress, to regulate the laws and turn them toward moderation. Such moderation is required of men of heroic and exceptional stature."[63]

Such eruptions and fresh beginnings are characteristic of Luther's belief on creation, for the fact that God creates implies for Luther something that goes on ceaselessly, "to create is always to do something new" *(creare est semper novum facere).*[64] The unifying bond in God's ongoing creation is his love. It is of course God's love that breaks forth in the life of the new man, which is born of the gospel. "Thus through faith a Christian becomes a creator."[65] It is God's love which, by way of fairness, opens rifts in the law and effects new relations in the home, in places of labor, and in courts, where decisions are arrived at. It is God's

[61] *WA* 51, 212-213.
[62] *WA* 44, 706 (*Commentary on Genesis,* 1535-45).
[63] *WA* 42, 503-504 (*ibid.*).
[64] *WA* 1, 563 (*Resolutiones disputationum de indulgentiarum virtute,* 1518).
[65] *WA* 27, 399 (*Sermons,* 1528; Rörer).

love which drives a "heroic man" on to trail blazing and bold enterprise, through which new relations in society are formed. Luther never gives up the thesis, developed in *The Magnificat* in 1521, that it is just in man's need, in times and occasions which look hopeless, that God out of such helplessness, out of "nothing," creates something new.[66]

In his view of society Luther stresses strongly the significant factor of change in God's creative work on earth, which seems like pure aestheticism, except for the fact that the struggle between God and the devil supplies the background, and the reason why a new creative act is necessary.

God by himself would be able to let the world continue as it is, steady, unchanging, and without fresh beginnings; but the devil does not permit it. We live in a world that is always being destroyed and always being made new. Fresh creation takes place all the time *contra diabolum*, against the devil. God's new measures in the external world are combative actions, and as such they are unexpected and sudden, springing forth from *Gottes Freiheit,* from God's freedom which is not fenced in by any lines laid down in advance.[67]

The freedom of God means that no rule or law can be set up as norm for his action; and that freedom is carried over into God's fresh creative work in and through human beings. God's freedom is made concrete in both natural fairness and Christian love, both of which rise in sovereignty above all rules and laws. In like manner, God's freedom is manifest through "heroic men," who act contrary to all that is conventional.[68] All these works of God have their mutual

[66] *WA* 7, 547-549. Here is the basis of Luther's entire view of history.

[67] *WA* 10^I, 1, 618-619 (*Kirchenpostille*, 1522), *WA* 18, 712 (*The Bondage of the Will*, 1525), *WA* 51, 255 (*Exposition of Psalm 101*, 1534-35).

[68] *WA* 51, 209 (*ibid*).

160

oneness only in that they all flow forth from the being of God, "simple, inexpressible love," and not because they could be subsumed under a law or rule. It follows that no man has access to a gauge by which he could judge the actions of God, to be loving or otherwise.[69] He gives access to himself to all who come in faith, which does not see or scrutinize God, but which suffers him and prays.

By willingness to receive God, whatever he may do, this open faith, though it has not yet seen, accepts it as true that God is always love. God enters in with a person with an open faith like this, who thus shares with God. When God begins to act in this person, he so directs everything that happens, even what is hard, that it all becomes expressive of his love. Furthermore, through such a man God reaches out to still other men, for man cannot close his heart against his neighbor without at the same time closing his heart against what God does with him himself. So it happens that new actions are constantly being brought forth. He who by faith is open to God is by love open to his neighbor. Since God directs what is happening, my neighbor becomes an instrument in God's hand for what he is doing with me. I cannot turn my neighbor away without thereby turning God away—and that is falling into unbelief. In faith all good works are encompassed.

Through a person who is receptive to what is laid upon him, and prays, God's actions are effected in vocation. The next chapter will be about the individual human being, man as he lives on earth, while he waits for death, who finds himself in his daily work in the midst of the conflict between God and the devil.

[69] Cf. *WA* 18, 784 (*The Bondage of the Will*, 1525). About God as love in his outward action in creation, see *WA* 36, 426 (*Sermons*, 1532; Cruciger).

III

Man

1. *His Situation*

Luther's concept of the world and his view of life are characterized by the dualism between God and Satan on the one hand, and on the other, eschatology or the tension between earth and heaven.[1] Our first chapter, "Earth and Heaven," discussed eschatology. Man lives on earth for a short time, in his vocation and with his neighbor, till death comes. Everything on earth is transitory. What is enduring and eternal is the kingdom after death, heaven. Our second chapter, "God and the Devil," discussed dualism. Man is created by God and has received God's Word, which is both promise of life in heaven (the gospel) and command concerning life on earth (the law). The devil seeks to lead man astray on earth, away from his vocation, in which the law is embodied, and to deprive him of salvation by destroying his faith in the gospel. From the devil comes death and destruction; with God there is life and salvation.

Here is the point to which we have come in our presentation. This third chapter is entitled "Man." Heaven is not for geese, animals, or wood; the resurrection world is specifically for human beings, for man.[2] Of all earthly beings

---

[1] Luther expected the final judgment to come soon, basing his expectation on observation of demonic activity and the action of Antichrist in his day.

[2] *WA* 18, 636 (*The Bondage of the Will*, 1525).

it is only man whose objective is heaven. And of all earthly creatures it is man who is the object of the struggle between God and Satan.

When evil has captured a man, no animal can vie with him in fiendishness; he is leavened throughout with Satan.[3] But a human being is also the only creature in which the miracle of being born again or made new can take place. Every animal is created by God; but he does not make a new creature of it. The new man is a new creation, with no counterpart in nature. He is a new creature in conflict with the powers of sin and death, in conflict against the devil.

In the foregoing, man's situation has been presented. It is characterized by the twofold fact that he stands between earth and heaven, and between God and the devil. The first of these implies that, whatever a man's age, on earth he always has the most important events of his life ahead of him, namely, death and that which follows. Inescapably he travels on toward that. The second implies that he is placed in a field of force, that he is never autonomous or isolated but stands ceaselessly in the midst of an invisible conflict.

An anthropology which first describes man and subsequently takes up his relation to God, is for Luther an absurdity. There is no such thing as a human being who stands by himself, not yet projected between God and the devil. From Luther's point of view, anthropology in the theological sense can only mean God's work with man looked at from man's point of view, from below, with the eyes of a concrete man, of one who always stands alone in his spiritual trial.

[3] WA 5, 38 (Operationes in Psalmos, 1519-21).

We shall not present any such comprehensive discussion of man in relation to God. This would require a thorough Luther research, and it is a very difficult task. In this chapter on man, we shall touch only on aspects which are connected with vocation. In our first chapter we considered vocation in relation to the two kingdoms: the realm of the works of the law on earth, where vocation is located, and the realm of the gospel of grace, in heaven, where man does not build on fidelity to his vocation or on works in general. In our second chapter we viewed vocation in relation to the two powers: God, whose weapon vocation is, and the devil, who attacks man's life in vocation. In both chapters vocation was viewed in cosmic perspectives, and such total views must be complemented by subordinate characterizations on a more intimate and consciously limited consideration, at closer range.

These aspects might seem to be selected at random, but they belong together because as far as possible we visualize the problem from the position of a single person occupying his place in vocation. As an introduction to the complex of details to be studied in this chapter, it may be helpful if we note the general lines in man's situation between earth and heaven, and between God and the devil.

Man's position between earth and heaven implies that he does not expect only good fortune on earth, but is prepared in advance to suffer "the cross" and tribulations of this world.

Some refrain from marriage and live in whoredom, thus assuming less responsibility. "That is true enough. For he who assumes that there will be no other life after this one, as some do, acts sensibly enough to seek satisfaction in promiscuous prostitution, rather than take upon himself the cares of the married state." But a Christian is happy to take a wife. "For since a Christian expects another life to follow this one, it is very sensible for him to accept here days that are less good, and thereby to have eternally the purest good of the days that are to be in the life to come. God himself recognized that when he made man and woman and brought them together."[4]

The promise of heaven is given by the word of Christ; but the way to this kingdom after death is through calm in vocation, through patient faithfulness to responsibility in evil and good days; "that is the right street that . . . leads to heaven."[5] Characteristic of this is the significance given to the body.

Luther often says, as we have recognized, that the conscience is already in heaven, or is enlightened by the gospel, while the body, on the other hand, is on earth and must be disciplined by the law. The freedom from law belonging to the conscience is a manifestation of the Christian's participation in Christ's resurrection, while the body's bondage to law (station, office) is connected with the fact that the body has not yet been raised. For the present the body is bound by sundry ties and must live a life of toil, with suffering and crosses. The Christian's conviction that he is "in Christ" is connected with this specific view of the cross, and this conviction cannot be separated from a simple faith in an actual resurrection after death. This faith is joined with a longing for death and readiness for it. Finally man yearns to pass from crosses to resurrection, from earth to heaven.

[4] WA 12, 93 (Exposition of I Corinthians 7, 1523). Cf. WA 2, 734 (Treatise on the Sacrament of Baptism, 1519) and WA 30^{II}, 175-180 (Heerpredigt wider den Türken, 1529).
[5] WA 6, 264 (Treatise on Good Works, 1520).

So faith in creation and eschatology belong together. Man has been created by God with body and soul, and after death he will arise with body and soul. Between creation and resurrection lies life on earth and vocation. Vocation bears witness to the belief that the body is to be raised, since vocation lays the law and the cross on the body, while the body is on earth, where the cross of Christ stood. To this view of life it is conceivable that vocation may appear in the form of what may be a heavy and troublous engagement in one's station. One does not demand that a work be "interesting" before accepting it as vocation. For this life view the sacraments too are comprehensible. Between creation and resurrection lies man's reception of baptism and communion, and in the visibility and outwardness of the sacraments lies the same witness to vocation; the testimony that the body too is to be borne on toward eternal life. Through vocation the law bears witness to the resurrection; through the sacraments the gospel bears witness to the same.

In other contexts Luther has said that the old man, the man of sin, is to be disciplined, whereas the new man is righteous and free from the law. This is another nuance. Luther's differentiation between body and conscience is an expression of the concept of the two kingdoms; conscience belongs to the heavenly kingdom, and the body to the earthly kingdom. In the concept of the old, sinful man in juxtaposition to the new, referring to the fact that the two are in mutual conflict, the opposition between God and the devil begins to emerge. The old man is not bodily but sinful. His sinfulness expresses itself in both soul and body, totally. "The old man, as he is born of Adam, is not according to nature, but according to the corruption of nature. He is called the 'old man,' not as he does the works of the flesh, but even when he does right, acts in wisdom, and exercises himself in all spiritual good."[6]

In like manner, the righteousness of the new man is conceived as a complete reality, manifesting itself also in outward, bodily actions, free from the law which would otherwise direct the body, according to the duality rooted in the concept of the two kingdoms.

These two ideas belong together: the continuing duality of body and conscience, derived from the concept of the two kingdoms, and the division derived from the dualism between God and Satan, which continually tends toward a total view of man. The entire man is bound in sin, through the fall, but the redemptive work, by which God liberates man from sin, is dual; it is both law and gospel. The gospel assures man of God's forgiveness, *favor Dei*, and thereby removes fear of the final judgment. He has a free conscience who does not fear the final judgment but trusts in God's promise. But his body is nevertheless bound. Sin still remains in his members, i.e. in external, empirical existence; conscience simply knows that this will not result in one's rejection by God. The responsibility remains to drive sin out of one's members too, but it is effected slowly and never perfected in anyone before the death of the body. To the body, which by itself does not will the good, the office applies, the station, created by God and compelling man to render useful service on earth. There he experiences his "crosses," borne on toward death and heaven at the same time as his God-given work moves tenaciously and victoriously against sin, against the devil, in the life of human

[6] *WA* 56, 325-326 (*Commentary on Romans*, 1515-16). See also *WA* 6, 246 (*Treatise on Good Works*, 1520).

society.[7] Sometimes the regulative view for Luther is that of the two kingdoms, both of which are God's even though earth is transitory and heaven eternal. Then he says that station and vocation are ended after death, because the transitory has passed away in heaven.

"Therefore you ought to learn well the difference between the two persons a Christian must bear within himself on this earth. He is living among other people and, even like the Gentiles, he has to use the goods of the world and of the emperor. For he is made of the same flesh and blood and has to sustain it. He does this, not by means of the spiritual realm, but by the field and the land which belongs to the emperor, etc., until he departs bodily from this life and enters the next."[8]

Sometimes the dominant idea is the opposition, the war, in fact, between God and sin. Then he says that station and office cease, after death, because sin, the body of sin, is vanquished and destroyed.[9]

These two ways of thinking are so interwoven that one cannot discuss man's position between earth and heaven without at the same time considering his position in the line of battle between God and Satan. We have noted repeatedly that both God and the devil breach the boundary line between the two kingdoms. The devil tries to thrust

[7] All without exception are set in this world of responsibilities. Man is unable to avoid them entirely, even by entering the cloister. "For you are a son, or a servant, or you have neighbors, free or bound, or you are in some other status in home or the society of men." WA 40[III], 210. On this rests the fact that there is a vocation for every human being. Cf. WA 40[III], 207-208 (Exposition of Psalm 127, 1532-33). In the same act both service to others and subjugation of one's own body are effected. WA 8, 607 (De votis monasticis, 1521).

[8] WA 32, 391 (The Sermon on the Mount, 1532).

[9] This is more common. Here is stressed the necessity for struggle against "the outer man." See, e.g., WA 17[II], 62 (Fastenpostille, 1525) and WA 12, 108 (Exposition of I Corinthians 7, 1523).

the law and works into heaven, so that man boasts of his own righteousness, or makes claims before God. On his side, God can let the law distress man's conscience, so as to bring man to anxiety and humility, and to repel wickedness and pride (the devil). The law has left its proper place in man's external relationships, and engulfed the entire person, who, before God, is altogether carnal and condemned.

Again the gospel which God addresses to every quaking conscience can be received in faith, and by the Spirit beget love to others and inclination toward what one's office requires, fulfilling it in freedom from the law. There too the law retreats from its proper role, in external matters, in the bodily. What is spoken of as the aspect of totality regarding man, so characteristic of Luther, seems to be related to the dualism between God and the devil, just as the duality of body and conscience belongs with Luther's doctrine of the two kingdoms. The boundary between the two kingdoms is constantly broken through in the conflict between God and the devil. Likewise the duality in man passes over into the aspect of totality. Man is a unity, even though he stands between earth and heaven, and the living unity, the totality which he is, cannot escape the conflict between God and the devil or take a third position in neutrality, neither spirit nor flesh, neither faith nor unbelief. Man is a beast of burden, ridden by one rider or the other.

In our discussion of co-operation we pointed out that the direction of the work of vocation, downward toward need, and the serving in which no one glories, is correlative with the fact that our work goes on in a world where the devil effects his devastation.[10] Christian love is poured out and lost in the world. It is fitting here to complete the

[10] See, above, Chapter II, sec. 4.

picture of *die verlorene Liebe* (the lost love), since this aspect of Luther's view is closely connected with the situation of the Christian between God and the devil, now under consideration. The devil impels his victim to misuse the external good, to the *abusus* of his office, of strength, of wealth, and of all of God's creation.[11] Christian goodness and willingness is such a freely offered good that it invites the egoistic to misuse it. Since this Christian willingness to serve others belongs to one's vocation, in the midst of a world harried by greed, it is open and without defense against being exploited and stepped on, at any time at all.

In his exposition of Romans 8:20ff, about creation's "longing," Luther proceeds from the statement, "the creation was subjected to futility," and asks what this perishableness, this "vanity" is. He answers that it is man who is vanity, sinful man. Everything good is misused by human beings, and the whole outer creation sighs under its yoke, longing to be free from man's misuse. Nature desires that humans should become good again; it reaches forward to the revelation of the children of God and their glorious liberty in the right use of creation's gifts.[12] As examples of such good gifts so ruthlessly misused, Luther mentions the sun which shines even for the evil, and the rain which gladdens the unrighteous too.[13] Despite their sighing, the sun and the rain nevertheless obey God, who is unstinting love and scatters his gifts upon an ungrateful world. Likewise the Creator is heeded by flowers, berries, trees, and singing birds; they bestow their gifts on any who pass by, even though it be the world's worst cheat or knave. "It is

[11] See, for example, Chapter II, sec. 1, above. Cf. *WA* 30[II], 572-573 (*Sermon on Keeping Children in School*, 1530).

[12] *WA* 56, 372-373 (*Commentary on Romans*, 1515-16).

[13] *WA* 56, 80-81 (*ibid.*).

written on all leaves and on every blade of grass; no bird, no fruit, no berry, no kernel of grain is too small to show this and to say, 'For whom do I bear my delicious fruit or berry? For the worst rogues and rascals on earth!' "[14] This is a pattern for Christian love, which must be willing to be misused, and to be "a lost love." Just as God scatters other gifts, so he also scatters this creation of his, for Christian love itself is the creation of God's Spirit.

The aspect of the work of one's vocation that labor is given forth and lost is very important; and it is a great temptation for the individual as he confronts his vocation. He is tempted to do something other than his vocation, something that has more meaning and receives some measure of recognition from the world. But the conflict between God and the devil demands that God's work have appearances against it in a world deranged by sin; and all false byways have appearances in their favor. This must involve an inner struggle for one who is employed in his vocation. He often stands alone with the day's task, without guidance from God's people, with God's command as his only support and prayer as his only resource. Having sketched, in bold outline, the meaning of life in vocation, we shall discuss some of its aspects in more detail in the section that follows. We begin with Luther's contrast of the life of vocation with monasticism's imitation of saints.

2. Vocation—Imitation

Luther places vocation in sharp contrast with imitation. His strong emphasis on fairness, for instance, on the grounds that every situation is unique, already gives intimation of

[14] *WA* 32, 404 (*The Sermon on the Mount,* 1532).

such a contrast. This consideration individualizes action and creates it to some degree with each situation. In decisions of great and important moment, the action is a bold venture to which one has to commit oneself in faith. It is therefore typical that Luther's letters are as important a source for his view of society as are his treatises. The letters were written in definite situations and contain counsel for the handling of given situations, whose elements are known and subject to study. High esteem for the capacity of some people to give counsel in all kinds of situations has about it something quite Lutheran. The local character of vocation shows the same contrast with imitation. He whose conduct copies some pattern seeks to act independently not only of the time, but also of the place.

Vocation means that those who are closest at hand, family and fellow-workers, are given by God: it is one's neighbor whom one is to love. Therein vocation points toward a world which is not the same for all people. The same course does not fit all circumstances. Each of the social factors arising through the vocational actions of different people has its own character; and the life of society in this way develops in rich variety. As for external relations on earth Luther personally certainly found pleasure in the many. Luther himself had a clear sense of vocation for his work of reformation; and to that end he found special support in the oath he took when he was made a doctor of theology. Each is to do his own work, without eyeing others or trying to copy them. Christ is not to be imitated by us, but rather to be accepted in faith, because Christ also had his special office for the salvation of man, an office which no one else has. "If a station or office were not good for the reason that Christ did not carry it on, what would become of all stations and offices except the office of preaching, which is the only one he practiced? Christ carried on his own office and station, but he has not for that reason rejected anyone else's office. . . . Everyone must tend his own vocation and work."[15]

"It is God's firm intention," we read in a famous passage in Luther's *De votis monasticis,* "that all the saints are to live in the same faith, and be moved and guided by the same Spirit; but in external matters carry out different works." God does not do the same works through all people, nor does he effect them "at the same time, or in the same place, or before the same people; but, directing them ever by the same Spirit and faith, he is active in different times, places, works, and persons." God's paths are hidden, and men cannot uncover his footsteps again. To each he gives his exercise "with a different work, in a different place, at a different time, and before different people, from what one has seen and heard about other saints." Thus man is forced to "follow the God who directs and leads, through works, places, times, persons, and situations which were previously unknown to him. This is the instruction of faith, in which all the saints have been taught, each according to his particular vocation." This statement is part of a general criticism of the ideal of imitation.[16]

It is clear that the background of such statements is the doctrine of the two kingdoms. It is in faith that all are alike, before God or in heaven, where man can depend on no work of his. But there are great differences in works which are directed toward one's neighbor on earth. Here the offices and stations, which count for nothing in heaven,

[15] *WA* 11, 258 (*Treatise on Secular Authority,* 1523).
[16] *WA* 8, 588 (1521).

have their place.[17] Luther uses the sun to illustrate how Christ wipes out all differences in the kingdom of heaven. The sun shines in exactly the same way on all: the peasant and the king, the thorn and the rose, the pig in the alley and the lovely girl. They all receive alike of the sun's light and warmth. But the works and actions which such diverse creatures carry on in the sunlight are widely different, and must be so. Likewise, all people are alike before Christ, who, like the sun, gives himself alike to all. All receive the body and blood of Christ in the Lord's Supper; and all hear the same gospel. As for the reality which makes us Christians there is not the slightest difference between man and woman, young and old, learned and unlearned, great saint and frail character. The differences among persons all lie in the things which they can severally do, a capacity or a work, and these activities are directed "downward" to the service of others. Before God in heaven there are no differences; all are simply human beings and sinners, to whom Christ is given, just like the sun that sheds its light on all without discrimination.[18] Luther's great emphasis on faith is unintelligible without that background. Faith is receptivity, openness to God's giving, present only when man knows of nothing by which he can lift himself up before God above any other human being. So man can only receive when he sees his sin.[19]

In earthly actions differences continue, with dissimilarities in authority and subordination, for in earthly relationships, aside from faith and receptivity, man is to render service and to effect something. In view of the fact that a Christian simply wants to serve, he accepts such worldly

[17] *WA* 40[I], 544-545 (*Commentary on Galatians,* 1535).
[18] *WA* 32, 536-537 (*The Sermon on the Mount,* 1532).
[19] *WA* 32, 540 (*ibid.*).

differences with simple joy, not complaining about his station if it is lowly, and not puffed up if it is lofty.[20] Since before God there are no absolute differences among men, a Christian can assent to the differences that obtain in relations among men in this world of social gradations, without making them an issue within his own heart. He does not idolize power and wealth when he sees them. On the other hand, he does not pretend to himself that poverty, the ascetic life, and the furrowed countenance have a monopoly on the filial relation to God; he is not tempted by the attitude of the monk and the pose of the fanatic, when that is what he sees. In his faith in Christ he has lost regard for all fronts, all masks.

"If it comes to pass that I see a husband or a maiden, a lord or a servant, a scholar or a layman, clad in grey or clad in red, eating or fasting, sad or laughing, what difference does that make to me? In a word, these differences which greet my eyes are all the same to me. For as I understand it, a maiden in her red coat or a prince with his golden vestment can be just as Christian as a beggar in his grey coat or a monk wearing woollen or hair shirt. By this understanding I am well protected against all kinds of outward masks."[21]

The earth is a shifting and variegated place, and mankind can never abolish its profusion of changes.[22] We shall consider the significance of these differences in outer cir-

[20] See, for example, *WA* 49, 606-610 (*Sermons*, 1544; Rörer). Luther does not advise anyone to give up a lofty office in order to teach himself humility. On the contrary he counsels everyone to fulfil the office which he has received, thereby serving others. If a man holds high office, that means that he has more people to serve than he who holds a lower office. If one would be humble, let him fill the office which God has given him, as long as he has strength to do so.

[21] *WA* 32, 510 (*The Sermon on the Mount*, 1532).

[22] *WA* 51, 214 (*Exposition of Psalm 101*, 1534-35).

cumstances, but before we do, we must make it clear that they have no significance in heaven, before God. In receiving the grace of God all are alike.[23]

But if salvation is sought by the way of good works, the result is that the differentiation which God himself has established in outer relationships necessarily becomes divisive, disrupting society. If the foundation, justification through faith, is removed, then justification must be sought through something that man does; but by unavoidable necessity men do different things. Each one looks upon his own way as the condition for right relationship with God. They who are justified by their works cannot think otherwise than that they themselves, because of their splendid works, are the saved, and that others, whose way of life is manifestly different, are not saved. "Paul teaches that such occasions of discord are to be avoided, and he shows how they may be avoided. This, he says, is the way to concord: Let everyone, in his manner of life, fill the office to which God has called him. Let him not exalt himself above others, nor find fault with other men's work and commend his own more highly. Let everyone serve other men in love. This is the true and simple doctrine about good works."[24]

As men develop new modes of life and custom, they thereby intensify the divisions; one religious peculiarity stands over against another. In his *Kirchenpostille* Luther develops this division in his explanation of the name of Judas Iscariot, which is said to mean "one who follows for gain," in contrast with "the disciple whom Jesus loved." The name of the latter is not given, and Luther attaches

[23] *WA* 32, 476 (*The Sermon on the Mount*, 1532). See also the passage immediately preceding.
[24] *WA* 40[II], 75-77 (*Commentary on Galatians*, 1535). See also the passage following after this; also 114.

great weight to this fact. "Notice now why St. John does not give his name; faith makes no sects, no differences, as works do. For that reason there is required of faith no specific work, which can be pointed out by name; for faith does all sorts of works best suited to the situation. To faith one good work is as acceptable as another. But it is the nature of Judas Iscariot to split up in works without faith. One is called bishop, by reason of his miter and staff, not because of his faith. Another is recognized as a barefooted friar, because of his gown and wooden shoes. Another is known as an Augustinian monk by his black robe, and so forth. One gets his name from this, another from something else. But faith is not recognized by external actions or stations; and for that very reason it is faith that produces disciples whom Jesus loves."[25]

If a man believes in salvation by works, he focuses holiness in some outward conduct and demands that others imitate it. Thereby society is split up into groups, each of which follows some pattern of holiness. Their concern is neither the good of all nor the well-being of the neighbor, whose life goes on under outward conditions that are completely different from those of such narrow and specific limits of holiness. Men have chosen some external thing and let their own earthly behavior serve for righteousness in heaven, where none of men's works can be effective. Thus they have put simple earthly society out of commission. What one does is for one's own profit, not for the good of others.

All this the gospel changes. Salvation is by grace, not by works. All works count for nothing in heaven; their sphere is on earth. What man does is directed "downward," to

[25] *WA* 10¹, 1, 322-323 (1522). Cf. also 132.

serve others here on earth. No particular form of conduct is fixed in advance as holy. A person has to wait and see what others need; and do just that in a particular situation. Another time something quite different may be necessary.

Consequently man now looks over changing social relations in a way quite different from that mentioned above. Differences in action remain; that is inescapable. But they no longer seem a confusion of activities and modes of life in mutual contradiction. The various actions are quite in accord. When the purpose of men's efforts is that they should serve others, serve all people, it follows naturally that their works will differ widely.[26] Differentiations are willed by God himself as a wealth of gifts which are spread abroad through the system of earthly vocations. To express this Luther has a special liking for Paul's figure of the body and its members (Rom. 12 and I Cor. 12).

On earth actions vary in glory and importance. "But the eyes of God regard not works but our obedience in them. Therefore it is his will that we also have regard for his command and vocation." In this connection Luther, as usual, refers to I Corinthians 7:20. By giving heed to the duties imposed by one's vocation a person becomes a useful member of the whole body. Its different members serve different functions; but its unity and co-ordination are not disrupted because of this. "What a fine condition it would be if it so happened that everyone looked after his own responsibilities, and yet thereby served his neighbor, so that together they traveled on the right road to heaven. So St. Paul writes in

---

[26] *WA* 49, 610f (*Sermons*, 1544; Rörer). The difference is needed in order that mutual service may be all-inclusive. Differentiation in outward pursuits that rests only on the desire to be saintly in some special way (e.g. the peculiarities of monks in garb, mode of living, and such) does not arise out of love for one's neighbor or from God's will.

Romans 12 and I Corinthians 12: The body has many members, but not all members have the same work. So we are many members of one Christian congregation, but not all of us have the same work. Everyone ought to look after his own work, and not that of another; so we should live together in simple obedience, in a harmony of many missions and manifold works."[27]

On the contrary, the unified and healthy life of the body is sustained through the fact that each member performs its proper function, which is not the same as that of other members. All functions would perish if one member were to demand that all other members perform the same function as it does. If one member, in solicitude for its own sanctity, were to cut itself off from the others, it would cut itself off from life and injure all the rest; for the body needs every member.

In Luther's exposition of this figure, it is of particular importance that no member of the body directs its effort toward becoming a member or sharing in the body. I already am a member! That is effected through the work of Christ; so my effort can now be directed entirely toward serving the body and its members, "my dear brethren and fellow-members," i.e. my neighbors.[28] Special emphasis is placed on the fact that a Christian does not select what he will do, nor does he start any divisions.[29] He contents himself with his vocation, even though it be humble and of low esteem. In faith all are alike; for faith is simply the fact that one

[27] *WA* 10[I], 1, 310-311 (*Kirchenpostille*, 1522). In this immediate context vocation is set up in contrast with the imitation of saints.

[28] *WA* 17[II], 37 (*Fastenpostille*, 1525). The life of the body is simultaneously God's and the life of the entire human society. One's fellow human beings are bearers of God's action, masks for God. Fellowship with God cannot be separated from fellowship with men.

[29] *WA* 17[II], 37 *(ibid.)*.

179

belongs to the body, and one member belongs to it as much
as another. In that they are all alike, even though their
functions are different.

Accordingly differences in the earthly realm do not imply
factions, for all orders and vocations are bound together
from above. Behind all of them is a common point from
which they issue—God—and they are all "masks" of his.
From this common center their functions are directed outward. Man's co-operation with God is not directed towards
God, but outward, toward his neighbor.

Man's action is a medium for God's love to others. The
life of the whole body is involved in the functioning of each
member. In the exercise of his vocation man becomes a
mask for God. It is significant that Luther's judgment of
imitatio is negative; one is not to put confidence in anything
external, but to act impartially before all human appearances.[30] But he presents man's vocation as something positive, saying that man, by labor and prayer, can serve as a
mask for God, a coworker with him, through which God
effects his will in external affairs. Viewed from the earthly
point of view, man's action is never to be the object of his
trust, so there is no danger in according it positive meaning.

If one who is mindful of his vocation looks heavenward,
he sees only the gospel between God and himself, and not
so much as one of his own good works. His works, his vocation, involve his relation to his neighbor. His conscience
rests in his faith in the gospel, while his love, with body
and might, is committed to his vocation. As his labor
reaches outward it is a mask for God; but at the same time
no value is attached to it because of the trust of the conscience in the gospel, and the attendant distrust of all good

[30] *WA* 32, 510 (*The Sermon on the Mount*, 1532).

works. It does not seem to the Christian that all other Christians must do just he as does, give just as he gives, suffer just as he suffers. Each has his own service to render.

The ethics of love lacks the severe and pathetic character which marks nearly all other ethics, deriving from the fact that they impose the same course on all. As he looks at everyday people the Christian who is faithful to his vocation readily believes that they also bear the burdens of their vocations, even though that may not be self-evident. A Lutheran Christian is pre-eminently disposed to believe that there is seriousness even when appearances may not show it, and to see a proper ethical course behind commonplace actions. The sign of a right ethics is not found in a certain fixed outward behavior, but in the ability to meet, in calmness and faith, whatever may come.

"God has given to every saint a special grace by which to live according to his baptism. But baptism and its significance he has set as a common standard for all men, so that every man is to examine himself according to his station in life, to find what is the best way for him to fulfil the work and purpose of his baptism, that is, to slay sin and to die."[31]

This is the background of Luther's attack on imitation. He regards it as the result of deficient ethical earnestness. The motive of imitation is not to serve others and to lose oneself, but to be just as holy as somebody else one knows. In imitation one's aim is steadily centered in oneself. The object sought is one's own achievement of personality; and

---

[31] *WA* 2, 735 (*Treatise on the Sacrament of Baptism*, 1519). See also *WA* 56, 276-277 and 417, where vocation is directly and expressly set in contrast with imitation (*Commentary on Romans*, 1515-16), *WA* 57, 87 (*Commentary on Hebrews*, 1517-18). When Luther recommends the reading of the psalter in place of the study of the legends about saints, that is another expression of the same underlying thought.

one's spiritual condition is not the fountain of one's action but the objective of it.

But for him who gives himself to his vocation, the gospel is the fountain; action flows from the fact of having been saved. The gospel says expressly that one's person is saved in an eternal kingdom after death, even if it is spent and cannot be "saved" in one's vocation because it is completely devoted to one's responsibilities and tasks. It is one's neighbor, not one's sanctification, which stands at the heart of the ethics of vocation. By that fact all imitation is excluded. The only saint who could in any sense be the proper object of my imitation would be one who had precisely the same neighbor as I and stood in the same relation to him as I do. But no saint has ever stood precisely where I stand. Only I stand there. The saints are patterns for us only in that we should resemble them in their faithfulness to their tasks, not that we should make their tasks ours. We must show our faithfulness in our own tasks.[32]

Thus we are prevented from judging others. The testings in my life are mine, and in the final analysis inapplicable to others; accordingly it is impossible for me to see through the lives of others and their trials. The final judgment is God's, and all will be surprised at his judgment. Sanctification is hidden and unknown to the world; it occurs in the vocations of men, which are many and different. No man has a yardstick by which he can measure another and in that way mark out a visible and calculable company of true Christians here on earth.

We shall first be able to see the holy church in the resur-

[32] In his *Kirchenpostille*, 1522, there are many illuminating passages as to this. See, for example, *WA* 10^I, 1, 306-308, or 311-312, and still more clearly 412-414. This last named is a cardinal reference about vocation. See also *WA* 56, 418 (*Commentary on Romans*, 1515-16).

rection kingdom, after final judgment. On earth the word of the Creed is valid, "I believe in the holy church." Faith is convinced that there are sanctified Christians, even though it knows that they look after their vocations "in the midst of the common throng."[33] Only the Lord knows those who are his; and according to the Scriptures it happens very often that God's friends and chosen ones are hidden in vocations that are ordinary and little noticed by human eyes. The Bethlehem shepherds went back to their flocks, though they had been the first of all to see the Savior; and, according to Luther, the Virgin Mary doubtless did her housework as usual after the annunciation, without letting her neighbors know anything about it. "See how purely she bears all things in God, that she claims no works, no honor, and no fame. She acts as she did before, when she had none of this. She does not ask for more honor than before. She does not plume herself, nor vaunt herself, nor proclaim that she has become the Mother of God. She demands no glory, but goes on working in the house as before. She milks the cows, cooks, washes the dishes, cleans, performing the work of a housemaid or housewife in lowly and despised tasks. . . . She is esteemed among other women and her neighbors no more highly than before, nor did she desire to be. She remained a poor townswoman, among the lowly crowd."[34]

Luther liked to think that the most commonplace matters in the world of men often contain just such invisible and hidden secrets, where man least expects it. God abides in the deep, and he makes his noblest jewels of "nothing," of that which is poor and rejected.

[33] *WA* 40[II], 104-106 (*Commentary on Galatians*, 1535).

[34] Concerning the mother of Jesus, see *WA* 7, 575 (*The Magnificat*, 1521). Cf. *WA* 10[I], 1, 323 (*Kirchenpostille*, 1522).

But since vocation bars imitation, it involves loneliness
and despair for him who faces his task without a single
pattern to follow. "For occasions of faith are without pattern, let patterns be as many as you please; for in faith
there are always new occasions, new situations, new persons. . . . To sum up, we are subjected to varying trials.
Varying occasions arise, from which we are freed, and they
are occasions that cannot be anticipated by human reason
or sense. Then things that can be seen arise out of the
invisible, and those that are evident from things that do
not appear. . . . This is the nature of faith, to make something of the highest out of nothing."[35]

God is Creator, and he steadily brings forth new crea-
tions, giving new forms to the exercise of the vocations of
men. Therefore man must always keep the door open for
God, as in hesitancy and desperation he seeks guidance
from God through prayer. "Note that faith is always constrained to prayer. It must walk in desperation and many
groanings, then closing its eyes and saying 'Lord, Thou
wilt do that which is good.' "[36] Instead of seeking help
from other people, who counsel repetition and imitation
of works that are past and dead, one ought to turn to God
in prayer, who can effect new and living works even in
difficult situations.

3. Prayer

Normally man works together with God by using with
all his power and understanding the things which God has
created. It happens in home, field, workshop, and govern-

[35] *WA* 31^II, 543-544 (*Lectures on Isaiah*, 1527-30; Lauterbach). Cf.
WA 8, 588 (*De votis monasticis*, 1521).

[36] *WA* 31^II, 543 (*Lectures on Isaiah*, 1527-30; Lauterbach). Cf. *WA* 12,
106-107 (*Exposition of I Corinthians*, 1523).

ment. He who does not utilize all available possibilities to achieve a good result, "tempts God."[37] In the exposition of Israel's instructions concerning war (Deut. 20) the particular preparations for battle are said to be a mask, behind which God veils himself that he himself may give victory. If man does not prepare himself well before the strife, he has tempted God; he is guilty of "putting God to the test, failing to use the things which God gave for use in battle."[38]

This neglect of preparations Luther saw in his own country, when the Turks approached toward the end of 1520. Luther is aware that he cannot pray with power that God will prosper action against the Turk. The German princes have tempted God, and there is danger that God will no longer hear their prayer. "It will be a weak prayer, and I cannot believe it will be heard. Because such weighty matters are taken up so childishly, presumptuously, and without care, I know God is being tempted by this, and he will not be pleased by it."[39] He who has not done what he can with creation's gifts does not have the firm faith that can confront God and pray for more. In answer to such lazy petitions God only points to the gifts already given in creation and says, "Thou shalt labor."

He who labors knows that there are times when all human ways are blocked. In a special sense this is the time for prayer. To be sure, Luther pleads for regular devotions, for morning and evening prayers, and not only for prayer in manifest need. But we have good reason to note Luther's

[37] Cf. *WA* 44, 648 (*Commentary on Genesis*, 1535-45).

[38] *WA* 14, 691-692 (*Exposition of Deuteronomy*, 1525).

[39] *WA* 30[II], 147 (*Vom Kriege wider den Türken*, 1529). Cf. *WA Tischreden*[II], 217: "I would that Charles should overthrow the Turk. For this I pray God with deepest emotions. But if I do, my prayer falls back, because our sins are too great" (No. 1797, 1532). See also *WA* 30[II], 585-586 (*Sermon on Keeping Children in School*, 1530).

words on prayer in special exigencies, for he gives special place to this, and writes again and again on this subject in a number of his writings. For instance, in his exegesis of the pericope about the three wise men, Luther explains why God appeared to them in a dream, revealing that they should not return to Herod, after their visit to Bethlehem. God could surely have protected the child Jesus even if Herod had learned where the infant was, could he not? This was done that we may learn not to put God to the test. What man can do "through creaturely means," he must not fail to do. "To what purpose are created things, if you refuse to use them?" As long as man can manage with the help of things about him, there is no word or promise to which he can appeal, to free him from taking thought and effort, or to permit him, in passivity and blind faith, to lay everything on God. When no help is to be found on earth, necessity has its hour, "the time of need"; for this there is word and promise.[40]

The exposition of the Gospel for Epiphany expresses the essential point: "But when the time and the situation come, in which created things can no longer give adequate help and all your effort falls short, behold, God's Word immediately steps in. . . ." Here Luther refers to the First Commandment which calls for absolute trust in God, and which first makes itself known in earnest in anguish; and here he cites Psalm 50:15: "Call upon me in the day of trouble, and I will deliver you."[41] He who in his need doubts God's help, regards God as a liar in the Word he has given. To cast one's cares totally and unreservedly on God is not to

[40] WA 10^I, 1, 615-616 (*Kirchenpostille*, 1522).
[41] *Ibid.*, 616.

tempt God; it is rather to heed his clear and manifest command.

In this connection we must observe certain statements in *The Magnificat,* of 1521. Explained there, among other things, is what Luke 1:51 says about the mighty works which God has done "with his arm." Actually, what is "God's arm"? In Scripture "God's arm" means the very power of God by which he acts without created means. God's action proceeds quietly and secretly, so that no one becomes aware of it before it has taken place. When God acts "through creaturely means," his action is not secret: all can see where strength and weakness lie. For example, the prince who is armed most adequately wins the victory over his inferior foe. That is God's work too, effected by the strength which is a mask of God. But in that case God is not acting "with his arm." When God acts "with his arm," he who is weak and despised gains the victory, and triumphs in the hour when his situation appears most doubtful and hopeless. It is thus, for instance, that God acts in Christ on the cross and in the martyrs. Thus he acts today too, in all who suffer and are oppressed, if only they have faith and do not fall away. "For where the strength of man fails, there the strength of God enters, if faith is there with such expectation."[42]

This is where the reality of prayer comes in. Prayer and faith become identical. For one in need and lowliness of spirit to expect, to await, to be receptive to what God does, while one endures injustice without resistance, that is the work of faith, and such a faith is in itself prayer. If a man has that faith, God does "mighty works" in him "with his

[42] *WA* 7, 585-586 (*The Magnificat,* 1521).

arm." Unexpected and new solutions come for one's tribulations. There noteworthy and new acts of God occur.

Where the faith that prays is lacking, there God does nothing "with his arm." There he acts "openly through the creaturely." There God usually acts through the medium of man's power, so that what is strong on earth triumphs over weakness. In such a case it is often possible for men to see in advance what the outcome will be. There is generally no miracle in a situation like that. In it there is no praying faith that opens the door to what God does "with his arm." "Where there is no faith, God does not perform such works; he withdraws his arm and works openly by means of the creatures, as was said above. But these are not his proper works, by which he may be known, for the powers of the creatures are in them mingled with his. They are not simply God's own works, as is the case when no one collaborates with him, and he alone does the works. This he does when we become powerless and our rights or our existence are oppressed. Then we allow God's power to work in us. These works are precious."[43]

A like thought certainly lies behind Luther's explanation of the Lord's Prayer: "The kingdom of God comes indeed of itself, without our prayer; but we pray in this petition that it may come unto us also."[44] In and through prayer God does something other than that done without prayer. In him who prays a special work of God occurs, a work which subsequently finds expression outwardly.

[43] *WA* 7, 588 (*ibid.*). Cf. 553-554 where it is affirmed that the work of God finds its course over the faith of men and proceeds through faith; for divine action moves on outside of the man who does not reach out to God in firm faith. By unbelief a person deprives himself of the works of God.
[44] The explanation of the third petition might be an even better illustration: God's will is indeed done . . . but we pray that it be done "in us also."

Particularly important is Luther's pointing out that prayer like this, potent and transforming, can hardly be made by anyone who is not in deep need and desperation. "For what sort of prayer would it be if need were not present and pressing upon us . . . that prayer be thereby the stronger?"[45] Likewise it is significant that there are two conditions for prevailing prayer: the first is certainty about Christ or the gospel; the second is certainty that one is in the "right station in life."[46] In one's vocation desperation comes and it is as one continues and is steadfast in one's vocation that God hears prayer. To await help from the Lord means not turning aside before adversities and forsaking one's vocation, but continuing in faith and prayer. The demand which vocation makes could be overwhelming to man, so that in his vocation the law presses down on him and smites his conscience (the second use of the law); and the inner freedom and joy which is the fruit of the Spirit may burst forth in man's specific daily work and in his relation with others, a fresh and unexpected transformation of the old and trying responsibilities of his station (the love manifested in the new man). Vital prayer stands between these two.[47]

Prayer is in direct relation to desperation and the second use of the law, the fruit of which should be humility and yearning for the gospel of God.[48] Man's exigencies, including outward conditions like war, sickness, and the cruelty of tyrants, has in the Christian life the essential func-

[45] See *WA* 32, 492. Just before, the matter of faith's desperation was discussed, including the burdens of vocation. Cf. 489 and particularly 490 (*The Sermon on the Mount,* 1532).

[46] *WA* 32, 493 *(ibid.).* It is specifically persons with such certainty upon whom the devil's onslaught falls; for that reason they must live in prayer, step by step. Cf. 491-492

[47] *WA* 6, 249 (*Treatise on Good Works,* 1520).

[48] This relationship appears clearly in *WA* 19, 223-224 (*Exposition of Jonah,* 1526).

tion of bringing to penitence and prayer the heart tempted
to pride and complacency.[49] With an uneasy conscience man
is under the yoke of the law, but God's law leaps over the
law to reach man, i.e. God commands man to turn from all
confidence in himself and, instead, to fear God and pray.
Luther ascribes the role of this burden of soul to the First
Commandment; therein God's injunction to pray is found.[50]
In his work on Luther's Small Catechism, Nathan Söderblom
rightly holds that Luther bases prayer on God's commandment, as God bids us in so many words, to pray in every
time of need. This is closely related to Luther's view on the
role of the law in man's turmoil of soul; for in his view the
First Commandment is a garb for God's love, as we can
see from Luther's thoughts about prayer. In the dread and
disquietude which man's straits cause, man looks for ways
of deliverance; then it becomes evident what his false gods
are. The commandment, "Thou shalt have no other gods
before me," contains a mandate that man is to turn to God;
that is, to pray. Prayer is regarded as an adequately functioning power through which man's relation to God is changed
from despair to freedom.

In his exposition of Jonah, Luther develops this point
very clearly: "As soon as Jonah had come to the point
where he called on the Lord (Jonah 2:3), he had attained
the victory. Realize that and do likewise. Do not bow low
and flee. Look up to God! . . . To the Lord, to the Lord,
and to none other than to him who is angered and punishes;
not to any other! Your answer will be that matters will soon

[49] WA 18, 317-321 (Admonition to Peace, 1525); WA 30[II], 116-120
(Vom Kriege wider den Türken, 1529); the extraordinary passage in
WA 40[I], 579-585 (Commentary on Galatians, 1535) where Israel's cry of
need by the Red Sea is discussed; also WA 51, 597-610 (Vermahnung zum
Gebet wider den Türken, 1541).

[50] WA 51, 204 (Exposition of Psalm 101, 1534-35).

be better, and that you shall know forthwith how wrath is softened and punishment lightened. He will not leave you unanswered, if only you call to him; but all you are to do is to cry out to him; he does not ask about your merits. He surely knows that you are a sinner, and that what you deserve is wrath. . . . Human nature is not satisfied to let it go at that; man always wants to appear with something of his own that can reconcile God. But he has nothing of the kind. He can neither believe nor understand that only crying out to God is enough to allay the wrath of God, as Jonah teaches us here."[51]

Prayer is not possible by our own power; it is the Holy Spirit who groans within us. For that very reason man is not always aware that he is praying. It may be that he notices only that adversities swarm about him; and he knows that he has lived in a way as to deserve adversities. Yet he dares to hope for God's help, only because God has promised to be merciful, and not for any other reason. A groan of that kind does not get much attention here on earth, by him who prays or by another. But in heaven the Father says, "I hear nothing else in all the world except that groan. In my ears it is so earnest a cry that it fills heaven and earth, rising above the many pleas raised from all other situations."[52]

The fact is that everything in our environment is encompassed in our relation with God: everything we deal with, every task, every person, can become an instrument for God's wrath and occasion for despair. This is all vocation. He who looks back sees how different things have been a

[51] WA 19, 223 (1526). Therefore nature cannot bring forth this vigorous prayer; that comes through the help of the Spirit. Prayer implies the same dialectic as faith.

[52] WA 40ᴵ, 585 (Commentary on Galatians, 1535).

burden and a "cross," and thus an occasion for prayer.
Afterward the problem is solved but new problems arise to
take its place. There are always places in one's vocation
where disturbance appears, and prayer is needed. Therefore vocation, which involves the total of a person's relationships in his situation, can be properly fulfilled only by
constantly renewed prayer. That is given conspicuous emphasis in the Latin exposition of Psalm 127. Inwardly one
must always be passive and prayerful, while the body labors.
Prayer in the work of one's vocation, Luther sums up in this
way: "While the outward man is busy with labor, the heart
or the new man makes his entreaties in the place of his
cares, and says, 'Lord, I follow Thy call. Let me therefore
do all in Thy name; and do Thou rule, etc.' "[53] We ought
to labor and spend ourselves, that we may not make trial
of God. In our work the soul must be "empty and free,"
not trusting in the work of our hands.

Desperation arises in our vocation, and stimulates prayer.
But God's answer to prayer also comes in our vocation; and
the divine intervention which answers prayer is closely
related to what has often been referred to as the transformation of the work of our vocation. In a monograph on Luther's
concept of prayer, answer to prayer in many other ways
(in inner peace, light on the meaning of Scripture, and
material gifts without direct relation to work in one's office)
would necessarily receive much attention. But in the present
connection we must limit our consideration to the answer
to prayer which directly affects the fulfilment of our vocation. A most characteristic thought of Luther's is that

[53] *WA* 40[III], 206, 233-234. Cf. 206 and 216. Cf. also 228 (1532-33).
As to prayer in outer stress, see *WA* 38, 361 and 368 (*Eine einfaeltige
Weise zu beten fuer einen guten Freund*, 1535).

through prayer the orders in which life is set are renewed by God.

Luther uses very telling expressions to describe what happens when people rush into earthly tasks without recourse to prayer. That means that God is "barred" from their labor. "It is most certain that without prayer you never effect anything, because government is something divine in its power; and therefore God is the Magistrate who calls all magistrates, not by the fact that he created them, but because he gives them the power, which belongs to God alone. For that reason he who is in the place of authority is as if he were God incarnate. But if heedlessly and, as it were, with unwashed hands they seize upon government, whether of church, of state or of family, and shut God out, do not pray or consider God, but wish to rule all things by their own counsels and powers, then the result finally is that in their economy they make the worst harlot out of an honest and chaste wife. In the political realm the state will be disturbed. There will be heresies in the church. Why? Because such a head of a family, prince, or pastor does not know God, the Author of all counsel and rule."[54]

In Luther's exposition of Psalm 101, the isolating of God in heaven is pictured in vigorous anthropomorphism. The prince and his sage counselors deliberate on earth; but God has no part in it, for among these mighty ones there is none who calls upon heaven to seek counsel and help from him. These lords are accustomed to decide everything themselves, without prayer. "Therefore our Lord God, as their deliberations proceed, must sit up there with nothing to do. He dare not take a hand in the counsels of such wise people. Meanwhile he chats with his angel Gabriel, and says, 'What do

[54] *WA* 43, 514 (*Commentary on Genesis, 1535-45*).

you think these wise people are doing in their council chamber, since they do not see fit to include us in their deliberating? It looks as if they would once more build a tower of Babel. Dear Gabriel, go down there and read a portion of Isaiah, which you can carry with you through the window into their presence. Read this: With seeing eyes ye shall not see, and with hearing ears ye shall not hear, etc. Or: Lay your plans, but they shall effect nothing. Make your agreements, but nothing will happen. For both belong to me, both to counsel and to do.' "[55]

Prayer is the door through which God, Creator and Lord, enters creatively into home, community, and labor. Man simultaneously directs his effort downward and his faith upward, thus becoming a colaborer with God and a mask for him. "Work, and let him give the fruits thereof! Rule, and let him prosper it! Battle, and let him give victory! Preach, and let him make hearts devout! Marry, and let him give you children! Eat and drink, and let him give you health and strength. Then it will follow that, whatever we do, he will effect everything through us; and to him alone shall be the glory."[56] When a person has spent his strength in work, and can do no more, he leaves in God's hands the undertaking in which he is engaged, and God enters in and gives the matter the advance and outcome which is best and most needed.[57] Here God enters into the situation immediately, without the use of human strength. We must examine this thought of Luther's more closely.

Certain statements in the Latin exposition of Psalm 127

[55] WA 51, 203-204 (1534-35). The references to Isaiah are to 6:10 and 8:10.
[56] WA 31[I], 436-437. Cf. 436 and 437 (*Exposition of Psalm 147*, 1532). "We are to work faithfully and zealously, each in his own vocation and office; then he will give blessing and good issue to it."
[57] WA 44, 648 (*Commentary on Genesis*, 1535-45).

are very instructive. A careful distinction is made between chance misfortunes in one's vocation and reverses in enterprises which lie outside of our vocation. If one meets with reverses in a matter which lies entirely outside of one's vocation, it will avail nothing to pray; for God gives no help in this, nor has he ever promised to do so.

"If anyone lives in marriage, in a certain way of life, he has his vocation. When this is interfered with—by Satan, or neighbors, or family, or even by one's own weakness of mind—it ought not to yield or to be broken in spirit. Rather, if any difficulty impedes, let one call on the Lord, and let both me and David be proved liars, if God in his own time does not bring help. For it is sure that here, in fidelity to vocation, God has insisted on hope and trust in his help. But when a work outside of vocation is chosen, in which it is certain that you are not able to please God, there is no hope, but on the contrary presumption and tempting of God; and in that you cannot be happy."[58]

Indeed it is impossible to pray effectively in such a case, since a man does not stand on firm ground when he moves against God. Prayer rests on firm foundation only if man stands where God has placed him and commanded him to stand. We know that our vocation has simply been given to us without our option, and in it we can claim God's help when we reach the end of our own ability. Then, according to the word and promise of God, his help is absolutely certain. The accounts of Peter's sinking into the water (Matt.

[58] *WA* 40III, 155-156 (*Exposition of Psalm 127*, 1532-33). Cf. 157: "So it can be seen that the article about faith in God's mercy and help ought not to be corrupted by presumption or tempting God, such as is present in a false vocation. In this one is certain to fail and to perish. But on the other hand, he who, obedient to his vocation, has hope and trust, will abide unmoved even as Mt. Zion, even if Satan attacks and makes attempts everywhere."

14:29ff) and of Jesus stilling the storm (Matt.8:23ff) show that such divine deliverance can come in the moment of apparent undoing.[59]

But in any case man must utilize all his own strength, if special divine aid is to be given.[60] Before that is done, prayer cannot have the force of a genuine appeal. The more unreservedly man has labored, the more powerfully can he pray, i.e. the more creatively God's miraculous works can be brought to man's aid in his vocation. There is an inconceivable dynamic in this interaction between prayer and labor. The miraculous work of God and the daily toil of man join and grow together in a unity of *co-operation,* in the proper sense of the term.[61] Our work in our vocation becomes a mask of God in a unique sense.

Creative action by God thus stands, according to Luther, in intimate connection with prayer by us. All transforming action of God is incalculable and surprising, springing forth out of the freedom of God without criterion or rule. Accordingly prayer must not bind God to a fixed resolution of man's outward difficulties. Prayer must always come to grips with God's "passivity" and cry out for help; but it must never prescribe how God is to help. If man does that, he does not pray; he "sets purpose, place, time, and manner" for God. He does not live in faith, he knows not what faith is. If God does not answer prayer as the petitioner expects, all expectation of divine help vanishes. Faith is immovable trust

[59] *WA* 40[III], 157.

[60] *WA* 40[III], 157: "But as long as it seems that the peril can be removed by our own counsel, there is no need for divine help." Cf. *WA* 30[II], 147 about feeble prayers and lack of divine help because of man's neglect of the responsibilities of vocation (*Vom Kriege wider den Türken,* 1529).

[61] *WA* 5, 580 (*Operationes in Psalmos,* 1519-21), concerning passionate and intense outpouring of prayer by him who knows that he is in co-operation with God.

in God; it is upward-looking receptivity in certainty that help is coming, but without a fixed preconception as to how God shall proceed. Faith leaves God free to keep his promise of help according to his own will and pleasure, "when, how, whom, and through whom he will."[62] This kind of faith and prayer is entirely in harmony with the nature of God. He is everlasting mercy, so it is right to trust without doubt, and to pray down here on earth to which his love descends. And he is the hidden God, to whose secrets man does not have the key, so it is right for man to restrain himself as he prays, not fixing a way in which God must act. Faith is certain that God is love. God himself must decide what he will do; he must decide what is to happen in an occurrence in man's life, of which faith will say, after it has occurred, "This was surely the love of God."

To apply, in the concrete situation, the affirmation that God is love is the continuing significance of faith's battle. Since prayer leaves God free, faith can actually see whatever happens as the answer to prayer in some form. Since God is hidden, whatever happens does not present itself as a self-evident expression of God's love. Faith always has to work at believing. This admonition against imposing conditions on God's answer to prayer Luther is always expressing whenever he speaks specifically about proper prayer.[63]

Answered prayer is not only intervention and changes in the external conditions surrounding man. In some respects it is more important, for our purpose, that by prayer clarity may be gained as to how one ought to act in a given situa-

[62] *WA* 10^I, 1, 618 (*Kirchenpostille,* 1522); Cf. *WA* 17^{II}, 67-68 (*Fastenpostille,* 1525).

[63] See, for example, *WA* 6, 233 (*Treatise on Good Works,* 1520) and *WA* 51, 606 (*Vermahnung zum Gebet wider den Türken,* 1541).

tion. The starting point for consideration of prayer was in the conclusion of the preceding section; the way of imitation is closed, and man, without following formulas, must venture new expression of his own.[64] It is then, as he faces this necessity for expression, that he begins to pray, seeking clear directions from God in the situation that confronts him. Luther gives a good illustration of such prayer in *On Secular Authority*. There he presents pointedly his customary affirmation that a prince must have the ability to hold strictly to the law and at the same time make exception to the law; he must be master of the noble art of moderation and be something of a superman in lesser matters, if all is to go well.[65] But if the prince is only an ordinary man, how can this be? Prayer, seeking counsel from God, will be a constant necessity.

"Where he [namely, the prince] is not wise enough himself to govern like courts of law and his counselors, there the word of Solomon comes true, 'Woe to the land whose king is a child.' Solomon recognized this himself. Therefore he despaired of all law, even of that which Moses, through God, had prescribed for him and of all princes and counselors; he himself turned to God and asked for a wise heart to rule the people. A prince should follow this example, proceed with fear, and rely neither on dead books nor on living heads, but cling to God alone, cry into God's ear, and plead for a right understanding, above all books and masters, to rule his subjects wisely. Therefore I know no law to prescribe for a prince, but will only instruct his heart, how it ought to be disposed and prepared regarding all laws, counsels, judgments, and causes, so that if he

[64] See, above, the end of the last section, and the passages referred to there in *WA* 31[II], 543f.
[65] *WA* 11, 272 (*Treatise on Secular Authority*, 1523).

govern himself thereby, God will surely grant him ability to administer all laws, counsels, and actions in a proper and godly way."[66]

God answers prayer by giving man certainty as to the right course, the right use of his office, certainty of God's direction. With this we pass over the line to our next section.

4. God's Commandment

The word "law" has for Luther a much more hostile quality than "God's instruction" and "God's commandment." The latter expression in particular, *mandatum Dei* or *was uns befohlen ist,* has a definitely evangelical meaning and is used in reference to a person of faith and his action; but on the other hand a legalistic person is said to violate "God's commands." Even the word "law" is sometimes used by Luther in a positive and favorable sense, as it refers to temporal government and its fruitage in external affairs on earth or in the realm of "the bodily": order and justice, external peace, possibility of working, home-building. But in the relationship between God and man, the "law" generally becomes an evil power which has wrongfully left its limited functions on earth and climbed up to heaven. Peculiarly enough that is not true of "God's command."

When a person believes the gospel, his relationship with God rests on God's action, not on his own. He is freed from any idea that he can base his righteousness before God on his religion or his character. That is, before God he is free from the law. Only then does he see what God actually commands. The command does not disappear when legalistic relationship with God is left behind. On the con-

[66] *WA* 11, 272 *(ibid.).* Cf. 278.

trary, when conscience finally comes to repose in trust in the gospel of God, man understands that he has hitherto not asked simply what God wants and commands; he has constantly been driven from one vain act to another in his pains to become adequately religious. But when he has come to faith, there lies a single command before him.

Legalism is a continual flight from God's command. Faith is a way toward understanding God's command. This insight into God's commandment, gained through faith, is a by-product of faith. A man does not believe with the purpose of attaining this ethical insight and in this indirect way reaching the envisioned goal of becoming a better person. If that is his intention, he is still held by the law. Such a man strives to believe, but does not believe with the heart.

Faith receives a gift which is not to be "used" toward something else; it is simply a gift, a promise of participation in Christ's eternal kingdom. Faith is joy at a gift which man received without becoming as good as he hoped (the gospel is for sinners). When he also receives God's commandment, he heeds it, not that he may thereby become a better person—that would still be bondage to the law— but simply because God commands it. Such "single" obedience is the work of the Holy Spirit.

The monastic life is a typical form of bondage to law. A precise outward mode of life is set up as especially acceptable to God. Effort is pointed toward God and heaven, not toward earth and one's neighbor. That mode of life stands under a fivefold condemnation: it is against God's Word, against faith, against evangelical liberty, against reason, and against God's command (against love).[67] The question

[67] See the rubrics in *De votis monasticis*, 1521 (*WA* 8, 578, 591, 605, 617, 623, 629). Love enters as a subheading under God's command, since love is the sum of the commandment.

as to what God has really commanded plays the dominant role in Luther's large treatise against monastic vows; the very first lines set this forth as its special theme.[68] Luther confesses that in his youth he had never clearly understood that God requires precise obedience; he thought that religion was something that one could take up and subsequently go on to greater rigorousness. Now he discerns that all promises of sacrifice are for one's own sake and arise out of self-seeking. They are deaf to what God commands and blind to the need of one's neighbor. Since a man promises to be a monk permanently, it cannot be for the sake of his neighbor.[69] What love of my neighbor will ask of me next year, I cannot know this year. For the sake of one's neighbor, according to Luther, one makes no holy and binding vows. Precisely for the neighbor's sake, one ought to be free to do what becomes necessary, free from vows (the law), to obey the command.

Bondage to the law is against and disturbs both faith and obedience. It involves a simultaneous deviation from the gospel and from God's command. He who does not have faith does not really face the future in peace. In the widest sense he must always "be anxious for the morrow," and base his security on his own efforts; and for that reason he is never master of the present.[70] He must hurry past his neighbor. The man of faith knows that in God he has

[68] Luther addresses his introduction to his father, since it was particularly the Fourth Commandment which he spurned when he vowed to become a monk, despite his father's opposition. He says, "I want you to know that your son has come to the point where he is now of the strongest conviction that nothing ought to be regarded as more sacred, more important or more religious than the divine commandment," 573.

[69] If the monk had not believed that the monastic life would bring him to eternal happiness, he would never have made his vow. See WA 8, 620 and 595 (De votis monasticis, 1521).

[70] WA 40III, 241 (Exposition of Psalm 127, 1532-33). Cf. WA 6, 272 (Treatise on Good Works, 1520).

enough for all eternity. Therefore he can desist from great, systematic efforts toward being holy. He can attend to that which needs righting in relation to other people's need, in the context of his life. It is of no moment to him whether or not his actions look spiritual.[71] He does not act in order to strengthen his religious life, but rather for the sake of his neighbor. These are the actions commanded.

We often come upon Luther's varied efforts to make it clear that man's outward conduct must not be bound and fixed by any scheme determined in advance. Such concepts as "freedom in externals," "freedom to do or to leave undone," "fairness," etc., can all be comprehended within the idea of God's ceaseless recreation of earthly relationships. Through such concepts the system is kept open for ever new beginnings.

There is no law for the conduct of life, no law which can be learned as a future requirement or as a standard of saintliness, whereby the ethical life of "the converted" can be guided into the right furrow.[72] In the relationship of faith the Spirit acts as an active force, bringing forth new works from the attitude of love, free from the law even in external matters. It is of utmost importance that this discussion about God's command does not rescind what was said earlier about "liberty to do or to leave undone," "fairness," etc. On the contrary, the truth is that the *divinum mandatum* as a demand now for love to this neighbor of mine demolishes the tyrant law which would fetter me with sustained concern for my own holiness, while I evade my neighbor's daily petty needs for help and support. God's command serves that which is creatively new. God's com-

[71] *WA* 27, 380-382 (*Sermons,* 1528; Rörer).
[72] Similar modes of thought alien to Luther underlie later views on the third use of the law.

mand is a weapon by which we break through the law.[73]

For every man his neighbor is a moving reality to which God's command is joined, "Thou shalt love thy neighbor as thyself." Without his having any choice, his neighbor is given to him.[74]

Despite the fact that love of one's neighbor has the character of something imposed upon us, it is not a matter of a law from which we could deduce in advance what is right. What the command means depends on each man's living neighbor and his varying needs. Since it is in my situation on earth that I meet my neighbor, my vocation comprehends all my relations with different "neighbors"; indeed, my vocation can be said to consist of those relations. Just as the expression "God's command" is directly coupled with love to one's neighbor, so it is directly coupled with vocation: *Beruf und Befehl* (vocation and command) is, for Luther, a natural combination of terms.

"Regardless of the lives and examples of all saints, each man ought to learn patiently what God commands him, and to discharge faithfully his own vocation. . . . See, you find many people who do all sorts of things, but not what they have been commanded to do. Someone hears that some saints went on a pilgrimage and were praised for that. Then this fool goes ahead, leaves behind the wife and child for whom God has made him responsible, runs to St. James, or here or there, and does not realize that his vocation and

[73] Luther gives typical examples of what is thus required, in *WA* 10I, 2, 175-177, at the same time pleading eagerly for the "freedom to do or to leave undone." That freedom means the freedom to do what love requires, or to obey God's commandment (*Adventspostille,* 1522). Of value in this connection is the exposition of Romans 13:9, in *WA* 17II, 100-103 (*Fastenpostille,* 1525). See also sec. 5 below.

[74] How the requirement of love for one's neighbor constitutes a disturbing factor for the legalistic ecclesiastical ethics found in Romanism is clearly seen, e.g., in *WA* 10I, 1, 256-257 (*Kirchenpostille,* 1522).

command are completely different from that given to the saint he is following."[75]

The command is an order regarding the "right use" of one's office, for the use must be modified by fairness, that is, by regard for different people, different "neighbors." In the light of this, we can understand that every action has its hour, its time—an idea with which we must deal in the next section.

When love breaks through law, it is a spontaneous action, done in the freedom of faith, effected in pure gladness toward one's neighbor. How can such a course straightway be coupled with a command and characterized as obedience to commandment? It is due to the fact that man is at the same time both old man and new. It is the new man who is spontaneous, free and outgoing, for the new man is a divine reality. His freedom is God's own freedom from rules. His love is Christ working through him. His joy is the Holy Spirit dwelling in his heart.

Christian love is not an untroubled spontaneity in the psychological sense. The devil always has a hold on man as long as he lives; and divine love has to make its way through a sinful medium, in which it encounters obstacles and resistance. In every self-sacrificing act which man would do for his neighbor, the old man asks what the self will get from it. The old man is slack and hostile in the things the new man does gladly. It follows then that all good appears psychologically to be something commanded. In the new creature, the breakthrough of the law takes place

[75] *WA* 10^I, 1, 306, 307. See also the discussion continuing from that point *(Kirchenpostille)*. The vocation is given, commanded, committed, but for that reason the work of the given vocation is also commanded, required. Cf. *WA* 51, 615-616 *(Vermahnung zum Gebet wider den Türken, 1541)*.

in divine freedom. Yet, from man's point of view, it presents itself as simple obedience to commandment, because free, creative action must make its way squarely against opposition from the body of sin. He is aware that he obeys gladly, though in the face of resistance.

From this point of view, all that is the expression of life in God and from God is commanded. Faith is commanded. Prayer is commanded, thankfulness toward God is commanded (the role of the First Commandment in man's desperation). It must be so, since man stands at the line of battle between God and Satan. The present-day idea of a loose spontaneity assumes a nondualistic view of the world, in which man's life is not characterized by such a battle.

Freedom from the law does not mean total absence of the quality of effort and demand in the Christian life. Freedom from the law means that man asks what God commands. Inquiry into God's will and the neighbor's need, free from self-centered concern about one's own religion, presupposes by its very nature a heart which has found peace and lives in faith. Its inner peace and equilibrium appear in the ability to obey in small matters which are attended by no glory and do not enhance the holiness of the doer in the eyes of others. "As for things commanded absolutely nothing ought to be observed more than the form of the command and the will of him who commands; nor should it matter whether the works are small or large, lowly or outstanding, many or average, short or long, or of what form or name they are."[76] Such a course is simultaneously obedience to commandment and expression of faith in divine forgiveness.

How can the content of what is commanded be ever new

[76] *WA* 8, 637 (*De votis monasticis,* 1521).

and changing? It is not because there is in the Christian some inner voice which commands him always to look for new things to do. It is due to the fact that "life never rests." God is seen to be active even in the outward affairs of daily life, in which there is constant change and man is always facing new situations which he had not anticipated. The great, all-inclusive command, which comprehends all concrete commands, is that all must be done in faith. Everything new which arises must be met in sustained trust in God, i.e. one must so deal with everything that he abides in God. From this general demand all concrete demands necessarily issue.

"As human nature and being cannot be without activity or abatement, without suffering or avoidance, for a single moment (for life never rests, as we see), therefore lay hold, if you want to become devout and full of good works. Exercise yourself at all times in all living and working in this faith. Learn to regard all your doings continuously from this perspective. Then you will find how many things there are for you to do, and how everything has its center in faith."[77] When man obeys he continues in faith, still abiding in God's power, as a mask for God on earth. Such a person applies God's Word to the situation in which he is placed, and creatively puts that Word in practice.[78]

In such ways as these, decisive new steps can be taken. Complete change of occupation and work may come as a demand from which there is no escape. To be sure, anything like that is attended by uncertainty and peril, since God's will is veiled. In such a situation one must pray, "casting oneself into the arms of divine majesty, and trust."

[77] WA 6, 212 (Treatise on Good Works, 1520); cf. 249.
[78] WA 31[II], 543-545 (Lectures on Isaiah, 1527-30; Lauterbach).

(This is true in the choice of a wife, or the enactment of new laws, to mention an important decision in each of two earthly "hierarchies.") At the same time it happens through God's call, *vocante Deo*, i.e. the occurrence is both natural and given or commanded. "The Holy Spirit alone is the Teacher who instructs and admonishes that we should cast ourselves completely into the arms of divine majesty and trust him, and in his name marry, care for a family, govern the state, enact laws, etc. If such things turn out successfully, it is well. If they are not successful, it is still well; because it is his will that when, having been called by God, you have entered into state or an order of society, you continue and persevere therein anyway, calling on him."[79]

A sound reason carefully judges the outward situation, and prayer seeks guidance from God. In this double receptivity, toward God and vocation, one becomes certain that a particular thing ought to be done; and through this receptivity in both directions, man becomes "a medium which receives from above and gives forth downward—like a vessel or a pipe." The concept of man as a coworker and mask of God is in harmony with this.[80]

A good example of this is Luther's description of a Christian prince in his *Treatise on Secular Authority:* He is a prince who prays and labors, always open both to God's will from above and to the need of his subjects down where they live. What he does as ruler issues from this double

[79] *WA* 40III, 206 (*Exposition of Psalm 127,* 1532-33). In the course of life, vocations may change, and a person may be led out of one station into another. See, for example, *WA* 10I, 1, 413-414 about Hannah, in Luke 2:36f (*Kirchenpostille,* 1522). Quite a different matter, which also ought to be noted here, is the self-evident fact that a Christian must immediately give up a means of livelihood of whose manifest unrighteousness he is aware; see *WA* 10I, 1, 317 (*Kirchenpostille,* 1522) and *WA* 12, 132-133 (*Exposition of I Corinthians 7,* 1523).

[80] *WA* 10I, 1, 100 (*Kirchenpostille*).

responsiveness to things above and things below. This is the same as "faith and love."[81] In things which are commanded, God himself, drawn near through prayer, is at work as the Creator who comes anew into life on earth. When God gives a vocation, he also gives his promise to be with him who endures vocation's cross and cries to God. "God will be there with his help so that, by divine grace and help, those may be consoled and gladdened who in their vocations have to endure all kinds of danger and difficulty."[82] The idea that the Christian is free from the law and can break through its rigidity is not in conflict with the thought that the works of the Christian are commanded. God's command serves the new creation.

Freedom concerning the law is a real freedom, "the freedom to do or to refrain." The Christian can choose what is best for all concerned. As a new creature he is not compelled to suspend law, as one always required to soften justice. That in itself would be a new bondage to law, the law that one must never be stern and particular, even though one can see that mildness would work harm to all. Slack softness is not freedom, even as fanatical justice is not freedom. One may egocentrically seek one's own saintliness by always yielding sentimentally and ignoring justice, even as one can be in the grip of selfishness in insisting on meticulous fulfilment of the letter of the law. In neither case is a man inwardly free, and in both cases he is lacking in interest for his neighbor and for that which is best for him. The Christian is free either to insist sternly on justice or to deal mildly, according to what love dictates, i.e. according to what God commands; for to discern that something

[81] *WA* 11, 272-274 (1523). As we know, Luther thinks it is very seldom that a prince is such a Christian.
[82] *WA* 16, 47 (*Sermons on Exodus*, 1524; Aurifaber).

is required by love to one's neighbor is the same as being commanded by God to do that. Such a Christian has an elastic constancy toward others. He is in God's hand, and does the right thing at the right time.

In that way even severe and apparently merciless things may be commanded by God and done gladly.[83] Men and women, not merely soldiers, must, as they are able, take an active hand in defense against the Turks, without any leniency toward the enemy.[84] Parents who, in greed for authority, hinder their children from marrying, or manifestly injure them in some other way, should not be heeded; and it is the minister's duty to release the children from the obligation to obey their parents in this.[85] Luther is especially eager to give a good conscience to those whose offices require them constantly to resist evil with force, to judges and soldiers. These offices are created by God for the maintenance of society, and the requirement of the office is God's own requirement. Severity is necessary for the right administration of worldly government.[86]

Somewhat of a tangent here, yet worth our attention, is Luther's distinction between sinners "in doctrine" and sinners "in life." He who falls into sin through weakness and

[83] *WA* 30[II], 184-185 (*Heerpredigt wider den Türken*, 1529).

[84] *WA* 18, 358 (*Against the Murdering and Robbing Hordes of Peasants*, 1525) and *WA* 18, 397-399 (*An Open Letter Concerning the Hard Book Against the Peasants*, 1525).

[85] *WA* 30[III], 239 (*Von Ehesachen*, 1530). Freedom from the authorities receives, on the whole, unusually frequent expression in this little brochure on marriage; see, for example, 245f.

[86] See *WA* 11, 278 (*Treatise on Secular Authority*, 1523), where the inclusive characteristic of a good prince is presented in four points: prayer and faith, love and service, judgment and common sense, earnestness and strictness. Such a prince is true to his vocation, and for that reason he can be sure he will have his "cross" to bear: "He will have to encounter much envy and suffering on that account. A cross will very soon be lying on the shoulders of such an undertaking."

desire sins "in life." Such a one is to be treated with love, by the Christian, with gentleness and readiness to forgive, though he be deceived again and again. But he who in pride attacks God and his gospel, misleading others and distorting God's word, sins "in doctrine" and clashes with the Christian's faith, which is unyielding and forgives nothing.

Love yields, but faith gives battle. Love must only bless, but faith has the right to curse.[87] Luther would be happy if the world could say that, against the pope, he had been the world's most unbending human being. That is his vocation and God's command to him as a preacher. Love works with things which God allows it to administer freely and to give away, even to evil men. But on the other hand, faith treats of God and his word, over which faith does not have authority, but to which it is subject itself. Faith cannot concede anything or permit attack upon the gospel; that would be doing violence to the Majesty of God. Since the gospel is the bearer of salvation, even this severity against false doctrine is a work of love, for it is a battle to maintain God's proffer of grace undiminished, for the peace and comfort of human beings.

If a Christian is sometimes severe and sometimes mild, he is expressing his freedom to do or to refrain; and that freedom is, in turn, a reflection of "God's freedom." Since God is both wrath and love, the concept of man as a mask of God implies that man can be a mask for the wrath of God, and not just for his love. Every action has its "time." We shall take up this very profound concept forthwith in the next section, on *Stündelein*.

[87] Regarding this see *WA* 17^{II}, 53-54 and 114 (*Fastenpostille*, 1525), *WA* 18, 651-652 (*The Bondage of the Will*, 1525), and the following passages in the *Commentary on Galatians* (1535): *WA* 40^{I}, 181-182, *WA* 40^{II}, 48-52, and 139-140.

God's wrath is an instrument of his love. To be sure, there can never be a clearly evident relation between divine wrath and love, but when cross and suffering come upon man he has to believe that God's love is concealed in his wrath. He will be able to see the connection only after death. As an officeholder he is often in a situation where he has to bring cross and suffering upon others; that is, he has to serve as a point through which God's stern law and punitive wrath break through. The reaction is like that which occurs when a man himself is smitten by God's wrath; reason cannot see how this wrath can be an instrument of God's love. Then man is usually unwilling to give himself to an office in which he must bring suffering on others, as, for instance, in military service or judicial action, in the work of a soldier or an agent of justice. Faith, however, is willing to serve this way, for it has learned that God's love is veiled under law. Faith trusts that the mandate of a man's vocation leads to something good; behind all stations and offices stands the Creator, who is none other than the God of the gospel. So even severe action is something which a Christian can freely will, certain about God's command.

Even if a man could educe from within himself a correct judgment about what ought to be done, that would not necessarily be the same as having God's command and the direction of an actual order. The vocation to which one is called and the command attendant upon it witness to what the gospel also says: We are in a dark world, yet God is not far away but near at hand. Therefore it is a joy for man's action to be under commandment. Man does not have to grope, for he has a vocation. "Should not the heart

211

leap and melt with joy, when one goes to a task and does what is commanded?"[88] An unexpected power flows forth in work when a man knows that he is truly under divine command in discharging the vocation at hand, a power greater than any to be found in the words of orators. "It is most true that when one is persuaded about one's vocation that God wills it, and that by his Word he has commanded what one is doing, then one feels such power and drive in that divine mandate as one will find in the speech of no orator, be it a Demosthenes or a Cicero."[89]

This side of the command, the side that looks to the gospel, must always be stressed in presenting Luther's doctrine of vocation. But it is just as important to emphasize that this power and joy, given by the command, is power and joy for this world. About life after death I find no certainty in "the gospel of earthly vocation." The gospel is, in its proper meaning, something quite different from the commands of one's vocation. The gospel speaks about the eternal kingdom in the resurrection, where Christ rules without law.[90] In that kingdom the old man, with his resistance to God's will, is no longer to be found. There is only the new, spiritual, risen man. There Christ can be Lord without commands.

[88] *WA* 30[I], 149 (*The Large Catechism*, 1529).

[89] *WA* 43, 210 (*Commentary on Genesis*, 1535-1545).

[90] The gospel, which brings peace with God, is contrasted with vocation's command, which gives a confidence of another sort. See *WA* 40[II], 155 (*Commentary on Galatians*, 1535). Even more eloquent is the terminologically distinctive reference in *WA* 29, 566, where it is said that "the gospel" gives us confident certainty in how we are to act in our vocation: "If therefore the gospel were nothing else, etc. nevertheless it would be the supreme gift which makes us certain with that very certitude." Cf. the context (*Sermons*, 1529; Poach). There it is shown that the specific content of the gospel is something quite different. The message of the gospel is eschatological.

5. *Stündelein*

Luther's expressions of "the time" and "the hour" are part of his general view of God's sovereignty and of man as "fellow-worker" with God. In brief, they mean that man cannot determine the moment for an action, since everything happens according to God's will (this is one side, an expression of man's bondage before God). In the hour God wills the action to be effected, man receives from God a creative freedom to carry the action through against all opposition (this is the other side, an expression of his freedom in outward matters, the down-reaching, form-giving freedom as God's coworker on earth). Man is free in his outward action when he is bound in God, as a veil for God's creative action, which, when the hour has come, breaks forth in an unpredictable way. What Luther says about "the time" is related to his concept of freedom and bondage, and sheds further light on his view of creation. This may clarify the role played by him who is faithful to his vocation as the point where God's action breaks through.

A prime reference, in this connection, is Luther's 1532 treatment of Ecclesiastes, specifically his interpretation of 3:1-17 and 9:11. From the very beginning, as he exposits 3:1 ("For everything there is a season, and a time for every matter under heaven"), Luther declares that this affirmation is in direct contradiction to the free will. All human labors and efforts have their fixed time to be started, to be effected, and to be concluded. That time cannot be known in advance by man. The moment of all happenings is in God's power. Therefore all anticipatory anxieties and all precise planning for the future are fruitless and meaningless. Man cannot escape that which is to be. But there is no power on earth which can prevent us in the hour when we carry out a work which God wants done, i.e. in the hour when we do that hour's work. "Here, as has been said before, Solomon is speaking about the works of men, i.e. works started by human counsels. . . . Therefore know this: All human works and endeavors have certain and definite time for their doing, their beginning and ending; and this lies beyond the power of man, as has been said against freedom of will—that it is not for us to prescribe time, manner, and operation of things to be done. Here our desires and efforts are plainly frustrated, since God has determined all things that are to go or come [referring to Ecclesiastes 3:2-8]. That he clearly shows by examples of men's works the times of which are beyond human choice, so that he concludes: It is vain for men to be tortured by their desires, and not to accomplish anything—even they are broken thereby —unless that time and hour fixed by God has come. . . . Thus the power of God embraces all definite times, so that they can be impeded by nothing."[91]

When a man makes up his mind to do as simple a thing as seeking amusement, he finds that joy is not won this way. Joy has its hour, which is not at man's command: *habet ergo laeticia suam horam*. From that we might learn that we cannot control matters by our own decisions. Man is not to rack his brain about the future, but live in the hour that has come.[92] That is the same as living in faith, receptive to God, who is present now and has something he will do now.

This concept of "times" is very close to that of "heroic

[91] *WA* 20, 58.

[92] *WA* 20, 61 (*Annotationes in Ecclesiasten*, 1532). Concerning the time of misfortune see *WA* 51, 212f (*Exposition of Psalm 101*, 1534-35); cf. *WA* 15, 300 (*On Trading and Usury*, 1524), where the fact is stressed that man must live in constant uncertainty about the future, praying for his daily bread, but not reaching beyond that.

men." Just as God has his special people, so he also has his special times. It is typical of Luther that in the appearance of special people, "heroic men," he finds evidence against man's freedom of will. Just anyone who would cannot play the hero's role; and he who can carry it has not taken it up of his own free will—he is driven to it.[93] This must be kept clear in order to understand Luther's thought of "the time," and the ambivalence of his concept of freedom. Outwardly a "superman" conducts himself not according to a pattern but freely, unbound by regard for all traditions; yet his will is bound, for he is driven by God. Similarly, in "the time" there is a sparkling freedom. When one is doing that for which "the time" has come, everything proceeds with light and easy pace, as if man were all-powerful; and man himself is surprised how well everything is going, how unhindered and speedily the work advances.

All of this is the expression of a complete bondage, for it is because of "the time," not man's power, that the work prospers. Perhaps the person who is succeeding so well has tried for years to carry through the same work, but with no success at all. God can make a brief moment of time freighted with significance, because he is sovereign and effects as much as he will whenever he will, through a minimum of human effort. When a person experiences such a "time" he stands before the incredible. God can also, on the other hand, empty a long period of time of significance, perhaps a time which, though it abounds in human striving, is nevertheless left empty by God because the Creator is bound by no rules.

"If God favors some person and grants him fortune, he

[93] *WA* 51, 224 (*Exposition of Psalm 101*, 1534-35).

can ofttimes accomplish more in an hour than another can
with great labor and trouble, in four whole days.... Nobody
is able to accomplish anything until the right hour comes,
which is given by God without our seeking after it. It is
vain for you to try to succeed before the time, achieving
your purpose by great pains and wise (as you think) planning. For God knows the art of secretly hastening or post-
poning the time and hour, so that to one an hour becomes
a fortnight; and on the other hand one does not accomplish more through long labor and pains than someone else
does by short and easy work.... God so handles things
that our pains are not necessarily blessed; for we do not
want to wait till such blessings come to us from God, but
want to find them by ourselves before God bestows them."[94]
As an example Luther uses man's varying success in min-
ing. Nature's treasures are unevenly distributed; and behind
that fact lies the sovereignty of God, which never allows
itself to be subject to man's plans.

A conspicuous example of this concept of "the time" is
found in the exposition of John 7:30, in Luther's *Wochen-
predigten über Joh. 6-8,* presented in 1530-1532. With
simple examples he sets forth even more positively the thesis
that the bondage of all actions to time is a death blow to
freedom of the will. The clock cannot strike one before it
has struck twelve; there cannot be any summer until winter
is past, nor can it be evening until it has been day; one
cannot be old until one has been a child. "Everything is
fixed in a time.... It is not man's thought that rules. God
must give to everything its time."[95] We cannot go out and
pick berries at Christmas; we must wait till they are in

[94] *WA* 32, 471 (*The Sermon on the Mount,* 1532).
[95] *WA* 33, 407 (manuscript).

season.[96] Hence it is the time that gives the fruit, rather than the field or the garden; for the field is there all year, "but if its season has not come, there is no yield; that must have its time."[97] With special emphasis Luther insists that man's thoughts are impotent; before God there is no free will. Man cannot evolve his life from within his own ego, or plan it in any kind of elevation above time. He is at the mercy of realities over which he is not master. Man has to accept life from God's hands, for it is definitely God who stands behind all that different times bring him. Man is at the mercy of this almighty God.

"For God has ordained and apportioned everything so precisely that he wills to keep all thoughts and works in his hand. There will be no progress unless the hour comes which God has appointed. . . . Thus God has kept everything in his hands; and so no one on earth can carry through his plans, yea, plans will effect nothing, if one does not first seek his counsel."[98]

The final sentence, about taking counsel with God, of course refers to prayer, which is a sign that man is under bondage to God. On the other hand, it is through prayer that God enters into man and makes him a willing instrument for the task of the hour. Regeneration and prayer are bound together.

There are similar statements in Luther's *Table Talk*, where he presents the concept of the "opportune occasion," the Latin *occasio*. There the same argument from the world

[96] *WA* 33, 404. The minister in the congregation cannot outrun the time either; he must wait till the day of harvest arrives.
[97] *WA* 33, 405.
[98] *WA* 33, 403, 404 (the printed text; Aurifaber).

217

of nature is his point of departure in demonstrating that man is bound and not free.[99]

But then we come to the other side, man's freedom in external affairs. In his exposition of Ecclesiastes are unusually clear expressions of man's freedom. Having established man's bondage, Luther asks how man can have dominion over creation, as the biblical account of creation says he does. His answer is that we can make use of things in the now. We can only wait for the future; but right where the future becomes the present, we can act. As always, in the same breath Luther introduces the word of command, the law in its proper function on earth, as a complement to man's freedom in his down-reaching activities: man is free to live according to God's will as a worker together with God in vocation, in the interest of service to his neighbor.

"But you say, 'In what way was man made the lord of things (Gen. 2), if he is not able to govern them according to his will and use them as he wishes?' Answer: We have been made lords of things in that we are able to use them in the present. But we are not able to govern them by our efforts and wishes. No one is able by his wishes to effect anything that is still to come. For how could anyone who does not know what is to come determine the future? Therefore God wishes us to make use of creaturely things freely, but as he gives them, without our prescribing regarding time, measure or hour. For these are in the hand of God; and we are not to think that it lies in our hand to use things when we wish, if he does not give them. Thus Ecclesiasticus says, 'God has left man in the hand of his own counsels'; but he adds the precepts according to which

[99] *WA Tischreden*[VI], 358f (No. 7050).

he directs his counsels and actions."[100] Man is an active instrument in the hand of God.

So freedom is found in the act of co-operating. Freedom is the bondservant's freedom to move as he wills in his lord's service, in the activity to which his orders drive him. This freedom in his possession of created things man uses in the course, the station, which the Creator gives him, and in which God is present with him, constantly adding to life on earth things that are fresh and new. It is not only a farmer's vocation which is subject to changes, bound as it is to the course of the year. Every human work is subject to a thousand modifications. One time gives results different from those of another. God has his purpose for every hour, and his direction is constant, for we can never free ourselves from our neighbor and our vocation. In the execution of the action which is given and commanded for the time, there is a creative freedom which makes the action irresistible, for God is irresistible, and he has set a "nice and free time" for everything that is to occur.[1] The God whose commands are made concrete in different laws is the same God who holds the outward course of events in his hands and thus prepares the opportune occasions in which the things commanded are to fit.

"He who neglects the opportunity is passed by it; for it is said, 'Lay hold while it is time. Now, now, while it is now.' . . . When our Lord God calls on one, one should give thanks to him. It has very truly been said that our Lord

---

[100] *WA* 20, 58-59 (1532). The passage referred to is in Sirach 15:14—the same one which played such an important role in what he wrote in opposition to Erasmus, see *WA* 18, 666f.

[1] *WA* 33, 405 (*Sermons on John 6-8*, 1530-32, in manuscript. The printed text possibly rests on a misunderstanding of the manuscript). About God's demanding something new by the time, and the situation itself, see letter to Wenzeslaus Link on December 18, 1521, *WA Briefwechsel*[II], 415.

God gives the favorable moment."² Just as one can transgress God's command and doubt God's grace, so it is also possible for one to do something other than what one ought to do in that hour. One can stand apart from God's time and act independently, in separation from God. That is the same as being unsuccessful and unnatural, out of harmony with what is under way, as it proceeds according to God's time.

It may indeed happen that a man may prosper and gain possessions without giving heed to God, without submitting to the things which God would effect through him, but his existence will thereby be made lifeless: "It will hold nothing but emptiness." Wealth will slip out of his hands, and he will reap no genuine gain.

Both prayer and God's commandment are more clearly understandable in the light of the concept of "the time." These three concepts can be said to clarify each other. In prayer man commits all to God, lets God direct all events; man himself heeds God's command, the command which in that hour gives him the form of God's direction. God's work with the factors of man's environment and God's work through man, by way of commandment and the Spirit, coincide, so to speak, in "the time." It may be an hour of defeat for man if he is to be disciplined and brought to naught. It may be an hour of strength and freedom if he is to effect something which in one way or another helps others. In any case, he is in God's power and pliant to God's will in his contact with that which transpires in his life. According to Luther man must live in faith and prayer, that

² *WA Tischreden*ⱽᴵ, 359-360. Illustrations of neglect of opportunity follow.

in this way he may be in God's hands. Otherwise he is closed to whatever God would do. In this way prayer does affect God's action, and in a certain way alters what happens step by step in man's situation. The answer to prayer is concrete.[3]

That man must leave anxiety about the future to God is stressed often in Luther's *Annotationes* of 1532. Apparently Luther means that it is easier to do the work of prayer in calmness and faith, if at the same time one also begins at the other end and gets under way with work and obedience to God's command concerning one's earthly task. Luther affirms that we must surrender uneasiness about the future to God, so that man himself no longer has that uneasiness, but lets God have it: "Therefore simply committing matters to God and making use of things present, one should abstain from coveting things that are future."[4] In reference to Ecclesiastes 3:13, he says that this inner security and freedom from apprehension comes as a gift from God.

"He [God] wants to say that nothing is better for man, in such tragic efforts, than to enjoy present things and with joyous and pleasant mind be without solicitude and care concerning things to come. That very thing can be the gift of God. I can teach what he says; but I am not able to effect or give what he does. He shows at the same time what should be done, and teaches when it should be taken up. He teaches that our cares fall heavily upon us; but he

[3] This does not mean that one prescribes for God how he ought to act. The manner of God's participation is left to his "freedom" by the praying believer. But God's participation is concrete. See the section above on "Prayer."

[4] *WA* 20, 59f. The passage begins by presenting precepts, i.e. God's instructions about our action in external matters.

admonishes us to call upon God, who may take away the cares and give success and peace of heart."[5]

Luther adds an express admonition to prayer, even though there is no basis for it in the verse of Scripture under consideration. Luther's own view demands that prayer have a place here. The prayer of faith and obedience to commandment belong together, and both of these in turn belong with the concept of "the time," the idea that every hour brings its demand, and every time is filled with God and something that God wills.[6] Prayer keeps man open upward toward God, and readiness to obey God's command keeps man alert to his neighbor. The work which God wants to do at the time to man's neighbor moves ahead through man. When one is at work on such a task, when one is only an instrument for God's work, prayer is strong and "ardent." "It is then that we pray most earnestly, when we are confident that the realm and portion of things are God's; for then we do not search for things which belong to us; and we are certain that we shall not have to turn away from that which is his and from the realm that belongs to him, especially since we call upon him."[7]

The command mentioned is the mandate of vocation. With undeviating regularity, Luther sets his view about "the time" alongside of his more inclusive teaching about

[5] *WA* 20, 64 *(Annotationes in Ecclesiasten)*.

[6] Regarding guidance from God through prayer, see *WA* 33, 403. We should refer to Isaiah 8:10 ("Take counsel together, but it will come to nought," etc.), which is cast up to the mighty (in the *Exposition of Psalm 101*) who make their plans without prayer by anyone, but presume to take God for granted in regard to the future. The same passage is also used in *Sermons on John 6-8* as supporting the thesis that God fixes an hour for everything. Cf. *WA* 33, 410-411 (1530-32) with *WA* 51, 203-204 (1534-35). See sec. 3 above.

[7] *WA* 5, 580 *(Operationes in Psalmos, 1519-21)*.

"vocation," "station," and "office." Four illustrations are illuminating.

In immediate connection with his discussion about God's ability to "foreshorten or to extend," Luther always includes an admonition to faithfulness (*Exposition of the Sermon on the Mount,* 1532). God fills some times with advance, and denies advance to others. Of what avail is it to strive to assure advance by one's own thought? Such anxiety profits nothing. Concern as to whether one has done one's duty is necessary and creative. God will bestow his gifts, "but not because of your solicitude, even though you labor. For such solicitude does not gain or accomplish anything. The kind of concern that is effective is that which belongs to your office and to God's kingdom, when you do what you are bidden to do, when you preach and insist on God's Word, serving your neighbor according to your vocation and accepting what God sends you. For the best blessings are those which are not sought after, but which come to one as they are given."[8]

God bestows his gifts on him who labors faithfully in his vocation and surrenders all attempt to determine the course of his life himself. Through such a person the gifts God gives are passed on to others as a matter of course, but he who is without faith is always marked by a tendency to keep God's gifts for himself, being anxious as he is for his own future. He dwells on the future, and is closed to the demand which the present makes on his action, and so he places himself as well outside of the divine gifts.

In his *Vermahnung zum Gebet wider den Türken,* Luther

[8] *WA* 32, 472. Just before this he discussed the question about "time and hour," 471. As he continues, he once again drives home the point that God refuses to bestow his gifts on him who wants to look out for himself, but gladly gives them to him who labors faithfully in his vocation and trusts himself to God's care.

considers the belief in fate. He affirms the idea that all is determined and that there is "a time" for everything to happen. Very characteristically, he proceeds, "I am not commanded to know what is foreordained; on the contrary I am forbidden to know what is foreordained. I am commanded to know what I am to do." For that we have received the Word of God. What is not communicated to us there we are not to brood over, "but leave that to God, and fulfil our commands, vocations, and offices." The point that man must bend himself to his work, busy with that which is in his power and about which his free will can decide, hangs with Luther's further statement that God is a hidden God, whose decisions man cannot penetrate. To the curious ponderer he says, "God knows what is foreordained, and he wills to be alone in that knowledge; you are not to know it."[9]

As gospel the Word of God impels man to faith, rather than to pious searching into God's plans; and as law the Word of God impels man to the work of his vocation. In the course of man's work in his vocation God's will is fulfilled step by step. Therein what God has willed is made evident. God's decree comes to light as one "time" follows the other; and through performance of his vocation man himself enters into God's work in its time, acting as an instrument of that which is to be. Then he does not, as before, stand in unbelief before God, wrenched loose from bondage to God and obeying his own will so as to squirm out of the grip of "the time," while attempting to learn in advance what God's will is. This person, who has religious questions and ideas but not faith, is by his very nature striving to be master over God, always searching for a timeless

[9] *WA* 51, 615 (1541).

knowledge about God, a knowledge without God's Word. He is in the power of the devil. In Luther's dualism one who attempts to have God at his disposal must be in the hands of God's enemy. Freedom before God exists only in the form of bondage to the devil. "We should address ourselves to our offices in this way, not prying into Providence, about which we have no word, no light and no knowledge; having put it out of our eyes, hearts, and all our senses, we should let it remain dark and secret. Do what you know, what God has commanded through his Word and the light he has given. Then maybe Providence will be made manifest of itself, without our prying, for it is not to be found in some other way. Such searching makes either vain Epicureans, Turks, bold and dumb fools or miserable, despondent and baffled people. The devil drives such people to think themselves clever and wise; so they do not see that this is the apple eaten by Adam and Eve and all their posterity to their own eternal death. They too wanted to know more than God had commanded; they tried to penetrate God's secret plans and Providence, and thus they tempted God and transgressed his holy commandment."[10]

God's Word is law and gospel; and the law includes the threat of final judgment, before which man must ever stand in fear, but the gospel is a promise that for Christ's sake man shall survive the judgment. The double-sidedness of God's Word cannot be resolved by man's penetration behind that double Word to God himself; for man has nothing beyond the Word. By reason of this double-sidedness (law and gospel) our knowledge never becomes timeless when it rests on the Word. Despair has its "hour," and rest in the gospel also has its "hour."

[10] *WA* 51, 616 (*Vermahnung zum Gebet wider den Türken*, 1541).

The third example of the combination of the concept of "the time" with the doctrine of vocation is in the exposition of Ecclesiastes 9:11, in the *Annotationes* of 1532. In this verse of Scripture the author advances the idea that victory, progress, and riches do not depend solely on a person's qualifications (strength, diligence, skill); but "all depends on time and chance." It is a fact that matters go well with some, but not with others. In his exegesis of this passage Luther immediately introduces the well-known message of I Samuel 10:7, which he has used so often in discussing vocation: Samuel says to Saul, "Do whatever your hand finds to do!" According to Luther, Solomon's wisdom in Ecclesiastes is precisely the same as Samuel's in his counsel to Saul. Since the course of our life is shaped by factors beyond our own plans and ideas, we are to address ourselves to the present hour, to whatever is at hand, to whatever is waiting for me now and belongs to my vocation.[11] What "your hand finds to do" has not just sprung forth by accident.

Since God is at work in the world about us, it is God who gives us the moment together with the relationships with others in our situation which the moment brings; and with these relationships he gives us our definite tasks. To use the moment and the time which God gives is to enter into one's vocation. It is in this way that what God ordains for "the time" is realized.

This is God's command. In this context in his *Annotationes* Luther sets this command in clear contrast with the law. "Therefore do not follow your own counsels and desires, but do what your hand finds before it. That is, continue in the definite work given you and commanded by

[11] *WA* 20, 163f.

God, eschewing such things as would hinder you. Thus Samuel said to Saul, 'You will be changed into a different man, and what your hand finds to do, do it, etc.' He did not prescribe a law to him, but whatever presented itself must be accepted, and there is the work to be done. And so Solomon speaks here: Always pursue that which is present to your hands and belongs to your vocation. If you are a preacher or a minister of the Word of God, continue in the reading of the Scripture and in the office of teaching, not wishing to be carried into something else till the Lord takes you. For whatever the Lord has not said or commanded will be of no advantage."[12]

Here law is not conceived as containing a similarly concrete and immediately accessible content. The law has a tendency to divorce a person from the moment and separate him from his neighbor and daily tasks. The objective of the law, as it binds man's conscience, is an apparent and obvious sanctity which will be effective before the judgment seat of God. Therein "ethics" becomes weightier than one's neighbor and God's command is brushed aside. Man ends up in a striving for self-fulfilment. Man determines his own ethical goal, which he aims to attain in a given time. As a result, he is cut off more and more from that which "your hand finds to do." He pursues his ethical goal apart from his daily work. In the midst of his straining ethics, he has a heart that is dead toward his neighbor. This legalistic life is a life that misses "the time." In contrast with that, God's command in vocation's concrete form leads a man into his "time."

This last point is made explicitly by Luther in his *Exposition of John 7:30*, to which we have already referred

[12] *WA* 20, 163.

several times. It supplies us with our fourth example of the
way Luther associates the concept of "the time" with that of
vocation. Here he says expressly that those who take care
of the responsibilities of the "stations" to which God calls
them do works when they are intended to be done. The
work takes its due course. In contrast, everything goes backward when a man decides by himself on a work for which
he has received no command. Such ventures do not advance;
they move "in crab-like fashion."

"It turns out so that the will of the world is not effected
unless God adds his commandment and order. What God
has ordained will follow his command and take its course,
for example, that parents bring up their children; for this
they have their time. Princes are to rule and punish
offenders; for that they have their time. For the farmer it
is cultivating the land. All this is contained in the word
'their time' (Stündelein). But everything which takes place
outside of God's Word and work, issuing from our own
ideas and not from his command, goes backward."[13]

To be sure, in another context Luther holds that it is
precisely the Christian who encounters the cross and defeat—which in the passage here cited would appear to be
the fate of one who enters into a venture which lies outside
of his vocation. The fact is that it is the unnaturalness of
such ventures that Luther wants to emphasize here. The
adversities encountered in such endeavors are self-chosen
crosses, which man has brought upon himself by a course
of his own design, in an hour when such adversities do not
rightfully belong to him. The cross of one's vocation comes
without man's own doing, in the hour when God wills it.

[13] WA 33, 406 (Sermons on John 6-8, 1530-32, manuscript; the printed
text adds little to clarity).

Faith can grow under vocation's cross; but it is weakened in him who labors under self-chosen adversities.

Luther mentions three different stations in which the correlative works are naturally done at the right time: parents who foster their children, rulers who fulfil their protective function against crime, and farmers at their work on the land.

In all three of these cases, actions are actually carried out which, in their respective areas, are appropriate to the several vocations. The vocation (i.e. God) impels one who labors in this kind of vocation to certain reactions toward what he is doing. Children grow up confronted with perils; and parents regulate the nurture of their children that they may go through life as they ought. The actions of rulers address themselves to unwholesome conditions under which people live. The work of farmers follows the occurrences in nature in the course of days and seasons. Of course there must be common understanding concerning what is sensible and wise in these offices, presented here only as illustrations. In that sense the works of vocation are entirely natural and reasonable, corresponding to the needs of the hour. At the same time they lack characteristics which outline them with any visible aura of sanctity, so they clash with natural feeling about religion.[14] These works, which are approved by a sound reason, are in opposition to the rational in the sense that the rational is the bearer of a

[14] This is, as we know, an abiding thesis in Luther's teaching about vocation, even though this special point in John 7:30 is not brought out in the passage cited from *WA* 33. The content of vocation is natural; but it is not for that reason at all easy for a person perverted in his religion. If this fact is not held firmly, one comes to an entirely false concept of the work of vocation presented in the statement from Luther just given, as if work is free of friction even from the point of view of the old man. On this, see *WA* 8, 629f, where the point is developed that the monastic life clashes with reason (*De votis monasticis*, 1521). But monastic ethics is an expression of a relation to God which rests on reason and not on faith.

MAN

religion excluding faith. The impression of the natural man, upon seeing these actions under vocation, would accordingly be that they constitute exactly the kind of conduct which is needed here on earth, but a religious person surely has to do something more, does he not?

A Christian, however, knows that what God wants is faith, whereas works belong to this world and are to be done for the sake of one's neighbor. These works are the expression of love which places others' well-being above one's own self-realization. We have already noted how, according to Luther, God uses the works of love, which one directs "downward" to one's neighbor, as an instrument in creating good gifts upon earth. All the Lutheran concepts which we noted in our discussion of God's new creation are intimately connected with the idea of "the time." A summary reference to this is in order.

The correlation between the concept of "supermen" and that of special "times" is manifest. When the whole external situation is in need of renewal, God sends his man. With regard both to "the time" and to these "workers of wonders" Luther confronts us with that which man cannot adequately deduce or bring about. Something suddenly appears, and for that reason witnesses steadily to the fact that God is Creator and Lord.[15] The same is true of Luther's well-known statements that God can unexpectedly give victory and advance to the weak, to those who have not, i.e. he can effect "by his arm" or "create out of nothing." Since God fills every time with the content he wills for it, history has to recognize the incalculable.[16]

Even more important is the fact that fairness is directly

[15] Cf. *WA* 51, 214-215 (*Exposition of Psalm 101*, 1534-35).
[16] Cf. *WA* 20, 163 (*Annotationes in Ecclesiasten*, 1532). The specific answering of prayer can be included here.

230

related to the idea that different times call for different actions. Of course, behind Luther's concept of fairness lies his basic thesis that a man's neighbor is the proper objective of his action. When a neighbor is given that place, change is introduced into ethics as a constitutive mark. His neighbor is now one person and now another. Now he is in need of one thing, and then of another.[17]

This line of thought is expressive of God's ongoing creative action. But the most important aspect of this creative work is man's life in love, or the Holy Spirit's work through man. The Spirit lays hold of just what God would effect in a given moment, for the Spirit is God himself. Through the Spirit man is brought into God's ongoing creativity. In a spontaneous and unsought way he lives in "the time," because he has been made new, while the old man has to labor at whatever the day brings, but looks upon it as a "cross."

The new man, whose heart rejoices in his neighbor, has freedom "to do or to leave undone," a freedom which the old man only claims to have. The freedom to do or not to do is closely associated with the concept of "the time." Man is free from a law which does not recognize different situations, free "to do" if that is what love requires at one time, and free "not to do" if that is what love dictates at another time. He is free to follow the law, or so to construe the law as to serve another new work. In other words, he is free from the law, that he may heed the command. "God's command" is of course at the service of the creatively new. It is a command given "now."

This short survey should show that, according to Luther, the varied expressions for God's ever new creativity, by

---

[17] As to "fairness" and "the time," see *WA* 51, 372-373 (*An die Pfarrherrn wider den Wucher zu predigen*, 1540).

their very nature, are coupled with the concept of "the time," in which the implication is that God's action is something factual which cannot be deduced from circumstances. It confronts man when he is not expecting it. God would not be God if man could know in advance what will occur next.

Even hard and severe measures may be commanded by God. Man is a "mask of God." But God is wrath as well as love, hence man may present himself as both demanding and giving in relation to others. At one time he may be a mask for God's goodness, at another for his severity.[18] In either case he is not striving to serve as a mask for God. He is only doing obediently what he is bidden to do. Living in vocation is so constituted that it includes both gentleness and severity. Because the Christian has a good conscience before God, yielding, irresponsible softness and supineness have no place with him, even as there is no place in the Christian order of life for the doctrinaire rigidity of a conscience caught in a closed system of ethics. This tension between necessary severity on the one hand and mildness on the other is of course very closely related to the point that different "times" call for different actions.[19] Both the love of God and the wrath of God step forth in visible form on earth in the fact that the exercise of vocation comprises this ambivalence.[20]

[18] See, above, sec. 2. About the Christian as an expression of God's love, see *WA* 36, 423-424; and about the same Christian person's apparently merciless actions in pursuit of his vocation, see *WA* 36, 427-428 (*Sermons, 1533;* Cruciger). There it is stressed that punishment is also a service to God's love.

[19] An example of this is given in *Fastenpostille, 1525,* where the change between these two is said to be the work of the Spirit—"Therefore the Spirit must be here"—and there the concept of "time" is also included in the presentation. *WA* 17[II], 53.

[20] Wrath and love also become evident in the course of nature: in catastrophes, sickness, sun, harvest, health.

Our exposition of Luther's ideas as to "the time" are thus concluded. From the vantage point to which we have come, we should look back at the route by which we came. The second, third, fourth, and fifth sections of Chapter III constitute a unity. The caption of the chapter is "Man," and through this central theme the detailed studies of the four sections show themselves to be parts of a whole.

In "Vocation—Imitation" we rejected the easy way of solving the ethical problem, the way of imitating an example. No single pattern can be adequate, for in the vocation he gives God calls for action that is new. Instead of the fixed way of imitation, there is the way of prayer which leads to God who wills to make all things new. So the next section considered prayer. He who prays stands between God and the vocation he faces. He is ready to act as God wills, and waits only to be sure what it is that God commands. In the succeeding section, in which we analyzed the term "God's command," we contrasted command and law. The command serves the new creation and breaks through the law. The law does not consider changing situations, but the command is addressed to the present need.

In a way, the law represents unchanging imitation, without regard for "the time," but the command calls man to his vocation, which is guided by the need of "the time." In imitation the individual person is just one more number, but in vocation, through prayer and divine command, he is the point where something more breaks in which is relevant to the occasion. He is a living instrument in the hand of the Creator.

The last of the four sections referred to considered "the time," when a particular course, coming from God through a given person, opens up as his calling from God. In "the time" man apprehends the course intended by God and given to man through divine command. Man sees it as an accomplished fact, launched at the proper time by God who uses man as a coworker. The problem of vocation is resolved without recourse to imitation.

6. *Hiddenness and Eschatology*

In the last four sections the free and creative side of vocation has been dominant. We might almost forget that vocation is also a cross, a burden, something which does not take shape from within, something that has to be accepted and borne as an unavoidable fact. The old man cannot escape the law; he always stands under it. He is to be crucified by having to do that which he would not. Only in that way can the body be borne on toward a future participation in Christ's everlasting kingdom after death. In this section about the hiddenness of God, and of his action as something always, in the last analysis, only preparatory to death and resurrection, we must finally consider the hard and burdensome side of vocation.

There are "times" when, by the will of God, failure, defeat, obstacles, and bitter things befall us.[21] In Christian experience there are times when the law is stern, when there is anguish, just as grace and joy also have their times.[22] Luther often emphasizes that troubles and tribulations are to drive us closer to God; they benefit rather than harm us. Here he accords to faith an unparalleled significance. Man

[21] See, for example, *WA* 33, 406-407 and 409f, where the expression used points to what Christ says to the mob which laid hands on him in Gethsemane and exercised violence against him, "This is your hour, and the power of darkness now rules" (Luke 22:53) (*Sermons on John 6-8,* 1530-32).

[22] *WA* 40^I, 524-526 (*Commentary on Galatians,* 1535).

can say that the hard times of life come to him as something evil, but his faith takes them in hand and turns them into something good. We must be reminded that faith is, by nature, laying hold of a promise, a future, the entrance into a kingdom now proffered to us in the gospel. The power of the kingdom will first be revealed after death, in the world of the resurrection. Faith moves life's center from earth to heaven. When the center is moved, the burden that falls upon us on earth appears in another light: it now presents itself as a "cross."

The all-inclusive, definite Christocentricity of the Lutheran faith is implicit here concerning the most matter-of-fact and tangible hardships of one's vocation. Christ came to earth and suffered the cross. He entered another kingdom by dying on the cross, then rising and ascending to heaven. In the gospel, which is by its nature a proclamation about this kingdom beyond death, faith can enter in now and shift life's center to heaven, to the resurrection kingdom, which Christ attained and set up by his triumph. In the gospel man possesses the power of Christ's resurrection. His simple occupation with his work on earth is to continue until death, and to be borne in faith. In that way one is really "in Christ." What is hard and burdensome is transmuted into good.[23] It is not a rationalization of the burdens of vocation; it is a genuine and real change. If faith does not believe it, life's bitterness is actually something evil. It testifies to God's wrath and hands man over to Satan's

---

[23] Statements bearing witness to this view could be adduced again from the following references, already cited in part heretofore: *WA* 9, 101-103 (marginal notes on Tauler, 1516), *WA* 57, 105, 122, 131, 132, 218, 232 (*Commentary on Hebrews,* 1517-18), *WA* 12, 93 (*Exposition of I Corinthians 7,* 1523), *WA* 15, 372 (*Exposition of Psalm 127,* 1524), *WA* 30^{II}, 176-179 (*Heerpredigt wider den Türken,* 1529), *WA* 32, 31-36 (*Sermon vom Leiden und Kreuz,* 1530), *WA* 40^{III}, 206 and 234-235 (*Exposition of Psalm 127,* 1532-33).

power, for he is constantly given to impatience, ill feeling and egocentricity. Through tribulations he is led not to heaven but to destruction. Faith is a course which transmutes all. As his faith, so is the man himself.

"This faith creates rest, satisfaction, and peace and dispels weariness. But where faith is lacking and man judges according to his own feelings, ideas, and perception, behold, weariness arises. Because he feels only his own misery and not that of his neighbor, he does not see his own privileges nor how unfortunate his neighbor is. The result of this unsatisfied feeling is aversion, trouble, and toil throughout life. He grows impatient and quarrels with God. God is not praised, and there is no love or gratitude to God. He remains a secret grumbler against God all his life, like the Jews in the wilderness. But he gains nothing thereby. He embitters his life, and hell is his reward. Here you see how faith is necessary in everything; how it makes all things easy, good, and pleasant, even in prison or in death, as the martyrs prove. But without faith all things are difficult, bad, and bitter, even if all the pleasures and joys of the whole world were yours, as is shown by all the mighty and the rich, who live the most miserable life all the time."[24]

We could make statements quite to the contrary. We could say that faith changes nothing, that it is only an acceptance of the reported facts that Christ died and rose again, that God is love. These are objective facts, which are not the product of faith. They remain what they are, whether I believe them or not. Faith lays hold of something that is true. How can these two views of faith both be accepted? How can we harmonize the view that faith

[24] *WA* 10^I, 1, 315-316 (*Kirchenpostille*, 1522).

changes things with the view that it is merely the acceptance of fact?

Luther himself answers that faith "perfects the divine and is, so to speak, the creator of the divine, not in God's substance, but in us." "Reason does not do this, but faith does. It is that which realizes divinity; and, as I might say, it is the creator of divinity, not in the substance of God, but in us."[25] Faith and prayer are possessed of one and the same power; they are really the same thing. Through faith and prayer a person opens the door to God and lets him come in. But one can neither believe or pray without the Spirit.

God is what he is. Faith rests on a fact which is affirmed by the Word of God. But in faith something new appears. Through faith God is what he is in the heart of man too. This is the meaning of Luther's repeated declaration that the entire efficacy of faith rests on a right use of the pronoun.[26] He who, by and large, only believes what Christianity says never discerns its power. But when I apply the Word to my sin, my suffering, my death, all the power of the Word flows into me and assumes a reality it did not have when faith was not present.

All this would be incomprehensible if we did not see it against the background of what was said earlier about the dualism between God and the devil. Without this dualism, we could think that he who does not have faith stands, for the time being, in a neutral and scrutinizing position, in an attitude of inquiry about God. In Luther's view lack of faith is in itself an active thing, for there can be no neutrality between faith and unbelief, between God and the devil. The vacuum, where there is no faith, is filled by unbelief,

[25] *WA* 40[I], 360 (*Commentary on Galatians*, 1535).
[26] *WA* 40[I], 85-86, 91, 299 (*ibid.*).

and that is action against God. Both God and the devil are objective realities outside of man. They are powers in battle against each other. The front between them shifts. Where there is unbelief, the devil advances his position. Where faith is present, God takes possession of an area which the devil once controlled. It is not faith that creates God's "substance"; God existed before faith arose. But faith lets God be "in us," present where he once was not.

His hiddenness is deeply involved here. What has been said implies that there is no possibility of excluding faith from man's relation to God. Reason wants knowledge about God apart from faith. It wants to talk objectively about God, to discuss what he is without involving the personal pronoun. Reason imagines that there is a God whom man does not know, but that it can learn to know him, and that this knowledge would be correct regardless of whether one accepted it or not. The fact is that man is involved in a constant struggle, in which faith advances and retreats with the positions of the contenders. If man does not really have his own personal faith, he is in the power of God's adversary, and he himself is the object of God's wrath. He cannot say that God is love (i.e. toward him). But when man has faith, the devil gives ground; God advances and is with the believer; for him it is true that God is love. Faith is an action. Knowledge about God is comprehended within faith, but without faith we do not have God.

At the same time it must be affirmed that faith is a work by God. The statement made above can be transposed to say that when God takes possession of a man, he believes. Furthermore such faith does not repose in "security"; it lives only in struggle and repentance.

Before we take up Luther's statements which disclose the connection between the concepts of faith and the hiddenness of God, it will be useful to raise the following question: In what way is the devil actively present with man, and in what way is God actively present with man in opposition to the devil? In answer to this question, what we have just said is coupled with the point that opened this section of the chapter, i.e. that man is a cross-bearer who lives under law. The answer to the first half of the question just stated is: the devil, sin, evil is actively present in the form of the old man. The answer to the second part is: God is actively present in his twofold work, as God of the law and as God of the gospel. The gospel acts in man's conscience, and extinguishes sin; wherefore the new man has no sin. The law acts in the body, and there it does not at once efface sin, but drives out sin slowly. The old man thus retains his sin till the death of the body, and in the meantime he is disciplined by the law, cross, and suffering. Law and gospel both come from God, and for God the two are one, a single reality. For man, however, the two cannot even appear to be in harmony until the old man is annihilated, that is, not at any time in this life, but only after the death of the body. "The law and the promise must be widely separated in the affections, although they are in reality closely joined together."[27]

We must look more closely at the function of the law. The law is primarily concerned with the body. It is limited to time in its relevancy; it is to rule only in this earthly, bodily life, as long as the flesh, the body of sin, continues. Therefore the law also belongs to the worldly realm which

[27] WA 40I, 490 (*Commentary on Galatians*, 1535).

is subject to earthly government, under law.[28] In terror of conscience, the second use of the law, the law reaches above the bodily and lays hold of the conscience. Since the conscience stands in relation to eternity, this means that when the law moves the conscience it is an action that reaches on ahead. In tribulation of conscience man sees no end to the law with the coming of bodily death, but sees the law as retaining its power beyond death, and being decisive in salvation, i.e. regarding eternity.[29]

Concerning this state of desperation, Luther says, in his *Large Commentary on Galatians,* that it is to "continue for a time," by the will of God, but it is not to last forever *(non debet esse perpetua)*.[30] Thus anxiety has its "time," just as do confidence and peace. Should it become definitive and continuous, man is doomed to desperation. Then God has not triumphed; his adversary, the devil, has won. If that state be permanent, it is evil and devilish; but if it be but for its "time," it is given by God. In the latter case it continues "till faith comes," or, as Luther also says, "till Christ comes." There the mission of the gospel enters and supplants that of the law.

We must remember that the devil can retain possession of a person. Man can come to eternal destruction. Concerning this it can only be said that this fate is the work of the law by itself, for the culmination of the law is final condemnation.

[28] This kingdom is the realm of death and transitoriness, brief and doomed to destruction. See *WA* 10^I, 1, 199-200 *(Kirchenpostille,* 1522). In this kingdom outpoured Christian love belongs. In this kingdom Christ's cross was once raised up; and in this same kingdom belongs vocation with its "cross."

[29] Luther says that "wrath" is present as a necessary constituent in the external order on earth. Cf. *WA* 40^I, 309f *(Commentary on Galatians,* 1535).

[30] *WA* 40^I, 522; and in nearly the same words, 528. Cf. 528 *(ibid.).*

The gospel is the proclamation about an eternal kingdom which God in pure mercy permits a person to share, excluding none who has sinned against the law, if only he will accept this kingdom, i.e. if he will believe the gospel. Faith is the anticipatory laying hold of heaven.[31] The gospel is preached by the church, which in this way shows the way to heaven and "bears children for the life eternal."[32] The work of the gospel advances in two stages, so to speak. First, faith is awakened (while a person is still on earth); secondly comes the resurrection (when the body has died and the person enters heaven).

Here we introduce the concept of "hiddenness." On earth we suffer much that is grievous and hard to bear. This is the work of God's law and of his wrath, for the discipline and crucifixion of the old man. About this Luther says (in *The Bondage of the Will*) that this tribulation is unexplainable "by the light of nature," i.e. by him who does not have faith, who has not heard the gospel. "By the light of grace" this riddle is solved: to faith this suffering is "the cross." Faith transmutes the bitter into the good, for faith shifts its center from earth to heaven. "Set three lights for me, the light of nature, the light of grace, and the light of glory, as the common and good distinction holds. In the light of nature it is insoluble how it is just that a good man

[31] Cf. *WA* 32, 468 (*The Sermon on the Mount*, 1532).

[32] *WA* 40I, 662-665 (*Commentary on Galatians*, 1535). It is the gospel alone which makes the church the church. The law is something which it has in common with the two earthly domains *oeconomia* and *politia*, but the church's essential message is the gospel, i.e. eschatology. One would expect Luther's vigorous eschatological outlook to obstruct a natural view of external relationships. Actually the opposite is the case. It is due to its anchoring in the eschatological gospel that there is freedom in man's outward life.

be afflicted and a bad man is well off. But the light of grace resolves this."[33]

In this sense, says Luther, faith lessens the hiddenness of God, but faith is only the first stage in the work of the gospel. Hiddenness still remains in that God can condemn him who by his own powers cannot do otherwise than sin and fall into guilt.[34] Once more we recognize the fact that this condemnation is the work of the law, which faith sets forth in clear light, in the gospel's first stage. Eternal condemnation is also the work of the law which has not yet been made clear, because the second stage of the work of the gospel has not yet been reached. Its culmination comes in the resurrection after death. "In the light of glory" even God's condemnation will be made clear, when man no longer lives in faith but beholds the face of God. Then there will be no further hiddenness. "The light of glory says something else: that God, who alone can judge with incomprehensible justice, shows himself to be of most righteous and manifest justice, insofar as we in the meantime believe this, being admonished and assured by the example of the light of grace, which fulfils a similar miracle in the light of nature."[35]

Since condemnation is the work of the law, our conclusion here is identical with the proposition stated earlier. Law and gospel cannot seem to be in harmony to one who still lives on earth. The harmony appears only after one has died and been raised from the dead.[36]

[33] WA 18, 784f (1525). Cf. WA 1, 208-209 (Die sieben Busspsalmen, 1517): the hiddenness is already lightened somewhat here on earth through faith. But it cannot disappear entirely as long as man lives in the flesh.

[34] WA 18, 785 (The Bondage of the Will): "In the light of grace it is inexplicable how God condemns him who by his own powers cannot do anything else but sin and be an evildoer." Cf. 685-686, 709 and 784.

[35] WA 18, 785 (ibid.).

[36] See the first part of this section.

Hiddenness is not a characteristic of God, along with others. It is due to the fact that a person still lives in the flesh, and has not yet died and been raised from the dead. For this reason we are discussing this phase of Luther's thought here. The hiddenness of God is not anything in itself. The truth of this is self-evident. If a matter is hidden, this is not a quality inherent in the matter; it is due to the position of the observer. The fact behind the hiddenness of God is this: man is on earth, where he is bound to sin by constant attack from the devil. He does not see God, but he believes that he will see him. After death he does see God. Then the observer comes into a new position. He attains to that which he formerly did not see. Then hiddenness comes to an end.

Not until now have we been ready to take up the point in connection with which we first brought up the question of hiddenness. In relation to God there is no way to escape the alternatives of faith and unbelief. He who wishes to be in positive relation to God must persevere in faith's constant struggle, never occupying a "surer" position than faith.[37]

One aspect of man's uncertainty in faith is the fact that the devil may get man into his power. Eternal condemnation may be man's end. It is incomprehensible how God can will that that should happen; but since Scripture says that that will happen for some, God must will it. Otherwise it could not happen. This incomprehensibility of the will of God is identical with the incomprehensibility of the fact that the devil is not immediately destroyed by God, but that life on earth must be served out in uncertain combat. In the resurrection it will be made clear why it must

[37] See the first part of this section.

243

be so, why the battle between God and the devil should be undecided so long.

The problem of predestination is not a separate problem in Luther's thought; it cannot in any way lie beyond the problem of law and gospel. It is exactly the same as the problem of law and gospel. If we had received only the law, we should end in eternal condemnation, without hope. If we had received only the gospel, we should be sure of heaven. But we have received both law and gospel, and in this life the two can never be one. Man must hear and receive both. He must believe that heaven is given by free grace; yet he has to battle against his sin. In his resistance to sin, he will have doubts at times about the gospel, feeling that for him evil is ineradicable, that in him the devil will gain the victory, not God. Then he is in hell, and suffers despair, which is the very ultimate in combat with the devil, the acme of the Christian's enduring of "the cross."

The place for fear that one is not one of the elect is not in a speculation abstracted from one's life on earth, pondering about predestination. The place for that fear is in the business of daily living, with its inevitable defeats in the battle against sin. The background of Luther's thought about this is his great basic thesis that Christian faith must always dwell, and Christian life must always be lived, in weakness, sin, shame, and the cross. "Therefore we rightly confess in our Creed that we believe in the Holy Church. For it is invisible, dwelling in the Spirit, in a place to which no one can attain; wherefore its holiness cannot be seen. For thus God hides it and covers it over with weaknesses, sins, errors, and various forms of the cross, that it may nowhere be manifest to observation."[38]

[38] Cf. *WA* 40^{I}, 106 (*Commentary on Galatians*, 1535).

The vital point is that even this dread of eternal condemnation faith sees as the cross, i.e. as real oneness with Christ. "For Christ is condemned and forsaken more than all the saints. Yet the course was not easy, as some imagine. He really and truly offered himself in eternal condemnation to God the Father for us. In his human nature he did not regard himself otherwise than as a man eternally condemned to hell."[39] When Christ died on his cross, he in his spotless holiness suffered the dread of condemnation: "My God, my God, why hast thou forsaken me?" (Matt. 27:46).

This is how fierce the battle is between God and the devil. Christ did not escape the cross, and the Christian does not escape desperation. Hiddenness lies in the two facts that God's own Son suffered agony on the cross, and that no man escapes death, fearing and dying in uncertainty. These are simple facts, and in them is hiddenness. The hiddenness is resolved in clear light both in the resurrection of Christ, which is victory over hell and the devil and transition from earth to heaven, and in man's resurrection when death has been vanquished. This kingdom, "heaven," exists after death because Christ arose. Through him this kingdom was established, and only through submission to cross and condemnation did he win his victory. Faith must likewise accept suffering and condemnation, for in that way these things become "the cross," i.e. a way to the resurrection. In faith and through faith Christ's victory becomes the believer's victory too.[40]

It can be said that faith joins together two different aspects of existence, which exist regardless of faith and are

[39] *WA* 56, 392 (*Commentary on Romans,* 1515-16).
[40] Cf. *WA* 56, 391.

real in themselves. The one is the work of Christ, his suffering and his vanquished grave, the work proffered to man through the gospel. The other reality consists of all the burdens which fall on man in this life. Faith joins these two together, and in so doing transmutes burdens into good things, into a way to the resurrection, even though to unbelief the same burdens remain evil and a way to condemnation. Everything depends on faith. It wavers when it is tried beyond measure, and it may fail; but if it endures, the way to heaven lies open. It rests on given realities, but it uses the "pronoun" correctly; the given realities take shape for him who believes. Through faith they become something which they are not if faith be lacking.

For this reason it is always a struggle to believe, and for this reason man's position in faith is never so secure that anxiety does not return. That secure position will not be reached before the resurrection. Prior to that man has to die, journeying on in uncertainty, depending on faith alone. Hiddenness may be said to lie in this fact.

Thus faith and hiddenness stand in positive and direct relationship. Because God is hidden, man has to believe. He believes only as long as hiddenness continues (until death). When hiddenness ends, he no longer believes; he sees (in the kingdom of the risen). Indeed, Luther can also move in the opposite direction. From the recognized fact that man lives in faith in God, he can deduce the fact, less often affirmed, that God is hidden. "In order that there may be place for faith, it is necessary that all that is the object of faith be hidden," he writes in his 1525 treatise, *The Bondage of the Will*. "Therefore in order that there may be a place for faith, it is necessary that all things

246

which are believed be hidden. However they are not hidden more deeply than under a contrary appearance, sense, and experience."[41]

In this connection Luther develops the thought that God veils all his actions. He conducts himself as if he were doing the opposite of what he actually does. When he brings to life, he does it through putting to death. When he justifies, he does it by making man guilty. When he bears man to heaven, he does it by bearing him to hell.[42] It looks as if the work of the law (to put to death, to make guilty, to carry to *infernum*) is set over against the work of the gospel (to make alive, to justify, to carry to heaven). The acme of the law appears in the fact that so many are condemned. If man could see God in such action, faith would not be necessary. But "since man cannot comprehend this, it becomes necessary to exercise faith." For "this is the highest degree of faith, to believe that he is gentle who saves so few and condemns so many."

"Thus he hides his eternal kindness and mercy under eternal wrath, his righteousness under unrighteousness. It is the supreme step of faith to believe him to be kind who saves so few and condemns so many. . . . If I were able for any reason to comprehend how that God is merciful and just who shows such wrath and unrighteousness, there would be no place for faith. Since this cannot be understood, there is place for the exercise of faith, while such things are proclaimed and declared—and not otherwise than that when God slays, life's faith is active in death."[43]

Faith is exercised in the same way, as we must believe

[41] *WA* 18, 633.
[42] *WA* 18, 633.
[43] *WA* 18, 633. Compare the final sentence with the previous passage.

that God gives us life by putting to death, effecting final judgment through the disciplinary action of the law.[44]

Since God veils his action behind its opposite, the reality of the Christian life is hidden behind that which is opposite to it. All divine power belonged to Christ; but he was scoffed at, derided and filled with agony on the cross. Christ reveals that God is hidden. In like manner, a Christian possesses righteousness, even in sin, want and agony.[45] The cry of the Spirit is never alone in the heart. There is always another cry present with it, sin's cry of "Murder!" which tries to outshout the Spirit. Only in the trembling conscience is Christ proceeding with his work.[46]

Man's vocation is involved in this hiddenness of the Christian life; in man's vocation the true "mortification" is to be carried through by God's will. There is none of the saintliness prized by men in the work of vocation. But when, after death and the resurrection, hiddenness ceases, the burden of labor in vocation will also cease. Then earth's time will be past, the devil defeated, and the old man who is to be put to death has died. There "offices" are to be no more; and "the law shall not rule up there."[47]

Summarized in three points, the condition before the

[44] See the conclusion of the quotation above the foregoing note. That by slaying, God gives life can become evident to faith, even here. That God is love even in judgment can never become clear as long as we live on earth. With God himself there is no cleavage between his love and his wrath. God in himself is not hidden.

[45] Cf. *WA* 32, 435-436 (*The Sermon on the Mount*, 1532).

[46] *WA* 10^{I}, 1, 372-373 (*Kirchenpostille*, 1522).

[47] *WA* 34^{II}, 27 (*Sermons*, 1531; Rörer). With Luther the terms *Stand* (station) and *Amt* (office) are more common than "vocation." That we now prefer the word "vocation" may be explained by the whole common social development away from society characterized by such "stations." This involves a certain danger of a modern "spiritualizing" of Luther's doctrine of vocation; but this is by no means necessary in its very nature. There is nothing to hinder us from regarding a business or work in modern society as a vocation in Luther's meaning.

resurrection consists of these concepts: We live on earth under the law, even while we believe the gospel. We are always confronted by an unconquered devil, even while we believe in God's victory through Christ. And we still have the old man in us, even while we believe we are the children of God. These three are different aspects of the same fact, for the law holds sway over man on earth because sin lingers in his flesh, and the sin of the old man is the presence of the unconquered devil. The old man does not vanish until death: "When I am reduced to dust, then my sins are at last entirely blotted out. In the meantime, as long as we live original sin also lives, as we constantly see, even among the saints, to our last breath. But we also say that that sin is forgiven to us. . . . Therefore it is remitted to us only by imputation; but when we die, it is actually removed."[48] God is hidden, and man bears his vocation as a cross.

The final eschatological consummation can be summarized in the following three points: The earthly realm and the sway of the law are past, for Christ's heavenly kingdom, which formerly existed only in the form of the gospel, has now come in power. The devil is conquered and Christ's mastery is revealed. The old man has died completely through the cross, and the entire man has been raised as a spiritual body without sin. These three points correspond exactly with the three points characterizing the condition

[48] *WA* 39^{I}, 95 (*Disputatio de iustificatione*, 1536). Regarding the presence of the devil as something actual in man's life on earth, see also *WA* 20, 565 (*Sermons*, 1526; Rörer). The devil's great power on earth, however, is only a sign that Christ will soon take all power away from him: "When Christ the strong One arrived for his first advent (up to that time the devil held sway over the whole world), the devil was weakened as a false prince. The same will take place in Christ's second advent." *WA* 10^{III}, 353 (*Sermons*, 1522).

before the resurrection and supply their resolution. These three, like the first three, constitute a unity, a single truth. For the law ceases where the old man ends; and this abolition of the old man is the same as the victory over the devil. In the divine hour when this occurs, hiddenness is ended and the toil of vocation is terminated. But that day cannot be hastened either by man's effort or his piety. "He is truly hidden, and yet he is not hidden. For the flesh stands in the way, so that we are less able to behold him. For it murmurs, laments, grumbles, is offended and cries out: 'I am most miserable, most abject, most despised.' " There follows a description of a minister's difficulties in making a living; then: "Therefore it seems that God forsakes and rejects us completely; because he has been hidden from us, and we are hidden along with him. But in faith, in the Word, in the sacraments, he is revealed and perceived. . . . Here indeed the Word draws near as a little flame that glows in the midst of the darkness; and as it spreads its gentle rays, through doctrine and the sacraments, God commands that they be apprehended. If we receive them, God is no longer hidden to us in Spirit, but only in the flesh."[49]

In these three points we recognize the captions of our three chapters in this study. Vocation belongs to man's situation before the resurrection, where there are two kingdoms, earth and heaven, two contending powers, God and the devil, and two antagonistic components in man, the old man and the new, related to the constant battle for man. The old man must bear vocation's cross as long as life on

[49] *WA* 44, 110 (*Commentary on Genesis,* 1535-45). This hiddenness "in the flesh" will not vanish before the resurrection. There is nothing dark in himself. Only to us is God hidden, as long as we live in the world of sin. In the world where we shall see, which comes after faith's battle, God is not hidden.

earth lasts and the battle against the devil continues. As long as he continues in his earthly vocation, there can be no end to the struggle. After death comes a new kingdom free from the cross; heaven has taken the place of earth, God has conquered the devil, and man has been raised from the dead. Then man's struggle is at an end.

Index

INDEX

256